Voices in the Wilderness

Voices in the Wilderness

Public Discourse and the
Paradox of Puritan Rhetoric

PATRICIA ROBERTS-MILLER

The University of Alabama Press
Tuscaloosa

Copyright © 1999
The University of Alabama Press
Tuscaloosa, Alabama 35487-0380
All rights reserved
Manufactured in the United States of America

Hardcover edition published 1999.
Paperback edition published 2014.
eBook edition published 2014.

Cover photograph: George Henry Boughton's *Early Puritans of New England Going to
Worship, 1872*, used by permission from The Toledo Museum of Art.
Cover design: Shari DeGraw

∞

The paper on which this book is printed meets the minimum requirements of American
National Standard for Information Science–Permanence of Paper for Printed Library
Materials, ANSI Z39.48-1984.

Paperback ISBN: 978-0-8173-5780-1
eBook ISBN: 978-0-8173-8758-7

A previous edition of this book has been catalogued by the Library of Congress as follows:

Library of Congress Cataloging-in-Publication Data

Roberts-Miller, Patricia, 1959–
Voices in the wilderness : public discourse and the paradox of
Puritan rhetoric / Patricia Roberts-Miller.
p. cm.
Includes bibliographical references (p. 193) and index.
ISBN 0-8173-0939-X (alk. paper)
1. American prose literature—Puritan authors—History and
criticism. 2. English language—Rhetoric—Study and
teaching—United States. 3. English language—New
England—Discourse analysis. 4. Rhetoric—Political aspects—New
England—History. 5. Rhetoric—Political aspects—United States.
6. Puritans—New England—Intellectual life. 7. English language—New
England—Rhetoric. 8. Language and culture—United States. 9. Puritan
movements—United States. I. Title.
PS153.P87 R63 1999
810.9'001—ddc21

98–25394

British Library Cataloguing-in-Publication Data available

Index prepared by Sheril Hook

To Elizabeth Killian Roberts,
whose courage she left to me

Contents

Preface

It's oddly appropriate that my interest in the American Puritans would have begun with a conversion experience. I do not mean that I was converted to Puritanism; on the contrary, it was to a distinctly non-Puritan way of imagining argument. I was converted to the rather simple notion that argument is best seen as a kind of inquiry. This is not an unheard of notion; philosophers ranging from Aristotle to Jürgen Habermas have promoted models of the public sphere that, although different in many important ways, share the assumption that the purpose of engaging in disagreement with other people is to learn as much as to persuade. That is, argument should be a kind of dialectic or dialogue in which people participate in order to change and be changed. In this view, disagreement is good, as it presents an opportunity to look at things from another perspective, one that one might end up adopting. As I said, this sort of approach to disagreement is far from rare among philosophers, and it even appears in popular culture in such concepts as empathic listening or "getting to yes."

Despite its many philosophical and popular proponents, however, it is not the dominant model of discourse, at least not in American culture. In the simplest sense, I have ended up writing about the American Puritans as a result of my puzzlement that dialogic rhetoric has failed to convert everyone.

Due to my conversion experience, I became a teacher of writing, and I have tried to persuade my students to see disagreement as an opportunity to learn. Like many other teachers who have been converted to some version of argument-as-inquiry (or what is often called dialogic rhetoric), I have found that most students respond positively, but some students find any such approach to disagreement actively threatening. In the simplest sense, I have ended up writing about the American Puritans because I was interested in that reaction. In more abstract terms, being genuinely committed to dialogic argument meant that I was obligated to understand why some students disagreed with me.

Why do some students express such deep hostility to seeing disagreement as a reason to listen?

That reaction is not purely negative—it is not simply that such students actively dislike dialogic rhetoric, but that they feel committed to their own approaches. Those approaches vary, but one of the more common is what is sometimes called monologic discourse. Monologic discourse presumes that public argument is (and should be) a form of combat or display. Like dialogic approaches to discourse, it has numerous forms in philosophy and popular culture, and it is neither simple nor simplistic, so it is difficult to summarize.

The most striking quality about this view is the generally unstated assumption that one should treat the public realm as an arena of real or symbolic domination. It is a field of combat or athletic contest that one enters with a commitment to an ideology that is both abstract and specific. That is, one is both committed to a general stance (one's country, one's team) and to very specific goals (killing the opponent, winning the game). These abstract and specific commitments have happened somewhere other than that arena; one does not enter the contest in order to discover what one believes, but to triumph over others. Just as it is considered treason for a military person to change sides, so many people see any kind of changing of a political position once one has entered the public realm as a sign of some deep moral weakness or evil. In such discourse, one announces a position at the beginning of the text so that the onlookers may immediately identify which team the speaker represents; the speaker remains committed to that thesis, at some point discussing and dismissing opposing points of view. Shifting in one's thesis is almost always interpreted by people who ascribe to this view as some kind of sloppiness at best and stupidity at worst. Often the speaker behaves much like an Old Testament prophet, not only damning the opposition (as fools if not sinners) but also presenting his or her own case as though it were self-evident to all right-minded people.

The comparison to prophets is not meant as a derisive comment but as an acknowledgement of how such speakers generally identify themselves. In fact, I was alerted to that analogy by how often these students or writers who participate in monologic discourse referred to themselves as "voices crying in the wilderness." Although the people who share this ethos also share other things, those things are not quite what one might predict. They are not necessarily religious or of a predictable political suasion or more likely to be male rather than female. They are often admirably concerned with ethics and frequently describe their opposition to dialogic rhetoric in moral terms. They do not want to adopt it because they think it is wrong.

Others have noted this tendency to make argument a contest between that which is obviously wrong and that which is obviously right, and it has been attributed to various causes. William Perry discusses the same phenomenon as dualism, and he argues that it is a stage in cognitive development. Habermas has referred to essentially the same quality as "strategic action" and attributed it to certain characteristics of post-Enlightenment Western society. Sacvan Bercovitch has noted the tendency in American culture to sacralize essentially secular issues, thereby leading to the Jeremiad being the form of political discourse in American politics—he blames it on the Americans' Puritan origins. The ways in which this approach to public disagreement simplifies complicated issues is extremely similar to what Richard Hofstadter has called anti-intellectualism, which he considers a recurrent melody in American thought. One could, I think, make an interesting case that the dominance of this approach to argument probably has to do with a particular reading of Aristotle, one which has long encouraged writing instructors to equate all forms of persuasion with forensic discourse, thereby unintentionally making modern notions of debate the model for all kinds of argument.

My approach is slightly different from the above, with the strongest resemblance to Bercovitch. Although one could probably make a causal argument—that current cultural tendencies were, to some degree or another, caused by Puritans—that is not my aim. I am interested in the Puritans as a kind of case study, as a highly intellectual and self-reflective group who consciously decided to create a public sphere of argument that was modeled on Old Testament rhetoric.

Again, I want to emphasize that I intend to critique but not to condemn this view of discourse. Although I think it is seriously problematic, I have also come to recognize the several very attractive aspects of it. And it would be foolish to condemn it as entirely destructive, because some of the most significantly constructive figures in American history have been strongly drawn to the ethos of the voice crying in the wilderness. Among my personal heroes are John Eliot, who used it to condemn Puritan treatment of Native Americans, Harriet Beecher Stowe, whose *Uncle Tom's Cabin* is clearly a Jeremiad, Henry David

Thoreau, who probably continues to do more for the cause of environmental protection than any other writer, and the man who got me started on my own errand in the wilderness, John Muir.

I have been far from isolated on this errand, receiving support of various forms from institutions and individuals. There are people who have been both friends and colleagues, providing emotional and editorial encouragement without which I would long ago have taken up dog training; I am especially indebted to Doug Hunt, Mike Bernard-Donals, Elaine Lawless, Trudy Lewis, Pat Okker, David Read, Hepsie Roskelly, Jeff Walker, and Nancy West. I am also indebted to a number of people with whom I have not had the pleasure of working, and who have provided astute readings of my work and helpful criticisms of conference presentations: especially Pat Bizzell, Gregory Clark, Jeanne Fahnestock, S. Michael Halloran, Nan Johnson, and Marie Secor. There are scholars whom I barely know, but whose elegant intelligence has been an inspiration: especially Sacvan Bercovitch, Jürgen Habermas, James Kastely, and Martha Nussbaum.

My continued interest in the project has been most helped by my students, who have repeatedly dragged me back toward what matters most. Some of those students, like Marsha Holmes and Ginny Jones, have also been helpful collaborators and readers. Sheril Hook's contributions have been extraordinary, finding lost citations, correcting mistranscriptions of Puritan passages, and tracking down vague memories of quotes. There are too many to name whose contributions are far more informal but absolutely necessary—especially the ones who cared enough to be carefully critical of the courses we shared.

I am most indebted to my teachers, especially Art Quinn. A scholar whose intellectual interests followed many currents, an administrator motivated by a desire to enable others to teach as well as he did, he was breathtaking in his ability to find the ethical rockshelf in the complicated shifting of specific situations. There were moments when I would certainly have concluded that academia was no place for a woman had he not simply insisted that I finish my dissertation.

My family and friends have been extremely patient, listening to rants and blatherings about Puritans and rhetoric when they must have been bored. My father gave me the wonderful advice of revising until the very sight of the writing is nauseating. Chester Burnette, Susan Dobra, Kylo Ginsberg, Carolyn Hill, Debbi McGath, Jim Miller, Molly Munro, Susan Pulliam, Jennifer Zarrelli, and the snigglers have been patient, encouraging, and cheering in the perfect combinations. Curtis

Clark and Suzette Griffith at The University of Alabama Press have been wonderful editors.

Portions of this work have been previously published (under the name Patricia Roberts) in "Habermas and the Puritans: Rationality and Exclusion in the Dialectical Public Sphere," *Rhetoric Society Quarterly* (winter 1996): 47–68; and "Habermas' Rational-Critical Sphere and the Problem of Criteria," in *The Role of Rhetoric in an Anti-Foundational World,* edited by Michael Bernard-Donals and Richard Glejzer (New Haven: Yale UP, 1998), 170–94.

1

Ghost in the Sphere

The time of his sicknes, nor the urgent cause, were not allowed to be urg'd for him; but whatsoever could be thought upon against him was urged, seeing hee was a carnall man of them, that are without. So that it seems by those proceedings there, the matter was adjudged before he came: Hee onely brought to heare his sentence in publicke: which was, to have his tongue bored through; his nose slit; his face branded; his eares cut; his body to be whip'd in every severall plantation of theire jurisdiction: and a fine of forty pounds impos'd with perpetuall banishment.   —Thomas Morton, 1637

Like a good Puritan minister, I will begin with my thesis. The paradoxical nature of the Puritan public sphere—that it was both authoritarian and democratic, hegemonic and individualistic—was the result of Puritan conceptions of how the truth is constituted, how one knows what is and is not true, how language can represent one's knowledge, and how the self is constituted and converted. In my exhortation, I will speculate that many of our current problems with argument, especially our cultural and pedagogical inabilities to enact a public sphere in which argument is a form of *inquiry,* can be explained as the ghost of the Puritan spirit that haunts our culture and classrooms.

Such an argument begs the rather obvious question: why study the Puritans at all? There are several answers to that question, ranging from the nearly pedantic (that the recent interest in the history of American rhetoric has left Puritanism strangely neglected) through arguments about the role of case studies in cultural criticism to my own idiosyncratic intellectual wanderings. Before going into more detail on those reasons, I'll mention that they are (more or less) compressed in the almost emblematic story that Thomas Morton tells of Faircloath (quoted above).[1]

The man whom Morton calls Faircloath, actually named Phillip Ratcliffe, was not a member of the church, so he was considered a sinner (or "carnall" man). He acted as agent for a man who lived in England, living off a portion of the money he was collecting on behalf of that man. He was having so much trouble collecting various debts that he was nearly reduced to starvation. When one church member refused to pay what was owed (on the grounds that debts to nonmembers could be ignored) Ratcliffe insulted him and any church that would have him as a member. In response, Ratcliffe was punished in the manner described in the epigraph above—fined, tortured, and banished. What one cannot help but wonder while reading the account is, why did the Puritans care so much about verbal abuse? Only people who took public discourse very, very seriously would feel so threatened by a conventional insult that they would respond in such a positively extravagant manner. Yet, they did not take public discourse so seriously that they thought a discursive answer would suffice. This incident is, in short, an emblem of the Puritan tendency to see language as simultaneously dangerously powerful and utterly ineffectual. And that is the paradox of Puritan rhetoric.

I

The recent resurgence of rhetoric has been coupled with an increased interest in the history of the discipline, but Puritanism—whether American, British, or Continental—is generally left out of such histories. Instead, these histories typically move from the Renaissance directly to the Enlightenment (Conley, Horner, Bizzell). If Puritanism is included, it is in the person of Peter Ramus in a chapter on Renaissance rhetoric, but this inclusion is itself somewhat odd. His inclusion in Renaissance rhetoric is jarring because—although chronologically correct—this puts him in exactly the category to which he was most hostile. He was, in fact, so antagonistic to rhetorical humanism that the triumph of his attitude has been posited as the primary cause of the death of Renaissance and humanist rhetoric (Ong, Sloane).[2]

As mentioned, it is most common simply to ignore Ramus and Puritan rhetoric altogether. For instance, most historians of the academic discipline of rhetoric in America begin in the nineteenth century, with, at most, some gesture toward the eighteenth (Berlin, Johnson, Horner). There are several scholars who have studied Puritan rhetoric, but their discussion usually remains within the seventeenth or early eighteenth centuries (Adams, Bercovitch, White).[3] There is, then, very little work that talks about Puritan rhetoric in the context of more recent scholarly debates regarding rhetoric, culture, and ideology. Simply because Puritanism has been ignored, then, it seems well worth investigating.

Ironically enough, in other aspects of Puritanism, scholars have often been criticized for overdetermining the significance of seventeenth-century New England culture for American history. Sacvan Bercovitch refers to the "American" Jeremiad (which encompasses nineteenth-century American literature), and the Puritan origins of "the American self." Other aspects of American culture and history have been tied to seventeenth-century New England: American political democracy (Shipton, Foster, J. Miller); American literary history with its tendency toward a particular kind of symbolism (Brumm, Feidelson); what has come to be called "the Antinomian strain" in American thought (Lang, Bercovitch); the importance of contract in American political thought (P. Miller); the American tradition of autobiography (Shea); the American inability to perceive difference of opinion as anything other than diabolical or degenerative (P. Miller, Bercovitch); and even the rhetoric used in the American Revolution (Stout). If these other scholars are correct in their presumption that American culture remains Puritan in significant ways, it seems reasonable to infer that Puritan notions of public discourse might continue to haunt the American public sphere.

The most intriguing possibility presented by the American Puritans is not, however, their possible causal relationship to current practice, but their status as a case study. Theirs was a conscious and highly educated attempt to form a public sphere of rational and ethical discourse—a place in which only good people would say only what is true. The ways and reasons that their attempts continually devolved into violence are important given current theoretical interests in discourse (as represented by, for instance, the communicative ethics controversy). In this regard, Charles Taylor has pointed out that historical explanation of a culturally powerful idea can be used to answer two similar, yet distinct, questions. The first is a question of historical genesis and tradition—what specific historical forces caused it to arise, dominate, and transform? This is largely a question of historical causation, of placing and tracing the history of the idea backward and forward. The second is not to insist on the long-term context for the idea, but for a deep analysis of the immediate context. An idea becomes a force not only because of its relation to earlier ideas but also because it explains something in ways that the people who hold it find powerful.

As Charles Taylor says, "What this question asks for is an interpretation of the identity (or of any cultural phenomenon which interests us) which will show why people found (or find) it convincing/inspiring/moving, which will identify what can be called the 'idée-forces' it contains" (Taylor 203). This method uses a historical period as a case study: an era or community becomes part of an analogy that might help to explain the same phenomenon in other eras and communities.

Taylor's two kinds of questions actually break into three here. The first is to show the chain of events that lead individuals to engage in unproductive methods of argument—to look at their training in public discourse. While this is not the approach I will take, it does seem an extremely important question to be pursued. After all, if there are serious problems with the American public sphere of argumentation, it is likely that there are equally serious problems with methods of teaching argument. The second is to look at the history of public discourse in America. Scholars who have examined this have, for the most part, excepted American Puritanism. The third method is to look closely at an individual or community that most promoted the paradox of public discourse as hyperbolic rationality and that would be a close and careful study of American Puritans.

My argument is that the Puritan failure to find discursive resolution of conflict was a failure of imagination in that their models of the mind, argumentation, the self, and language precluded their finding ways for people with genuinely different views on important issues to engage in dialogue. And I suggest that the history of rhetoric provides much richer fields for reimagining discourse, but this failure is not unique to the Puritans. My interest in this topic arose out of teaching argumentation in freshman composition courses, preparing graduate students to teach composition, and my alternating puzzlement and irritation with the way argumentation is typically discussed in contemporary composition journals and conferences. This book is not an attempt to link Puritan practices and the current status of argumentation through a historical genealogy of American rhetoric. Although such a study would be extremely valuable, it would also be extremely long. Later I will discuss Weber's metaphor of the ghost of Puritanism haunting the economic sphere in order to suggest that there is a similar ghost in our public sphere. But I am not saying that it is the only ghost or that the history of American discourse is some kind of linear progression from Puritanism. The Puritan failure of imagination haunts us, and it is probably an especially active ghost because of the influence of New England universities in the history of rhetoric, but it shares the house. In other words, the history of American attitudes toward public discourse is not itself monologic; there have always been other voices, and at times they have been much louder than Puritanism.

For instance, recent scholarship has emphasized the important shift that took place with the advent of Jacksonian democracy and American sentimentalism. Whereas the late-eighteenth and early-nineteenth-century public spheres promoted intellectualism, high style, and the aristocrat as the ideal rhetor, Jacksonian democracy relied on a kind of common man rhetor who was openly anti-intellectual (see especially Cmiel). Neither of these models was specifically Puritan, especially since they were promoted by people whose public ideals were often classical (Jefferson), Anglophile (Adams), or sentimental (Jackson). Nor were they the only models available—Gregory Clark and S. Michael Halloran have shown the variety of theories and practices operating within the oratorical culture of the nineteenth century. Some of these theories and practices (such as Timothy Dwight's) can accurately be called Calvinist (Clark and Halloran 57) but others are dependent upon post-seventeenth-century philosophical, literary, and educational movements (such as the notion of the picturesque, Clark and Halloran 226–46).

The history of rhetoric as an academic discipline in eighteenth- and nineteenth-century America is similarly variegated. As Nan Johnson, Winifred Horner, and others have argued, American pedagogies were strongly influenced by British (especially Scottish) movements. Hence, an argument that tried to make a direct and simple line of influence would have to explain the ways in which Campbell, Whateley, Locke, Hutcheson, and the other influential models were themselves influenced by the Calvinist origins of many American universities.

I do not want to be understood as arguing the opposite, however—that Puritanism had no influence on nineteenth- or twentieth-century American culture. Although other regions in America had other traditions (such as the Anglican tradition in the American South), and trends in eighteenth- and nineteenth-century American rhetorical practice were grounded in non-Puritan movements, Puritanism did not disappear. It is possible, for example, to point to the ways that those trends moved differently in America from similar trends in other cultures. American sentimentalism, for instance, was more explicitly (and institutionally) religious than English sentimentalism (which tended toward deism). American sentimentalism was also more explicitly political, and some of the great documents of American sentimentalism (such as *Uncle Tom's Cabin* and *Walden*) have justifiably been identified as instances of the American Jeremiad.[4] Other scholars have pointed to the strong influence exerted on American Romanticism by American Puritanism. As Mason Lowance has said, "The two vectors of historical influence between Puritanism and the American Renaissance may be seen in the connections between Edwards and Emerson in the area of epistemology, and between Edwards and Thoreau in the transforma-tion of the prophetic language of Canaan into a viable imagery for ex-pressing the hope of regeneration" (279).

Numerous other scholars have remarked on the Puritan origins of various more recent cultural traits. Mona Harrington has discussed "the myth of deliverance" that she defines as "the conviction that hu-man relations are, by their nature, harmonious, that *serious* conflict in human societies is unnatural and unnecessary" (16). She has argued that this myth, which she says is rooted in the American Puritans, has contributed to the American failure thus far to find solutions to com-plicated world and domestic problems. Perry Miller has described this same denial of difference as: "This habit of ambiguity [which] devel-oped out of New England's insecurity, out of its inability to face frankly its own internal divisions, out of its effort to maintain a sem-blance of unity even while unanimity was crumbling" (Miller, *From Colony to Province*, 199). Perhaps most famously, Robert N. Bellah et al.'s *Habits of the Heart* describes the essentially Puritan conflict between in-dividualism and community (see especially "Finding Oneself"). Amy Schrager Lang's argument regarding the Antinomian strain in Ameri-can literature emphasizes our tendency to admire the individual who relies on his/her own knowledge over and against what the crowd says. Bercovitch has argued that the American Jeremiad has resulted in the melding of sacred and secular issues in the sense of American identity. Garry Wills has suggested that the messianic tendency in Americans has been at the root of our interventionist foreign policy, and Frances Fitzgerald has argued that our Puritan heritage causes our continual creation of small communities intended to re-form the world.

In other words, Puritanism is one instance of monologism, and one might look at others. Puritanism is, however, distinguished from those others by how intellectually thorough it was. Whatever their faults, the Puritans were intellectually courageous, thinking through a system to logical conclusions that even they sometimes found frightening. For proponents of dialogism, then, it is an intelligent and informed opposition; it is monologism at its best. That is, the Puritans are a case study of a failed public sphere—failed in the sense that it did not encourage or permit people with different points of view to take stands on matters of community interest without incurring great risks, and it failed (I will argue) due to its monologic nature.

Jürgen Habermas's *Structural Transformation of the Public Sphere* has been characterized as posing the following question: "What are the social conditions, he asks, for a rational-critical debate about public issues conducted by private persons willing to let arguments and not statuses determine decisions?" (Calhoun 1). The question I am posing is only slightly different: What are the social and intellectual conditions that *prevent* a rational-critical debate about public issues conducted by private persons intending to let arguments and not statuses determine decisions? Or, to put it more simply: Why did a culture as self-consciously discursive as seventeenth-century New England have a public sphere in which differences of opinion frequently ended in banishment, torture, disenfranchisement, or confiscation? The Puritans' failure results, I will argue, from a variety of assumptions regarding ontology, epistemology, interpretation, and linguistic reference, or, more generally, from the Puritan denigration of rhetoric.

As James Berlin has famously argued, "A rhetoric is a social invention" (1). Berlin not only means that rhetoric is a social construct but also that it helps to reinvent what constitutes the realm of the social. Rhetoric, he says, is "implicated in all a society attempts. It is at the center of a culture's activities" (2). When students in a writing class learn a particular rhetoric, "They are learning assumptions about what is real and what is illusory, how to know one from the other, how to communicate the real, given the strengths and limitations of human nature, and finally, how language works" (2). These are precisely the kinds of assumptions that the various participants in Puritan controversies shared. Specifically, such apparently opposed figures as John Winthrop and Anne Hutchinson, or Roger Williams and John Cotton, had the same sense as to what the appropriate stance is for an individual to take when participating in public argumentation. Although they made different arguments, they made them in the same way: like an Old Testament prophet crying in the wilderness. In Puritanism, a good person will demonstrate his/her integrity by acting like Isaiah (or John the Baptist), announcing a hard truth to which all right-thinking people must assent.

I am concerned with rhetoric in Aristotle's sense—the ability to perceive the available means of persuasion—and the ways in which Puritan models of mind, God, and language restricted participation in public discourse to a single ethos and means of persuasion. In chapter 2, I focus on Puritan ontology, specifically the theory that reason is not a mental faculty but a thing that God has placed in Creation. This discussion necessitates some explication of the question of intention in distinguishing rhetoric from other forms of discourse, the Calvinist construction of predestination, and the distinction between informal reasoning (or probability-based argumentation) and demonstration. That relationship is further explained in the third chapter, in which I discuss Puritan epistemology and the purpose of sermons. As John Adams has argued, for the Puritans "linguistic values and religious interests were intertwined" ("Linguistic Values" 66). One can see the intertwining (if not entangling) especially in regard to Puritan metaphors for rhetoric—metaphors that effectively express the reasons for the Ramistic divisions of disciplines, Puritan assumptions about the writing process, and notions of clarity of meaning.

The fifth chapter begins with the following conundrum: one problem with dialogic theories of discourse is that they presume as a good (specifically skepticism) something that monologic discourse is committed to eradicating. There are two interesting implications: first, it limits the pragmatic consequences of traditional critiques of monologism (in that such critiques presume as goods things that which the Puritans would have found abhorrent, such as skepticism and religious tolerance); secondly (and consequently), it may therefore appear that dialogic and monologic discourse are simply two mutually exclusive but internally consistent systems. Although this conundrum points to one danger of various models of dialogic discourse (that they are themselves insufficiently dialogic) it is resolved by paying close attention to those parts of Puritanism—especially the sense of self implicit in conversion narratives—which presume skepticism, benefit of community conflict, and a polysemic view of language. Thus, the monologic discourse of the Puritans contains within it arguments for dialogism. In the conclusion, I return to the genealogy of my interest in this topic, in the ghost of Puritanism that haunts argumentation in the history of the American public sphere as well as the composition classroom.

Max Weber's *The Protestant Ethic and the Spirit of Capitalism* is an attempt to explain the patchwork origins of capitalism (that it flourished

in some countries and languished in others). It has become most famous as a critique of his own era. His argument was that something
that was conceived of as the heart of a reformed body of Christian
thought—the insistence on one's religious duty to pursue one's
worldly calling—caused a new way of thinking about one's participation in the economic sphere. Even when the body of Reformation
thought had died, this way of thinking continued, but in the form of a
kind of ghost: "The Puritan wanted to work in a calling; we are forced
to do so. For when asceticism was carried out of monastic cells into
everyday life, and began to dominate worldly morality, it did its part
in building the tremendous cosmos of the modern economic order"
(Weber 181). Weber has never been famous for elegant turns of phrase,
but it seems to me that central to his work is an especially nice use
of metaphor. He argues that a conception that had been a difficult but
powerful presence in the body of Protestant thought died, but the ghost
remained: "The rosy blush of [the Reformation's] laughing heir, the
Enlightenment, seems also to be irretrievably fading, and the idea of
duty in one's calling prowls about in our lives like the ghost of dead
religious beliefs" (Weber 182). Weber is playing with the productive
double reference of the German word "geist." Like the English word
"spirit" it means both mind (as in his title) and ghost (as in this passage). This play provides significant strengths to the method and nature of his interpretation of the continued Protestant presence. There is
something similar that one can see with the ethos of Puritan rhetoric.
Striving for monologism did not work especially well in early New
England, but it at least would have seemed a lively possibility in a
fairly homogeneous community (which was striving for even more ho-
mogeneity); it does not make sense in an avowedly pluralist culture.
Yet the ghost of Isaiah wanders through our public sphere.

2

The Ontic Logos, Predestination, and Aims of Probability

> Sorrow for sin, no good can win,
> to such as are rejected;
> Ne can they grieve, nor yet believe,
> that never were elected
>
> —"Day of Doom" stanza 145

The Puritan authorities of the seventeenth century have been described as the planters of the seeds of democracy who made persuasion the basis of society and, alternatively, founders of patriarchal oppression who grounded government in coercion.[1] Substantial evidence exists for both positions. Puritan authorities have been credited with promoting a democratic form of public discourse because of their continuous efforts to make public the decisions regarding public life: authorities often discussed their decisions in public meetings; church membership was dependent upon one's public declaration of faith; full members of the church had the opportunity to take a stand (quite literally) on issues regarding the community; ministers and other authorities were elected to office. The 1641 "Body of Liberties" guarantee that "Every man whether Inhabitant or fforreiner, free or not free shall have libertie to come to any publique Court, Councel, or Towne meeting, and either by speech or writing to move any lawfull, seasonable, and materiall question, or to present any necessary motion, complaint, petition, Bill or information" (35). As Stephen Foster says, "Though it sounds strange to say it, few societies in Western culture have ever depended more thoroughly or more self-consciously on the consent of their members than the allegedly repressive 'theocracies' of early New England" (156). Similarly, Joshua Miller has said that "the Puritan practice of allowing all adult male members of the community and church to vote for their magistrates and clergy made the bodies politic of New England among the most, if not the most, democratic in the world" (24).

The importance granted to public opinion (and the power granted to public discourse) is also indicated by the Puritans' tendency to invite the public to judge private controversies, not only through the specific dispute settlement arrangements but also through frequent appeals to the more abstract public sphere through publication of letters, pamphlets, and trial transcripts. Some scholars cite the sheer number of controversies as evidence of freedom of opinion; if, as Philip Gura argues, "*Heterogeneity*, not unanimity, actually characterized the colony's religious life" (emphasis in original, 7), then settlers were given the freedom necessary to follow their consciences. Finally, the central place accorded the sermon, the emphasis on training ministers, and the insistence on general literacy, all speak to the Puritan faith in public discourse. Such faith has caused some scholars to insist on the essentially democratic nature of the Puritan experiment. The strongest case has been made by Clifford Shipton, who is unstinting in his praise of the New England authorities: "One of the best criteria of the degree of democracy in any state is the amount of protection afforded by its laws to the individual; protection against the state itself, against other individuals, and against economic adversity. In this regard, the Massachusetts Code of 1648 was centuries ahead of the greater part of the world. The compilers, whetting their consciences to discover the will of God, selecting wisely, innovating when necessary, drew a document which is a milestone in the history of individual liberty" (140). As Foster notes, *Winthrop's Journals* contains many instances of Winthrop attempting to talk to people before punishing them. Mediation was one of the skills required of ministers, and courts and churches had various avenues of conflict resolution. But as William Nelson has shown, their methods of conflict resolution could only function under circumstances of high uniformity. Those methods broke down when the conflicts concerned wide differences of opinion or matters of important religious or political doctrine.[2]

In other words, Puritan methods of conflict resolution could not function when a deep conflict existed. The treatment of Friends is especially important to remember in the light of claims of Massachusetts being unique in its attention to individual freedom; as one scholar has noted, Massachusetts was unique from 1656–61 in a particularly ugly way: "Barring one Vatican-ordered Quaker execution during this period, the Massachusetts Bay authorities would stand alone as the only governing elite that found it necessary to condemn Quaker missionaries to death. . . . Whippings were extremely severe, banishments were often ordered in the dead of the Massachusetts winter, and imprisoned Quakers were in immediate danger of starving or freezing to death" (Pestana 325). Of the major discursive controversies of the seventeenth century, only the issue of the Halfway Covenant was resolved discursively; the others—such as those caused by Thomas Morton, the Antinomians, Roger Williams, and the Quakers—were almost all resolved through coercion of one sort or another.

That these incidents resulted in banishment and sometimes execution has caused some scholars to typify the Puritan authorities as only concerned with coercion: the trials, pamphlets, and speeches are then explained as more or less cynical attempts on the part of authorities to rationalize their behavior for themselves and the public. Scholars such as Ivy Schweitzer, Lad Tobin, and Ann Kibbey, for example, have insisted that the Puritans were authoritarians who engaged in what has come to be called hegemonic discourse: "[Cotton] preached hopeless obedience to a systematic prejudice. His apparently expansive prophecy of the Puritans' millennial rule narrowed to the belief that there was only a single locus of meaning, only one space and time, only one social category with the authority to determine meaning: the Puritan elite. . . . Appropriating the determination of meaning to themselves, they maintained their social power through their refusal to declare, and thereby limit, the significance of their own discourse, relying on the threat of violence, or the fact of it, to sustain the social conditions of their own imagining" (Kibbey 147–48). Hence, for Kibbey, the massacre of Indians at Fort Mystic and the repression of dissidents equally result from this refusal to recognize the multiplicity of the material world.

Bercovitch has argued that the American Jeremiad, an originally Puritan form of discourse, has historically enabled communities to enforce conformity and repress political change through refusing to acknowledge conflict: "Whether the writer focused on the individual or on history, whether he sought to vindicate society or to ingest society into the self, the radical energies he celebrated served to sustain the culture, because the same ideal that released those energies transformed radicalism itself into a mode of cultural cohesion and continuity" (*Jeremiad* 205).

This rather paradoxical point—that the American Jeremiad describes dissent in precisely the way that disables it—has been summarized by Joseph Alkana: "The logic of the American jeremiad demands that the centrality of the community routinely be reconceived by the marginalized individual consciousness. And the individual consciousness, authorized by the community, no longer appears as a detached and free point of origin for ethical action" (xii). In this view, Puritanism permits individualism only as long as individuals are behaving like one another.

In short, it appears that the central scholarly question in regard to the Puritan public sphere was whether it required conformity or permitted diversity. The proximate inquiry that must first be pursued is why the question of conformity versus diversity is generally answered in terms of the motives of the participants—that is, the issue of diversity is typically rephrased to the issue of whether the authorities who so frequently relied on violence to resolve initially discursive conflict *intended* to create or prevent freedom of thought.

I

The Antinomian controversy and the Roger Williams–John Cotton debate are two of the most documented discursive conflicts from the early era. Although they were the most famous, there is no good reason to believe that they were atypical in ways other than their notoriety. They shared a basic pattern with other (less famous) controversies: the authorities heard reports that someone was espousing heretical opinions; this situation was investigated (generally by an authority questioning the accused person); the person was invited to recant; if the person refused, authorities conferred with one another and began formal proceedings, which typically resulted in recantation and punishment.[3]

Because I will refer to these controversies throughout my argument, they should be briefly summarized. The Antinomian controversy was ostensibly over the correct way to describe the precise relationship among election, adherence to the law, and assurance of election without falling into Arminianism or Antinomianism. That is, one of the more vexing questions in regard to predestination is whether one can feel assured that one is elect by looking to certain signs—such as the ability to follow God's law. This is closely tied to the equally puzzling balance that Calvinists tried to maintain in describing the cause and effect relationship of behavior and grace. Calvinists condemned the

Catholic doctrine, which they described as "Arminianism" for seeming to suggest that engaging in godly behavior leads to grace—that one can cause grace through one's own will. Yet, Puritan authorities, for various reasons most likely related to social control, did not want to disengage behavior entirely from grace. By the time of the Antinomian controversy (1637), most ministers, with the exception of John Cotton, appear to have accepted two compromises: the doctrine of signs and the doctrine of preparation. They preached that the ability to adhere to God's law was the consequence of grace and therefore *might* be a sign of election (but it might also be hypocrisy), and it *might* be the way that the individual prepares for grace.

To various Puritans, including a woman named Anne Hutchinson and the Boston minister John Wheelwright, this latter explanation regarding preparation and grace sounded like Arminianism (or what was also called a "covenant of works"). For them, this reinterpretation of predestination seemed like a backsliding away from God's word into something less rigorous but more palatable, a sweetening of doctrine. They condemned this reinterpretation in various fora, including meetings in the Hutchinson home. Hutchinson, like many people, held informal meetings at her home at which community members discussed religious and political issues. At these meetings, she appears to have indicated her own views on the matter, and those views were deeply critical of most ministers. Hearing that they were being criticized, other ministers visited these meetings, and they seem to have tried to get her to repeat her criticisms.

It remains unclear the extent to which Hutchinson openly condemned other ministers (or whether she simply praised John Cotton at their expense). It is clear, however, that something was going on at those meetings, for there was growing dissatisfaction and mistrust in various congregations. The unrest either originated in or collected at Hutchinson's house. The unrest was so powerful that it resulted in the governorship being taken from Winthrop when an ally of Wheelwright was elected.

The authorities' main problem was that the Antinomians claimed the support of the influential minister John Cotton. Cotton had been a famous preacher in England, and he remained famous as a minister and thinker. He had praised Hutchinson, and she continually praised him. Furthermore, his own views on predestination remained strict, and his thinking contained a mystical element that was not unlike Hutchinson's. The distinct possibility existed that Hutchinson was doing nothing more than repeating what she had heard Cotton say. The authorities' response had two aspects, a theological and a political. They began by exchanging documents with Cotton in order to test the heterodoxy of his opinion. At the same time, they maneuvered to get the governorship away from Hutchinson's supporter Henry Vane. They held a synod that condemned the Antinomians and that had two consequences. It produced a report of sorts, a long list of heretical beliefs that may or may not have had anything to do with what Hutchinson or the people allied with her actually believed. More important, this synod brought Cotton onto the side of the authorities. Secure in their alliance, the authorities moved to banish the political leaders of the Antinomian party in November 1637.

But Hutchinson had not been one of the political leaders. In his preface to the collection of primary materials on this controversy, David D. Hall says that the authorities perceived Hutchinson to be the real root of the problem, but her failure to participate in the open political contests made it difficult for them to find a pretext to banish her. All she had done was to have meetings in her home at which she may or may not have criticized the established ministers. The authorities brought her before the General Court in proceedings that were somewhat irregular and that some scholars see as an attempt to trick her into some admission that would provide a pretext for banishing her. In the transcript of this examination, one sees a very bright woman debating with her accusers, and continually frustrating their attempts to make her views seem groundless. There is a moment, though, when things suddenly turn against Hutchinson (when she claims divine inspiration for her interpretation of Scripture). Winthrop describes that moment and what was so offensive about it: "And, after many speeches to and fro, at last she was so full as she could not contain, but venter her revelations; amongst which this was one, that she had it revealed to her, that she should come into New England, and should here be persecuted, and that God would ruin us and our posterity, and the whole state, for the same" (*Winthrop's Journals* 1: 240). She was condemned at this examination; then she was tried by the Boston Church and banished and excommunicated in March 1638. Her subsequent death in an Indian raid near Rye, New York, was interpreted as a providential sign of her guilt.

The Williams-Cotton debate is not quite as dramatic and is famous primarily because of the documents that were exchanged after Williams left Massachusetts. It began, however, in somewhat similar ways to the Antinomian controversy in that authorities heard that Williams was speaking out against certain points of doctrine—in this case, practices regarding ordination of ministers. Hearing that he was going to be arrested and banished, he left for Rhode Island. John Cotton wrote to him in 1636 to justify the decision of the authorities (and probably to defend his own participation in that decision). In this letter, the issues expand to include not only Cotton's behavior and the general issue of the legality of the proceedings against Williams, but other accusations, such as that Williams had been skeptical of the legality of the original Massachusetts charter. Cotton's letter was published in 1643 (possibly by Williams himself), and Williams published a rejoinder that more explicitly raised the question of prosecuting someone for saying things that are critical of the religious authorities. Williams published another (and longer) treatise on the subject of religious toleration that was partially a response to the 1635 statement by the Massachusetts clergy and partially a response to an essay by John Cotton that had not been formally published. This essay, which Williams called "The Bloody Tenent of Persecution," provoked a response on the part of Cotton in 1646, which he called "The Bloody Tenent, Washed and Made White in the Blood of the Lamb." The last document in the exchange, which Williams called "The Bloody Tenent Yet More Bloody," was published by Williams in 1652, the year that Cotton died.[4]

It is typical to say that Cotton and Williams were arguing about the freedom of conscience, which they were, but not in the sense that we might assume. Neither of them denied the importance of freedom of conscience, and both asserted that no government should infringe upon that freedom. They even agree on the definition of freedom of conscience, in the abstract—that no government has the right to force an individual to go against his or her conscience. They disagree as to whether Williams's situation, as well as the general Massachusetts practice of punishing dissenters, constitutes an instance of using the law to attempt to subvert conscience. Cotton's rather paradoxical but almost certainly quite sincere argument can be briefly paraphrased: the Massachusetts authorities used the law to attempt to force people to follow their own consciences. The Massachusetts authorities, Cotton argued, were motivated by the desire to ensure that people were free to do what they truly knew to be right.

The Antinomian controversy and the Williams-Cotton debate shared several points of issue. In both cases, the question of Scriptural interpretation was eventually raised as a kind of meta-discourse during the argument. That is, both participants used Scriptural citations as the bases for their arguments, so they had to reject the citations of the other. They typically did so by accusing the other person of using the wrong method of interpretation—of imposing upon the text something that existed in their own minds; that is, they were attempting to force the text to submit to human will, whereas the true method was to submit one's mind to what clearly resides in the text. This particular meta-argument was repeatedly connected to the other recurrent theme in Puritan public controversies: the question of what motivates dissent. This latter question has remained an issue in scholarship regarding Puritanism.

As previously mentioned, arguments regarding the degree of freedom in the Puritan public sphere are frequently stated in terms of the sincerity of the participants—whether the authorities genuinely intended to create a realm of perfect discursive freedom or whether they were actually motivated by a desire to establish and preserve their own authority. Defenders of the authorities often assert that Puritan ministers, whatever flaws they might have had, felt deep affection for their congregations and were, therefore, sincerely motivated. David Leverenz characterizes Thomas Hooker's attitude as pastoral love: "He knew his people, and yet he loved them (almost) as they were" (70), and Sargent Bush refers to Hooker's pastoral love that "made him want to affect these listeners in whatever way he could" (23). Hooker, whom Bush calls "a voice in the wilderness" (314), was filled with good intentions to his audience; determined to save them, he self-consciously shaped his sermons to be as effective as possible: "Hooker was not willing to let [sinners] go their way to hell if there was any chance of reaching them" (22). Nevertheless, such characterizations of the authorities' motives are somewhat troubling in that they are difficult to reconcile with the doctrine of predestination. In addition, attributing good intentions to the Puritan authorities ignores the ways that a very strong case can be made for insincerity on the part of the ministers and sincerity on the part of the dissidents.

Puritan authorities, many of whom were trained as attorneys, violated their own legal principles in order to secure conviction of Hutchinson, a violation that was even noted at the time. Winthrop's own transcript of the trial shows that observers complained that not only was the result of her "examination" a foregone conclusion but also that basic principles of justice were abrogated in order to ensure her banishment, such as permitting her accusers to act as her judges, permitting vague accusations, not requiring that her accusers testify under oath, and banishing her for actions that were not technically illegal.[5] Hutchinson complained, with some justice, that the accusations were based on misrepresentations of statements she had made in private and that the statements for which she was condemned were in response to direct questions. That is, she had been tricked into saying things that were then taken out of context to be used as incriminating. These procedural violations can be seen as evidence that the authorities were more concerned with silencing Hutchinson than with promoting or pursuing the truth. There is, then, a serious problem with asserting that the authorities were sincere: Certainly they believed in what they were doing, but the evidence strongly suggests that they were quite willing to engage in sophistries along the way.

Even more problematic is that attributing sincerity to the authorities implies insincerity of some form on the part of the dissidents. There appears to be a strong (and essentially Puritan) narrative that only one side in a controversy can be sincere. So, the narrative that asserts that the authorities were sincere appears to necessitate positing that the dissenters' protests were motivated by something other than sincere religious conviction. This viewpoint almost inevitably pathologizes the dissidents. The most famous is probably Emery Battis's argument that Hutchinson did not actually care about the religious issues in that she did not even really understand them: "Her emotional bent rendered her overly susceptible to some theological notions and shut her mind too firmly against others, so that she was, perhaps, unwarily drawn into a naive oversimplification of certain subtle and complex points of doctrine" (5). Battis's narrative is quite clear: an overly emotional woman, who did not fully understand the complex arguments of her intellectual betters, made trouble. Her emotional bent was caused, he has argued, by menopause, and it resulted in her desire for power; the particular theological controversy was less important than that desire: "She was a woman who . . . sought an emotional outlet which seemed to resolve itself most effectively in the acquisition of power and influence over the lives and spiritual destinies of her fellows. Had she been born into a later age, Mrs. Hutchinson might have crusaded for women's rights or even wielded a hatchet for temperance's sake" (6).

The rather obvious problem with this interpretation is that Hutchinson had a considerable number of followers, very few of whom could possibly have shared her menopause. He suggests that her followers felt that the movement "offered an outlet for the expression of latent hostilities against the society. Or it may have helped to confirm the individual's own self-evaluation, and to offer psychological compensation for an inferior status in the community" (261). Kai Erikson also pathologizes the dissidents, arguing that they were motivated by a desire to be martyred, so that the governmental persecution of them simply encouraged them. Others have assumed that Hutchinson, Williams, the Friends, and others were motivated purely by a desire to be in power, by pique or by sheer bad nature. This particular narrative (one used at the time by such participants as Winthrop) makes Hutchinson into a persecutor with perverse motives such as illness, desire for worldly gain, desire for power, or desire to protect her own sins, whereas the victims (the authorities like Winthrop) were motivated by a genuine concern for the community, by sincere religious conviction, by a knowledge of the needs of the public, and by their intellectual understandings of doctrine.

This narrative, oddly enough, is shared by those who take the sides of the dissidents, but the terms are simply reversed. Such narratives tend to assert that the persecutors (in this case, the authorities) were pathologically motivated, whereas the dissidents (the victims) were sincerely motivated. For example, it has been suggested that the authorities' actions were due to their hatred of the material world (Kibbey), their hostility to women's ways of knowing (Tobin), or their terror of female power (Lang). This narrative is common, and it is appropriately Puritan. As will be argued later, Puritans imagined only two possible identities in an audience: the reprobate and the elect. This binary opposition may explain their tendency to throw the kitchen sink at opponents: if one was on the other side, in one way, one was in the service of the devil and therefore in the same category as everyone else in his service. This tendency often resulted in sheer absurdity, as when Quakers were assumed to be in the service of Catholics or to have been converted through Catholic clerics. (For more on this equation of Quakers and Catholics, see Pestana, 339.) Again, this is a strangely Puritan way of telling the story. As Hall has pointed out in his unusually balanced account, both sides of the Antinomian controversy "relied on the same rhetorical pattern" (*Antinomian*, xiii), which he summarizes as "a sharply dualistic understanding of the good and the bad: orthodoxy and heresy, the forces of God on the one side, the forces of Satan on the other" (*Antinomian*, xii). In essence, secondary accounts of the controversy have retained that rhetorical pattern.

This dualistic understanding operates throughout Winthrop's account of the controversy, but it was also employed by Hutchinson and her allies. As Hall notes, "Wheelwright invoked the image of a holy war between the true followers of Christ and their enemies who taught a covenant of works" (xiii). The similarities in rhetoric are even more specific. Both sides characterized the other as insinuating subtle impurities into true doctrine, of making doctrine impure, motivated by a desire to make God's hard ways much easier. For instance, Winthrop says that the attraction of the Antinomian doctrine is that it opens "such a faire and easie way to Heaven, that men may passe without difficulty" ("Short Story" 203). As mentioned earlier, the objection to the covenant of works was that it made the way of heaven seem open to everyone.

The rhetorical similarities in the two sides is not merely rhetorical in that it was fundamental to their argument. Both sides carried the argument on through a set of dualistic categories. Wheelwright uses the standard Calvinist arguments against a covenant of works in his sermon, including ones that people such as Thomas Shepard used when they condemned the same doctrine. The authorities' point was that they were *not* preaching a covenant of works, but Wheelwright did not bother to introduce their arguments in full complexity. Similarly, the authorities like Winthrop appear to have emptied their luggage of epithets in describing Hutchinson and Wheelwright, pulling out every heresy of the previous several hundred years in looking for ways to characterize their opponents. It does seem fair to say that the authorities were almost, but not quite, preaching a covenant of works, and that the dissenters were almost, but not quite, preaching Antinomianism. The latter were most certainly not libertines or familists, and they were not advocating the kind of doctrine that would lead to the social uproar Winthrop and others predicted. Still, by placing Wheelwright and Hutchinson in the category of Antinomians, the accusers could invoke the fears raised by other spiritual extremists who had sometimes pillaged towns. The Antinomians, by placing the doctrines of preparation and signs in the category of Arminianism, could accuse the authorities of backsliding into Anglicanism—the rejection of which was the justification for the Puritan errand. Consequently, as Bercovitch notes is typical of American public discourse, each side could accuse the other of constituting a divergence from the true purpose of the Puritan errand.

It is important to consider the effect on the audience of such a strategy. Although this demonizing of the opposition may confirm the sentiments of those already in agreement, it irritates or enrages those who understand the complexity of the argument being oversimplified. As is shown by the reaction of readers sympathetic to Hutchinson, for example, Winthrop's account does not move her supporters to see her as dangerous, evil, or even especially heretical. Only someone unfamiliar with Hutchinson's complete argument or already highly sympathetic to Winthrop might be persuaded (or, more accurately, confirmed in the conviction) of her heresy. Similarly, the rhetoric in which Wheelwright engages provides no means to move his opposition. Whatever their faults, the Puritan authorities were no fools. The doctrine of preparation, whether or not it was a backsliding, merited a complex critique. But Wheelwright never provided that critique. In fact, the rhetorical pattern used by both sides in the controversy seems almost designed to alienate the opposition, for it continually involves characterizing oneself and one's supporters as martyrs for Christ, whereas anyone who disagrees is an enemy of Christ motivated by hatred of Christian doctrine.

There is, then, a way in which the rhetoric undermines itself. The rhetorical strategy of attributing bad motives to one side ensures that one cannot reach one's opposition discursively. Although it may help to confirm the opinions of some people, it guarantees that one cannot persuade others. This limitation points to one very significant problem with the theoretical aim of describing discourse by intention: it slips into the narrative of saints and sinners far too quickly.

The project of inferring motive is methodologically flawed at a deeper level as well. As long as the argument about whether the Puritans promoted persuasion or coercion is cast in terms of motives, it cannot be productively resolved because the argument tends to become circular: people who see Winthrop as a good man assume (and therefore assert) that he had good motives; his good motives are then used as evidence that he was a good man. People who admire Hutchinson's intelligence, wit, and courage assume that her motives were good; her good motives are used as evidence that she was a martyr for truth, not power. There is a rhetorical parallel in the primary and secondary material: just as making this assumption during the debate contributed to the inability to resolve the conflict in a noncoercive manner, so does making this assumption about the debate seem to necessitate scholars lining up on one side or the other.

II

Inferring motive, however unproductive, seems a necessary part of studying the rhetorical culture of early America, however, because some of the most influential theories of discourse make motive the central defining term. Habermas, for example, distinguishes consensual communication from strategic action on the basis of the intentions and desires of the speakers; in consensual communication the speaker "must have the intention of communicating a true proposition" and "the speaker must want to express his intentions truthfully" (*Communication* 2). In manipulative action a speaker may *appear* to engage in consensual communication but actually intends to deceive (see, for example, *Communication,* 210n2d). Another proponent of Habermas's project, Dietrich Böhler, has emphasized the role of intentions in dialogic discourse, explaining what it means internally for the dialogue to be reciprocal: "This means that 'I' must make clear to myself, must reflexively acquire a knowledge of what 'I' in my communicative role as a person arguing *owe* to the others as representatives of the community of argumentation. Then and only then can my acts of argumentation (not only fortuitously but regularly) succeed" (emphasis in original, 119–20). Ironically, Böhler's argument is extremely similar to the Puritan conception of a productive public sphere: everyone must have good intentions.

The tendency to discuss the criteria for dialogic public discourse in terms of participants' inner life is common.[6] As in Habermas and Böhler, descriptions of dialogue generally emphasize the "willingness" of participants to consider other points of view, to permit open-ended discussion, to critique their own position. Or forms of discourse are distinguished on the basis of speaker aim. John Gage defines rhetoric as discourse that "aims at producing mutual understandings" in contrast to eristic discourse that is "aimed at winning any given case, and knowledge of the truth [is] no more than a means to that end—to be used if warranted or hidden if necessary" (154). Whereas most of these theories make certain qualities of the interior life normative, the taxonomies of other theories rely on inferences regarding motive. For instance, James Kinneavy's influential *Theory of Discourse* asserts that "the aim of a discourse determines everything else in the process of discourse" (48), and he proceeds to define all the possible types of discourse—expressive, persuasive, informative, literary—on the basis of authorial aim. Expressive discourse is when language is used "as the simple vehicle of expression of some aspect of the personality of the encoder. . . . uses of language whereby an individual or a group expresses its intuitions and emotional aspirations. The expressor dominates the process" (38–39). Persuasive discourse is determined by the language use in which "encoder, reality, and language itself all become instrumental to the achievement of some practical effect in the decoder" (39). Informative discourse is primarily referential; it "stresses the ability of the language to designate or reproduce reality" (39). Literary discourse "calls attention to itself, to its own structures, not as references to reality or as expressions of personal aspirations or as instruments of persuasion, but as structures worthy of contemplation in their own right" (39).

A brief application of Kinneavy's taxonomy to Puritan discourse indicates a few of the problems with categorizing discourse on the basis of speaker intention. By this taxonomy, one would determine whether or not Puritanism promotes persuasive discourse by determining whether ministers, for instance, were simply expressing themselves, hoping to effect some kind of practical change, trying to reproduce reality, *or* drawing attention to the language itself. That is, speakers would decide the kind of discourse in which they were engaged by inferring their motives toward their audiences. However, in addition to the problems previously mentioned, using categories based on speaker motive in order to determine whether Puritanism promotes or prohibits public deliberation rests on a distinction (persuasion versus demonstration) that the Puritans themselves rejected.

One might make the following kind of common-sense critique about distinguishing rhetorical discourse on the basis of speaker motive: Because the most common approaches to characterizing Puritan discourse depend upon inferring speaker motive, the implicit taxonomies should involve distinctions that those speakers might also have made—that is, the conscious or semiconscious attitude that a rhetor has toward his/her audience while creating and presenting the discourse. Such a reliance on self-characterization is the method that Kinneavy himself uses to argue that all discourse is not rhetorical: "Otherwise everything is rhetoric; even Plato's dialogues and Aristotle's treatises and Baudelaire's poems are rhetoric—a thought which would cause all three of these gentlemen to turn over in their graves"

(217). So, the question is: How can we describe Puritan ministers' intentions in a way that would not cause them to stir in their graves?

The answer is that any argument that suggested that they were trying to persuade rather than demonstrate would have dismayed the Puritans because Kinneavy's taxonomy rests on a basic distinction that the Puritans themselves rejected. Puritan ministers explicitly rejected such a distinction because it relies on a series of assumptions—about causality, about proof, and about power—that would have been blasphemous. It seems highly unlikely that any Puritan minister would have described his motives as intending to effect a change, would have (consciously or semiconsciously) told himself he hoped to persuade his audience (as opposed to express himself, demonstrate a factual point, or confirm already present beliefs), since the practical ability of any individual to effect a change was severely limited by several Puritan theories of logic and power, the most obvious of which is predestination.

Predestination is often ridiculed, but as Calvin points out, predestination was always part of Christian theology, albeit tempered by various semantic or theological distinctions that leave human beings with some degree of free will.[7] Calvinists such as the American Puritans should not be discussed as though they were the inventors or sole believers in the doctrine; they were distinguished by their initial rigidity in regard to the doctrine but not in holding it at all. I must emphasize that this rigidity should not be pathologized: the strictness with which they drew certain conclusions regarding predestination is the result of their conviction that God's mind and therefore God's world is perfectly rational.

Puritan discussions of predestination indicate clear awareness of the emotional and intellectual objections to the decree. Calvin admits that "it is horrible to be heard, that of such an infinite multitude a small number only should be saved" (from Calvin, *Romans* 275).[8] John Norton refers to predestination as the "wonderful and dreadful administration of God" (73). Norton's discussion of predestination has a long series of objections and answers, as well as advice about how ministers should handle the admittedly difficult topic in their sermons (50–101). Michael Wigglesworth's poetical description of Judgment Day, "Day of Doom," consists mostly of sinners arguing with Jesus about the justice of their being sent to hell given predestination, and sermons on the subject always have a section in which the minister refutes various objections. Those objections can be classed into two general categories: arguments concerning the logical consequences (e.g., if God is the author of everything, then he must be the author of sin); and arguments concerning the rhetorical effect of insisting that humans have no will (i.e., that the doctrine is unappealing or discouraging).

The argument that God cannot be all-good and all-powerful in the face of evil has a long history in Christianity. It is particularly complicated given the Puritan unwillingness to let anything like a sharing of power be the basis of the explanation. The doctrine—what Norton calls the "Decree"—is fairly simple: "The Decree, is God by one eternal-free-constant act, absolutely determining the Futurition, i.e. the infallible future being of whatsoever is besides himself, unto the praise of his own Glory: the cause, and disposer of all things, the Antecedent and disposer of all events" (*Orthodox Evangelist* 51). This perception of God—as the un-moved Mover, the final cause of every being and every event—is explicitly a rejection of any kind of theological dualism, that is, an explanation of origins that would give any power to another entity (such as Satan).

The response to the argument that God is the author of sin is complicated for a modern audience to follow, since, at least as explained by Norton, it relies on two systems of thought—Augustine's definition of evil and Aristotelian categories of causality—that have since fallen from favor or been transmogrified. Yet, it is necessary to understand the explanation not only because predestination is so central in Puritan sermons but also because the Puritan explication of the doctrine highlights two premises of Puritan thinking: first, that everything, including God's will, can be rationally explained; second, as will be discussed later, that power is of limited amount, and it is diminished through sharing.

Norton's argument that God does not cause sin relies upon the Augustinian view of evil as being merely the absence of good: evil is not a thing that exists, that has some kind of actual presence or ontological being. Only goodness actually exists, and evil is merely the absence of good, a kind of defect. Because it has no real existence, Norton says, it has no efficient cause; since it is a defect, it can at most be granted a sort of "deficient" cause. He concludes that it is therefore logically impossible that God causes evil; something perfect and complete has no deficiencies and therefore cannot cause them: "The evil cleaving to the action is a defect, therefore hath no efficient, but a deficient Cause: Now God cannot be a deficient Cause, because he is the first and absolutely perfect Cause, therefore cannot be the cause of a *non-ens,* i.e., a nullity, or of that which is defective" (*Orthodox Evangelist* 63). In other words, God does not cause evil, because evil has no cause whatsoever.

It should be emphasized that this argument is logical, that is, it relies on careful use of the logical principle of noncontradiction: something cannot be A and the opposite of A at the same time (God cannot be an efficient and deficient cause at the same time). This use of logic for a theological (and ontological) issue typifies the Puritan belief that logic is true, that logic represents the actual structure of the universe, because God himself is the very source of reason: "REASON, what is it, but a *Faculty* formed by GOD, in the Mind of Man, enabling him to discern certain *Maxims of Truth,* which God himself has established, and to make true *Inferences* from them! In all the Dictates of *Reason,* there is *the Voice of God*" (emphasis in original, C. Mather, *Christian Philosopher* 283).[9] Alexander Richardson begins *The Logicians Schoolmaster* with an essentially Ramistic (albeit somewhat circular) argument on the logical structure of all Being: "Now then there must be reason in every thing, because I am to see every thing by my Logicke, which is the rule of reason, *ergo* all things must be lyable to it, *ergo* it must apprehend the *logismus* in everything" (emphasis in original, 9). William Perkins insists that the conscience, which always calls one to correct doctrine, is actually a part of the faculty of understanding, which "is that facultie in the soule, whereby we use reason" ("A Discourse of Conscience" 5). At least until the religious revival of the Great Awakening, Puritan sermons and documents rely on such logical principles and schema as the principle of noncontradiction, the syllogism, and the different kinds of causes—principles that would be taught in logic courses.

Norton's summary of his argument that God is not the author of sin (because there is no such thing as a deficient cause) is only intelligible in light of the distinctions involved in Aristotelian causality:

> Adam's transgression, was the eating of the forbidden fruit: The *external moving* cause, was the temptation of Eve, and instigation of Satan: The *efficient cause* was Adam's abusing of the liberty of his will, which yet is better called a *deficient,* then an efficient cause; because sin is a defect, not an effect. The will of man, as acting deficiently from the rule, was the cause of sin. The *material cause,* or rather the material of sin, is the entity or action wherein sin is found: Sin is an *accident,* and therefore can have no being, but in a Subject. . . . The *formal cause,* is its deformity, and aberration from the Law of God. Though Sin hath no *final*

cause (as neither indeed properly hath it any other) its end being more aptly called a *Term,* then an *End:* Because sin in itself is only evil; yet by *accident,* it becometh conducible unto a greater good: In that God hereby takes *occasion* to manifest his Glory, either by pardoning of it in a way of mercy, or by punishing of it in a way of justice.

(emphasis added, Orthodox Evangelist 71)

As difficult as it may be for a modern reader to follow Norton's argument, it is a highly rational answer to the argument that God causes sin in a world that accepts Aristotle's categories of causality. Norton's explanation that God is not the author of sin relies on distinguishing among five kinds of "causes" (external moving, efficient, material, formal, final) and distinguishing causes from things that might look like causes but are not (term, accident, and occasion). The external, material, and formal causes of an event do not properly answer the question "why did it happen?" as much as "what was the catalyst?" "what was the contributing matter?" and "what shape did it take?" respectively.[10] The efficient and final causes do answer the question "why," and they do so by indicating the specific agent and the final purpose. For Aristotelian causality, the final cause is always the most important.[11]

If all final and efficient causes come from God (or, more accurately stated, if God is the final and efficient cause of everything), and if sin does not properly have a final or efficient cause, then it is perfectly logical to conclude that God is not the cause (properly speaking) of sin. God does cause some people to remain reprobate, and people who are reprobate shall inevitably sin, but "Reprobation is not the cause, only the Antecedent of sin" (*Orthodox Evangelist* 66). It is not, therefore, that God causes sin, as much as that he permits some people to remain in a sinful state. Those people are then punished for sinning, not for being in a reprobate state.[12]

One sees a nearly identical defence of the logic of predestination in Wigglesworth's popular "Day of Doom," a poem that describes the scene on the Day of Judgment. Most of the poem consists of an interchange between various kinds of sinners (babies who died before baptism, heathens who never heard Scripture, people too stupid to understand doctrine, and so on) and Jesus. Each group of sinners puts forward some argument as to why they should not be sent to hell, and Jesus—as both judge and prosecutor—justifies doing so. One group, whom Wigglesworth calls "an impudenter sort," argues:

How could we cease thus to transgress?
      how could we Hell avoid,
Whom Gods Decree shut out from thee,
      and sign'd to be destroy'd?

Whom God ordains to endless pains,
      by Law unalterable,
Repentance true, Obedience new,
      to save such are unable:

Sorrow for sin, no good can win,
      to such as are rejected;
Ne can they grieve, nor yet believe,
      that never were elected.   (Wigglesworth 144–45)

Jesus' reply makes the same distinction as Norton's: "I damn you not because / You are rejected, or not elected, / but you have broke my Laws" ("Day of Doom" 147).

This issue is not simply a pedantic question about Aristotelian causality or the complicated logic of predestination. In addition to having profound implications for the limitations of human discourse, what makes this issue so interesting is that it is an emblem of Puritan theories of power. For the Puritans, to say that God causes everything necessitates saying that nothing else causes anything. Thus, the particular way that the American Calvinists discussed predestination is logically dependent upon the Puritan conception of power. Only if one takes the doctrine seriously as a logical doctrine can one understand the impact that it had on Puritan conceptions of community and discourse.[13]

Besides being an extremely limiting notion of power, this explanation of causality is teleological. Every thing and every event has a purpose, and that purpose is its true cause. It is typical in Christian uses of the Aristotelian causes to identify God's will as the final cause, as Norton does, and to thereby equate the cause of something with its function in God's plan. This equation is extremely important in Puritanism: God causes major events, like the smallpox epidemic that killed so many Native Americans, and he causes minor events like Samuel Sewall's chamberpot to break, and he does both for his own specific purposes. All events have a place in God's history. This sense of God's will being behind every incident has significant consequences for Puritan theories of history, literature, and interpretation, which will be discussed later. The concept of God's will also has very important, but complicated, consequences for theories of power. In order to explain those consequences, it is necessary to belabor some apparently obvious points whose significance can easily be overlooked.

For the Puritan explanation of causality, causes and origins are combined, as are consequences and purposes. One can especially see this combination in a private document, like Samuel Sewall's diary: He can interpret the spiritual significance of his chamberpot breaking during the night because the experience is a text that God has written—that is, God is the origin of the plan for it to break *and* of the action of its breaking. Because the origins of all actions reside in God's will, human beings cannot will anything: "The Will of God, is God himself willing, his Will is the Rule of our wills, Whose Will else should be the Rule? The Will of God is the cause of all things, the constituted Rule of Righteousness therefore being an effect, it must needs proceed from the Will of God, otherwise there should be an effect which were not resolved to the first cause" (Norton, *Orthodox Evangelist* 148). Seen in these terms, it becomes more clear that predestination is primarily a theory of power: If all causes resolve to God, all power to cause anything also lies with God.

Underlying this perception of causality and will is an important way of thinking about power: power is an entity of limited quantity that moves in one direction. That is, all power comes from God and is used by him on or through beings lower in a hierarchy. In this system, only two possible positions exist in regard to the possession and use of power: one holds it and uses it in order to compel obedience to one's will, or one is the object of someone else's use of power and obeys that person's will. I will discuss later the consequences of this hierarchical view of power for ways of imagining the relationship of minister and congregation, but here I want to point out that this perception of power leads one into a logical dilemma that can only be resolved by denying any power to humans: either God has all the power and human beings have none, or human beings have some power, in which case God is not omnipotent. It was perfectly logical, then, for the Puritans to conclude that human beings cannot exert power. All that they can do is be used by God in order for him to compel obedience on the part of someone else. One can also understand why the Puritan authorities did not describe themselves as using their power to exert their own wills; they defined themselves as powerless tools that God uses as he wills. Any coercion—physical or verbal—that might seem to come from them is merely flowing through them from God.

This way of perceiving power necessarily affected the place of dissent in the Puritan public sphere. Obviously, it severely restricted the ability of the American Puritans to imagine alternate areas or exertions of power in a community as anything other than a threat to (because necessarily a threat to reduce) the power of God's tools. In other words, with this view of power, dissent, difference of opinion, lack of agreement, and sedition are equally interpreted as attacks on God's power.[14] In addition, such a view of power ensured that the Puritans would think of power in terms of the ability to compel obedience, the ability of one person or group to get another person or group to behave a certain way. Because it thereby makes uniformity of behavior a sign of governmental authority, this sense of power guaranteed that the Puritans could only see difference (of opinion or behavior) as a sign of governmental weakness.

A hierarchial and reified sense of power was the foundation of the Puritan assumption that human discourse cannot be the cause of salvation. To give such power to the minister would be to take it from God, just as it would grant the minister the ability to will something. Perkins explains that it was sheer arrogance to think that a minister could give such an effective sermon as to save a sinner: "For by this means the voice of the church should be of greater force than the voice of God and the whole state of man's salvation should depend upon men; than which what can be said to be more miserable?" (*Work* 335–36).[15] Because only God can actually will the salvation of an individual, the sermon can simply bear witness to the truth: "The church also may bear witness of the canon, persuade she cannot" (*Work* 335).[16] To return to the question of intention, a Puritan minister could not consciously choose to do certain things that would *cause* a person to change. A minister, being a human being, cannot cause change of any sort. Obviously, as will be discussed in more detail later, this sense of the inability of human discourse to save a sinner has complicated consequences in a culture that makes the sermon the center of public discourse.

Some scholars have characterized Puritan rhetoric as essentially classical, but a brief comparison to classical rhetoric on this point of determinism shows how fundamentally misleading this characterization is. Whereas Calvinism explicitly denies human power, classical rhetoricians like Aristotle assume it. For Aristotle, the ability to deliberate well in inherently uncertain situations—the central virtue in his ethics and the most valuable skill in his rhetoric—is so important precisely because, in his view, there is so much about which one can and should deliberate: not only communal actions, but even such apparently individual decisions as the ethical course of action in a very particular situation. One of the reasons that Aristotle included invention and arrangement in *Rhetoric* (although these topics are also discussed in his works on dialectic) is that he insists that the kind of reasoning appropriate to public discourse is very different from that which is appropriate to a small group of specially trained philosophers. With a large crowd there is no point in arguing from first principles because such a group cannot follow a long chain of reasoning. Since the audience is not trained in dialectic, one cannot expect them to be able to follow the complicated rules of that art.

This is not to say, as did the Puritans, that the enthymeme is simply a compressed syllogism. One uses enthymemes and other forms of proof in rhetoric because rhetoric is a different way of knowing the world; it is and reinforces a different kind of knowledge. Dialectical reasoning is not appropriate in rhetoric because public deliberation relies on such realms of knowledge as politics and ethics, which Aristotle insists, are not susceptible to certainty (unlike, Aristotle says, mathematics.) Instead, such fields depend upon the quality of *phronesis*—the ability to take all sorts of information into consideration in order to determine the best course in the very particular instance at hand. It is because the particular is so important that *phronesis* is not a science: "Matters concerned with conduct and questions of what is good for us have no fixity, any more than matters of health. The general account being of this nature, the account of particular cases is yet more lacking in exactness; for they do not fall under any art or precept, but the agents themselves must in each case consider what is appropriate to the occasion" (*Nicomachean Ethics* 1104a). Because one cannot rely on certainty, one must be well trained in the art of evaluating uncertain arguments, that is, probability. Aristotle's only limitation of the realm of deliberation is pure common sense: we can only deliberate about things over which we actually have control ("We deliberate about things that are in our power and can be done" [*Nicomachean Ethics* 1112a]). We do not deliberate about mathematics or the past, for we cannot actually change either (the rules of mathematics are true regardless of whether or not we perceive them, just as we cannot change the past by arguing about it). Instead we pursue them in a scientific manner, looking for certainty.

This sense that some kinds of questions cannot be answered with certainty and require a different sort of pursuit is the origin of the classical distinction between probabilistic reasoning (or persuasion) and demonstration. This same notion is repeated among modern rhetoricians, as when Thomas Farrell argues that rhetoric is the central civic virtue because moral problems "can be resolved only through a willingness to extend our own energy through an unfinished, imperfectly understood episode" (100). In such a tradition, that ability for an individual or community to consider information in the realm of the probable is the ability to deliberate, and the process of inventing an argument is the process of deliberating over both the best policy *and* the most effective way to argue for that policy. So, as in humanist rhetoric, the skills taught in rhetoric are useful for learning as well as persuading. A belief in the value of deliberative rhetoric is closely associated with the sense that the most important topics are not subject to tests of truth and falsehood, but instead to utility or to explicitly contextual and contingent standards, so that as Charles Kneupper says, "In the rhetorical tradition, at least from Aristotle on, rhetoricians have been concerned with argument in the realm of the contingent. . . . Thus, by definition rhetorical argument has always dealt with matters of uncertainty" (117). Or, as is conventionally said, rhetoric is a way of thinking. More specifically, classical and humanist rhetoric presume that the art of creating probable arguments grounded in consensus is a way of knowing.

That presumption is precluded by Puritan theories of discourse because the basic distinction between demonstration and persuasion is itself rejected. Because of predestination, Calvinists put everything in the same category as the past or mathematics, that is, in the realm of demonstration. Deliberation, at least in Aristotle's sense, has no real place because human beings do not actually control anything. Since everything has been predetermined, determining a course of action requires discovering and obeying God's will, not making the future. Thus, as far as the Puritans were concerned, probability or rhetorical reasoning, the kind of reasoning used in Aristotle's deliberation, does not even exist, properly speaking.

The classical distinction between demonstration and persuasion is based on the idea that one knows different things in different ways—that demonstration is appropriate for areas in which certainty is possible, and persuasion is appropriate for areas in which one must rely on probability. The theorist of rhetoric who most strongly influenced the American Puritans—Peter Ramus—refused to acknowledge that such a difference in judgement might even exist: "Nor indeed should we consider it possible that rhetorical judgment is one thing and dialectical judgment another, since for evaluating whether something is truly useful, suitable, fitting, or has the qualities it seems to have, there is one faculty of judgment which the syllogism alone executes and accomplishes" (106). Therefore, those aspects of the rhetorical process that depend upon the faculty of judgment—invention and arrangement—are acquired through learning to create and criticize syllogisms, that is, in logic and theology. Ramism quickly spread among Puritans, and the major theorists of Protestant preaching (such as Gabriel Harvey, John Rainolds, and William Perkins) were strongly influenced by it.

One can recognize Ramus's influence in Puritan statements regarding probabilistic reasoning. Rainolds says, "Grant that proofs which produce persuasion and proofs which produce certain knowledge are not different. Grant that proofs must be sought from the same science of discussing, and not from various arts, so to speak" (205). Puritan logic stated unequivocally that there is, in all the subjects of human discourse, "a signal difference, while some are true and some are false; and therefore it belongs to Reason to make the choice" (Arnauld 1: 1–2). And the method that Reason uses is not the enthymeme (crucial to Aristotle's notion of rhetoric) but the syllogism. All reasoning, Norton argues, is by syllogism: "Men understand by way of syllogistical discourse, viz. by reasoning; that is, by deducing and gathering conclusions from principles" (*Orthodox Evangelist* 17). According to William Ames, even the kind of reasoning done by the conscience is syllogistic (see *Of Conscience* 3–5). The typical definition of enthymeme in Puritan logics is a syllogism with one premise not mentioned—Richardson calls it "nothing but a syllogisme wanting a leg" (295). Arnauld's dismissal of the places is typical of such logics; he says to think that one might actually find out "matter" through the places "is a meer falsity" (3: 78).[17] In Puritanism, what had been the central parts of rhetoric—the enthymeme and the places—are either compressed forms of dialectical reasoning or utterly useless.

Here one sees that what is at stake is not merely a question of academic disciplines or methods of speech training. The Puritan stances toward rhetoric, public discourse, and human endeavor are closely linked. Attempting to base all discourse in certainty, the Puritans grounded all reasoning in dialectic, and they therefore excised from the discipline of rhetoric any of the skills that might teach one how to articulate or evaluate conflicting proposals on a topic about which one cannot be certain. That is, they made rhetoric nothing but embellishment: the "embellishment of speech first in tropes and figures, second in dignified delivery" (Ramus 86). In addition, the Puritan restriction of rhetoric goes hand in hand with the sense that one does not deliberate about important matters; instead, one determines God's will. One might look to one's fellow citizens in order to deliberate, but one does not pay attention to them in order to find certainty about God because truth is not to be found through human deliberation.[18] The reason, then, that Puritan rhetoric and public discourse are not means to the truth on any given matter is that the Puritans would not permit them to be.

It may appear that I have wandered far afield from the question of categorizing discourse by speaker aim. My argument is that such categorizing leaves one with either of two equally counter-intuitive descriptions of Puritan public discourse: that the Puritan ministers secretly intended to persuade their audiences, regardless of whether or not such an intention contradicted several central tenets of Puritanism; or, that there was no rhetoric in Puritan New England.

III

Rhetoric's oft-invoked claim to be a way of knowing is generally connected to some sort of skeptical epistemology. Specifically, rhetoric is skeptical about the ability of an individual to know anything with certainty and in its entirety. Gregory Clark refers to the "constructed, and thus contingent, nature" of knowledge that becomes particularly apparent in rhetoric (16). Knowledge is contingent for two reasons: First, knowledge is itself a construction, the result of interpretation. John Gage refers to rhetoric's "legacy" "with which even the earliest theorists of rhetoric had to contend: that in the use of language to describe reality, reality undergoes interpretation" (153). That process of interpretation is likely to be influenced by various forces; as Thomas Sloane has said, "predicated on the idea that truth is probable, Ciceronian rhetoric is implicitly systematized epistemologically in its further insistence that probable truth is a function of public interaction, of verbal exchanges between people, of the construction of public form, and the search for advantage in persuasion" (143). But even if a person could perceive something in perfect accuracy, there is the problem of perspective: proponents of an active and diverse public sphere generally argue (or simply assume) that different perspectives are necessary because, as Hannah Arendt says, "Only where things can be seen by many in a variety of aspects without changing their identity, so that those who are gathered around them know they see sameness in utter diversity, can worldly reality truly and reliably appear. . . . The end of the common world has come when it is seen only under one aspect and is permitted to present itself in only one perspective" (52–53).

The second reason that knowledge is contingent in the rhetorical world is that rhetoric is skeptical about the ability of language to represent the world. This skepticism is, it has been argued, reflected in style. Thomas Sloane explains this attitude in the humanist rhetoricians: "That language is plastic was shown in puns and in verbal ironies. But this plasticity, this nominalism, was no more cause for despair than the contrarieties of living in a fluid and changeable world" (83). That is, rhetoricians play with language because language can never perfectly encapsulate truth. Even when trying to be absolutely literal and perfectly perspicacious, one is almost always talking around subjects, hinting toward meaning, and sometimes playing with language simply for joy. This is not to say that rhetoricians are necessarily nihilists about the capacity for language to be true, but that a rhetorical attitude toward language may well assume that language is most true when most playful. Later chapters will pursue the interactions of theories of knowledge and language implied by such antirhetorical theories of discourse as are assumed in Puritanism, but here the question concerns the different relation in regard to theories of reality.

Although it is conventional to connect rhetoric with a skeptical epistemology, there is not such a consensus about a necessary connection between rhetoric and any single ontology. The rhetorical tradition includes ontological nihilists like Gorgias and Christian foundationalists like John Donne. The Puritan denigration of the discipline of rhetoric, however, *is* necessarily tied to a particular theory of reality. Puritan ontology is relatively simple to describe (which is not to say that it is simplistic). Yet, to discuss Puritan ontology, it is necessary, once again, to anticipate the discussion of epistemology. Gage has distinguished two ways of perceiving knowledge: one, the rhetorical, is to see knowledge as the activity of knowing; the other view is to see it as object that someone may or may not have. In the rhetorical world, "knowledge can be considered as something that people *do* together rather than as something which any one person, outside of discourse, *has*" (156). Or, as Farrell describes the Aristotelian notion of rhetoric: It "is a sense of rhetoric as intrinsic to a conflicted, indeterminate human nature—a rhetoric not of being but of becoming" (103). It is a process and activity.

For the Puritans, knowledge is an object, and it resides in things. Furthermore, this object exists originally in God, who, in the act of creation, has placed it in the world: "Now man not being able to take this wisdome from God, which is most simple, therefore it hath pleased the Lord to place it in the things" (Richardson 18). Knowledge is carried from objects, like scent or light, to our minds: "as flowers doe send out a sent, or odor that doth affect our sense of smelling, so every precept of Art doth *spirare* a sweet science to our glasse of Understanding, which is indeed that irradiation, which we heard of in Divinity in the Creation of things" (Richardson 18). Knowledge is a material thing that moves from Creation (in which God has placed it) to the mind. The container for this thing, this knowledge, is logic: "So wee knowe that Logicke carries from the thing to man" (Richardson 8).[19] As odd as this notion may seem to the modern mind, it was quite common in pre-Cartesian philosophy. In such a world, one that contains what has been aptly called "the ontic logos," Reason is not merely a mental faculty that enables a person to order Being, nor to infer some more or less hidden taxonomy; instead, Reason *is* Being. Reason is the static hierarchy of things created by God; logic is the art that describes the true relationship of those things because it has the same set of relations within it. One of the sets of things in which God has placed this knowledge is the arts, or disciplines, which were themselves created by God. Because it is the art that is Reality, "Logicke is the most generall, and the first in order of the arts" (Richardson 11). Everything else is derivative of logic (grammar), a special application of it (geometry), or a way of presenting logic (rhetoric).

It is an understatement to say this ontology has important consequences for theories of public discourse, some of which I want to list briefly. First, and most obvious, it is a static sense of reality, so that knowing means submitting one's mind to the Reason that exists in things. Change, invention, and novelty are all disruptions of and deviations from the norm (which is, of course, normative). This has complicated implications for the rhetorical concept of invention and arrangement (which will be discussed later). There is one consequence of this static ontology that it is interesting to note here. It is, I suspect, this stasis that makes epistemological certainty possible—the number of things to be known is finite, and they will stay still eternally such that they can be known. A more dynamic ontology would logically necessitate a more skeptical epistemology, as a changing world must constantly be re-known. The reverse, however, is not true, in that although a dynamic ontology apparently requires a skeptical epistemology, a skeptical epistemology does not logically presume a dynamic ontology.[20]

In addition, this ontological and epistemological stasis is hierarchical; so that knowing anything, including one's self, means knowing its place in a static hierarchy. One can see here the source of Winthrop's considerable anxiety regarding social mobility, which is most famously expressed in his "Model of Christian Charity"—the sermon delivered aboard ship in which he describes the economic classes as intended by God and perfectly static. This sense of a static hierarchy extends to what it means to know a discipline: one knows the category of being that a discipline describes. The previously discussed equation of Logic, Reason, and Being, with its denial that knowledge might operate differently in different disciplines, means that, in all disciplines, to know is to be able to categorize, and vice versa. This equation of the ability to categorize and the ability to know shows the intricate distinction between ontology and epistemology: if Reason is in Creation, and Creation is itself a hierarchy of discrete entities, then to know anything is to know it clearly and distinctly. All meaningful language use is essentially a form of naming, and one can say that the name is true or false—that is, it does or does not correctly delineate the true boundaries of the Real identity. To know something is to know its name, and to know its name is to know its true place in Reality.

Finally, these categories—which include the categories of the disciplines—are Real and are created by God. Logic exists in the thing itself, so that the world is distributed into a hierarchy of categories; identity itself is static. It should be no surprise that the Ramistic teaching of logic (like most disciplines) relied on demanding that students memorize a taxonomy. Discovery of a particular argument is supposed to result (somehow) from knowing that universally applicable taxonomy. Although such reliance on memorization is a recurrent method in pedagogies of rhetoric, it is not inherently part of classical, humanist, or neoclassical rhetoric. On the contrary, many theorists of rhetoric insist upon or assume a dynamic model of categories, especially in regard to the invention stage. As Thomas Farrell states, "Rhetoric is, above or beneath all, an art of chance and circumstance" (97). When

Gage, for example, remarks that "intentions result from situations of conflict of knowledge, which are the mutual invention of the writer and the audience," he is assuming a model of creation that is unintelligible in Puritanism (167). He assumes that a writer's intention is created by the *particular* conflict, so a different conflict might have created a different intention; that is, the writer would have had different thoughts. Similarly, Farrell has noted the importance of the contingent and particular in rhetoric: "rhetoric is unavoidably biased toward the particulars—the persons, materials, and interests that are close at hand" (81). In a system that posits the eternity of knowledge, the particular is useless because thoughts that might change cannot be determined true or false; in fact, they are not properly thoughts at all—they are chimera with no real cognitive content.

As with Gage, rhetoricians tend to emphasize that knowledge is created by conflict, or, at least, the contrast of differences, so that it is impossible for anyone to learn without public discourse in which people genuinely disagree. Farrell has argued that rhetoric forces us to acknowledge that "there is need, at times, to firm up and complete our own reasoning practice through the intervention of competent, interested others" (73). In a static world, however, such controversies are useless, and deliberation need not involve any public at all: "A man may take counsell of himselfe, without counsellors" (Richardson 89). Participating in disputes, in fact, may be dangerous either because we may become emotionally involved—"It is a difficult thing not to loose the prospect of Truth in Disputes, there being nothing that more heats and exasperates all regulated Affections" (Arnauld 3: 130)—or because we may actually be corrupted by contact with sinful ideas. Nathaniel Ward warns that "prudent men, especially young, should doe well not to ingage themselves in conference with Errorists, without a good calling and great caution; their breath is contagious, their leprey spreading: receive not him that is weak, saith the Apostle to doubtfull disputations; much lesse may they run themselves into dangerous Sophistications. He usually hears best in their meetings, that stops his ears closest; he opens his mouth to best purpose, that keeps it shut, and he doth best of all, that declines their company as wisely as he may" (19). This sense that ideas are things that contact through touch is the origin of one part of the prophetic stance in monologic discourse: once one knows the truth, one speaks without listening to others because listening is dangerous.

The Puritan refusal to distinguish persuasion (based in probabilistic reasoning) from demonstration (based in proof)—"The arguments of orators do confirm and teach and explain, that is, they *demonstrate*" (emphasis in original, Rainolds 203)—contributed to the notion that the ideal public rhetor is a prophet. People are persuaded because they recognize that an argument is true; there is no experiential difference between knowing that a particular interpretation of Scripture is right and knowing that a mathematical answer is correct. Since certainty is the goal of all knowledge, and certainty is attainable, there is no reason to settle for anything less than certainty in public discourse. That is to say, the Puritans did not distinguish between the kind of intention that one might have in trying to persuade people toward a course of action and the kind of intention that one might have in demonstrating a geometrical proof. The function of sermons is to demonstrate the truth; the minister should strive "out of soundnesse of argument, and plaine evidence of the will of God, and the spirit of God, make truth knowne to the spirits of men: when a mans doctrine goeth so guarded and confirmed with Scripture, and sound and plaine demonstration of argument, that they stand as Mount Sion and are undeniable" (Hooker, *Implantation* 75–76).[21] If we categorize Puritan discourse on the basis of speaker aim, then, it is always demonstrative and never persuasive.

There is an apparent contradiction about Puritan attitudes toward rhetoric, which this rejection of persuasive discourse and probabilistic reasoning helps to explain. Puritanism was fundamentally hostile to rhetoric, but Puritan colleges continued to require that students take rhetoric courses. The explanation is that what the Puritans meant by "rhetoric" and what was taught in rhetoric courses was a pale version of what rhetoric had meant in the Renaissance. Hence, Miller's argument regarding the importance of rhetoric in the New England mind is slightly misleading. Although colleges did require that students take rhetoric courses, it was a very different discipline from, for instance, humanist rhetoric.

IV

I have left aside the question with which I began: was the Puritan public sphere open or repressive? I have only partially answered the rephrasing of the question: what were the aims of the most powerful members of that community of discourse? And my answer is essentially paradoxical: the rephrasing of the question, although common, precludes reaching a coherent answer because Puritan public sphere cannot be usefully characterized by taxonomies of discourse that emphasize intention. If one uses Kinneavy, one ends up with the conclusion that the Puritans never engaged in rhetorical discourse. This conclusion is odd in that one wonders why the Puritans would have engaged in so much of it under those circumstances, a question to be pursued in the next chapter. It also leaves one with an extremely broad sense of demonstrative discourse—one that does not particularly help resolve the initial question of whether Puritanism was coercive or democratizing. Obviously, then, the taxonomy is not helpful.

I have lumped together several taxonomies that more centrally address the issue of coercion, but, here again, the application is slightly puzzling. John Gage, Gregory Clark, Jeffrey Walker, and Maxine Hairston emphasize that the eristic or monologic discourse authoritatively tells the audience what to believe, but a dialogue involves the inclusion of different points of view. The problem is that the Puritan rhetor seems to have done both. As mentioned earlier, the majority of Wigglesworth's "Day of Doom" is a dialogue in which the criticisms of predestination are quite accurately voiced. Norton's *Orthodox Evangelist*, like many theoretical pieces of its era, uses the structure of objection and refutation, and as with Wigglesworth, the objections are not fallaciously oversimplified. Sermons, similarly, frequently include a section in which the minister lists counter-arguments to his proposition. Granted, these objections and counter-arguments are explicitly presented as evil-minded cavils, but they are *included.* So, inclusion and coercion are not mutually exclusive.

This criterion of inclusion, and its assumed opposition to coercion, is somewhat more complicated in regard to Habermas and it is worth exploring in some detail. In *Structural Transformation,* he defines the rational-critical public sphere as having three identifying characteristics: first, it is a realm that, at least in theory, disregards status in favor of rationality; second, the discussion within such a realm is the domain of "common concern," including criticism of the governmental authority; third, the realm is perfectly inclusive (at least in principle) "for it always understood and found itself immersed within a more inclusive public of all private people, persons who—insofar as they were propertied and educated—as readers, listeners, and spectators could avail themselves via the market of the objects that were subject to discussion" (37). It is the first claim that has both led to the most controversy and that has remained, more or less intact, throughout

Habermas's work (see, for example, "What Is Universal Pragmatics?" in *Communication*). In *Structural Transformation*, Habermas argues that the eighteenth-century *philosophes* articulated such a sphere, although they failed to enact it. In this regard, much criticism of Habermas is slightly off the point, in that he does not claim that the eighteenth-century *philosophes* actually created a perfectly inclusive realm of rational-critical discourse; they exemplify the reality of the goal, not the attainment of the state. He argues that at least in theory ideas were debated by anyone who chose to participate in the discussion by reading, writing, or speaking; he grants that in practice people were excluded on the basis of gender and class, "but as an idea it had become institutionalized and thereby stated as an objective claim. If not realized, it was at least consequential" (36). Because it was genuinely consequential, one cannot claim that it was merely an ideal; because it was not fully achieved, one cannot claim that it was a fact. It remains, therefore, in the borderland of substantive project.

One can see the problems in applying Habermas's argument to the Puritans. They were, as I have said, deeply concerned with ensuring that all discourse followed the rules of rationality. Sermons, for instance, were structured as logical demonstrations, theological issues used logical terms (such as Norton's discussion of predestination), and the study of logic was required for ministers. But logic was not restricted to the training of ministers; it was generally described as a necessary quality of piety. Pious living, as Cotton Mather said, means following the dictates of Reason: "Whatever I see to be *Reason*, I will comply with it, from this Consideration, *'tis what* GOD *calls me to! Reason* extends to Points of *Morality*, with as much Evidence as to those of *Mathematicks*" (emphasis in original, *Christian Philosopher* 283). The New England Puritans also, like the *philosophes*, claimed to value rationality over speaker status, and they were deeply suspicious of argument from authority. Arnauld's logic, for instance, says that individuals should feel free even to reject famous philosophers when such authorities veer from Reason (1: 36–37), and Richardson says that grounding an argument in authority is far inferior to direct proof (see, for example, 230). John C. Adams has argued that Richardson typifies the Puritan mistrust of argument from authority—it should, at least, have backing in individual experience or action ("Alexander Richardson's Puritan Theory" 259). Puritanism required that individuals not take their beliefs from institutionally constructed authority, but, instead, themselves reason to what is true and right: "Any permanent institution requiring his dependence upon others, or unquestioning obedience that is based upon any sense of a permanent defect in some men, was a form of bondage that kept him from becoming fully human" (Adams, "Alexander Richardson's Puritan Theory," 264). Obviously, it is absurd to suggest that the early American Puritans made an ideal public sphere, nor do I mean to suggest that they were, in practice, no more exclusionary or oppressive than the *philosophes*. Like the *philosophes*, however, they did *claim* to be a perfectly inclusive and rational community, and claim is the most important criteria for Habermas. Thus, at the very least one must say that his criteria are seriously flawed.

One might argue that Habermas's discussion of rationality in "Remarks on Discourse Ethics" and *The Theory of Communicative Action*, volume 1, restricts his argument to "justificatory discourses in which we test the validity of universal precepts" rather than discussions of practice (35). In other words, his criteria do not apply to the Puritans because they did not distinguish between purposive rationality and theoretical discourse, and his sense of the true nature of argumentation only applies to the latter. In such a case, the best that one might say is that Habermas's argument is relevant to a small part of the kind of arguments that any community might have: If the purpose of communicative ethics is not to determine what a community should do, but what values might serve as the universal basis for the decisions for that community, then it will be a long time before communicative ethics can provide the kind of discourse that might practically enable people to critique the practices of oppression of institutions. Restricting the argument only to theoretical discourse accordingly gives up half of what was the justification of the project—that it would define a perfectly inclusive and liberatory form of public discourse. It is not perfectly inclusive, because only people with a very narrow form of education appear able to participate; it is not liberatory, because it does not deal with topics related to practice.

How then does one distinguish a coercive public sphere from one that is genuinely open to disagreement? After all, the Puritans did not intend to create a coercive public sphere, but one in which any form of force would be a last resort. However, they also defined ideal discourse and the ideal individual in such a way that the community would frequently find itself in that last resort. Put simply, the Puritan public sphere was intended to be a region of dialectic deliberation, a purely inclusive arena in which matters of public import would be decided only on the basis of the rationality of the arguments presented. Exclusion or coercion would be used only in those circumstances when someone's carriage or arguments demonstrated an irrational refusal to abide by the rules of argument, those whose carriage or arguments clearly demonstrated ill will, irrationality, or dishonesty. This was the theory, and, at least insofar as one can infer motive, this was the intention of the Puritan authorities.

In practice, the Puritan public sphere was violently exclusive and heavily dependent upon various forms of coercion. So, the question becomes: what was wrong with the Puritan effort such that noble intentions resulted in a coercive public sphere? The short answer is that they tried to have discourse without rhetoric and demonstration without persuasion. I will argue that it was their attitude toward demonstration that blunted their efforts—the specific assumption that demonstration is preferable to persuasion as the basis of public discourse because demonstration is more true and equally effective. It seems to me that it is not enough to understand what was limiting in this attitude without also understanding how it came about, and as Charles Taylor has said in another context, "One has to understand people's self-interpretations and their visions of the good, if one is to explain how they arise" (204). Understanding how the Puritans defined themselves and what seemed to them so good about a demonstrative public sphere requires an exploration of several closely related concepts: their notion of the range of power and will exerted by any individual (i.e., the doctrine of predestination); their sense of what constitutes and what forms the identity of the regenerate; their theories of how reality is constructed and perceived; and their assumptions about how that reality is best represented in language.

3

The Place of the Opposition

Hence there is only one meaning for every place in Scripture. Otherwise the meaning of Scripture would not only be unclear and uncertain, but there would be no meaning at all—for anything which does not mean one thing surely means nothing.

—Ames, *The Marrow of Theology* 188

To belabor the obvious, if our definitions of dialogic discourse do not actually differentiate it from monologic discourse, we cannot know what theories or pedagogies promote one versus the other. Whether one's purposes in defining a noncoercive form of argumentation are historical-cultural or pedagogical, the criteria must effectively distinguish those methods that (however intended) tend to devolve into exclusion and violence from those that do not. I have suggested in the previous chapter that in either area—cultural or pedagogical—making the aims of the speaker the major criterion is deeply unsatisfactory because such a distinction requires that we define speaker aim in ways that the speakers themselves would not recognize. Speaker aim, always problematic, is especially so when attempting to work with people whose epistemology and ontology preclude their being able to recognize, let alone intend, dialogue. I have two intentions in this chapter: First, I want to follow more carefully a strand that was repeatedly pointed to in the previous chapter: the role that the Puritan epistemology played in the complicated seventeenth-century New England public sphere. Second, I will suggest that the humanist concept of "controversia" has many of the qualities of other forms of dialogic discourse but does not require the inference of speaker motive. Pursuing this discussion will involve a paradox that will not be fully examined until the fourth chapter: that many of the criticisms of Puritan discourse (such as that it is monologic) would not have seemed to the Puritans to be points of criticism, but congratulation.

I

Thomas Sloane has argued that rhetoric is unique in its reliance on "controversia"—a method of invention *and* presentation, a way of determining one's own position as well as considering how to present the argument. Sloane defines controversia as "a question in contention, one with (at least) two sides, and anyone who would think controversially must give some thought to *both* sides" (emphasis in original, 59). The two sides "exist simultaneously" (59); that is, one is not simply rejected in favor of the other, nor is either presented merely as part of an antithesis. Or, to put it another way, this rhetorical method is not merely a method of presenting or embellishing material, but a way of perceiving the world. Sloane argues that rhetorical humanists like John Donne present dualities (such as the flesh and the spirit, or reason and emotion) as concepts that must be simultaneously contemplated and equally privileged. Sloane's definition of rhetoric shares certain characteristics with several of the ones discussed in the previous chapter, but it is distinguished by its not depending upon guesses regarding speaker motive. One sees controversia in the texts themselves, by seeing that such texts end somewhere other than where they began, having moved through the inclusion of both sides of various apparently antithetical concepts.

Like Gage, Clark, Walker, and Hairston, Sloane links rhetoric to a skeptical epistemology: "Our claim is that nothing can be known with certainty, everything must be argued for. This claim does not prevent us from having opinions about the probable, but you cannot have an opinion about the probable until you put the facts in contention, argue all sides of any matter, and make a final judgment, which is like a comparative estimate" (115). And as with the others, this is not total skepticism, as much as an acceptance of the best argument contingently; whereas one does not accept any answer as closure to the controversy—"Suspension of judgment is the starting point and rationale of *controversia*" (emphasis in original, 115)—one does evaluate respective solutions. It is not, therefore, the sort of skepticism that forbids any answers at all, just answers that close the possibility of further debate. This openness to future answers contributes to a certain kind of inclusiveness. Because one must remember that what looks like the fullest answer now may seem incomplete at some future point, other answers are not exactly rejected as much as set aside. Most typically, they become part of the argument in that the thesis of the argument includes rather than simply rejects or ridicules the opposition(s). The notion of controversia helps to explain exactly what distinguishes dialogic rhetoric from monologic discourse. It is not simply whether or not the opposition is included, for such inclusion was a regular part of Puritan discourse.

Sermons and theological treatises often have a section that follows the dialectic model of "Objection" and "Answer" in which heretical views are presented and condemned. It was a common rhetorical strategy for ministers to use the second person in sermons, often apparently speaking directly to the sinners they were condemning. This pattern is even evident in Puritan literature—Wigglesworth's use of debate in "Day of Doom," for instance. Looking carefully at the contrast between controversia and the Puritan attitude toward the opposition enlightens what kind of inclusion of the opposition contributes to an open public sphere and what precludes nonviolent resolution of conflict.

Sloane's controversia presents rhetoric as an art with a cognitive function; one considers two opposing positions not in order to choose between the two as much as to come to a new understanding of the issue. Thus, controversia will result in all participants in the discourse reaching a third position not obviously present when the conversation began (such as an uncomfortable and tenuous balancing of both extremes, a compromise, or a synthesis). Rhetoric assumes that this new understanding could not have been reached without the conflict between the initial two. Without considering both sides, one would never have reached the third. This epistemological assumption has interesting pedagogical consequences: it requires, as I said above, a chaotic and recursive composing process. At various times in the history of rhetoric, pedagogues have been comfortable with this chaos. At other times, however, there has been an insistence on a linear and orderly process.

From the classical era on, the composing process has generally been divided into different stages (or steps or subprocesses): invention; disposition; style; memory; delivery. As with the Puritans, these steps are often described as cognitively and chronologically linear: one invents the argument through one's reading in Scripture and theology; then one discovers the arrangement most "natural" to the argument; then one adds the appropriate level of ornamentation; then one makes one's notes or writes one's script; and finally one delivers the sermon with the appropriate pronunciation and emphasis.

In contrast, the process of composing implied within controversia (and humanist rhetoric generally) is disorderly. One poses a question, considers both sides, and comes to some position (invention). But in the process of arranging the discourse (disposition), one must again consider both sides, which might cause one to reinvent one's own position. Even in what is supposed to be the final "stage," delivery, one might change one's argument because of audience reaction—spending longer on those sections that seem to puzzle the audience or adding additional arguments to those portions that fail to gain assent. This chaotic composing process was not new to Renaissance humanism.[1] Augustine, for example recommends that the speaker look to the audience to see how long to spend on a topic, continually handling the same topic in different ways until the audience signals that they have understood: "An attentive crowd eager to comprehend usually shows by its motion whether it understands, and until it signifies comprehension the matter being discussed should be considered and expanded in a variety of ways. . . . As soon as it is clear that the audience has understood, the discourse should be finished or another topic should be taken up" (134–35). Such attention to audience reaction precludes a strictly linear process of invention, especially one in which invention and disposition cease before the product is presented; presentation and invention are synchronous, and the product remains a process.

This recursive process involves not simply a reinvention of one's argument but of one's identity. There is, as Sloane notes, a continual reinvention of the self through a continual interweaving of the topic and how one feels about the argument: "The process is both mind- and mood-altering" (203). Similarly, Farrell argues that rhetoric requires that "character in public must constantly be re-formed and performed through the rhetorical choices we make in engaging responsible others" (80). The topic, argument, arrangement, and self are reinvented through a consideration of oppositions. Aristotle argues that this inclusion of opposition, especially in the process of inventing an argument, enables not only the rhetor but the community to identify the best arguments. The notion of "best" argument here is productively ambiguous—Aristotle's defence of oppositional thinking is not dependent merely on the rhetorical utility of the practice. He says that considering the other side enables one to get closer to what is true because "things that are true and things that are just have a natural tendency to prevail" (*Rhetoric* 1355a). This use of "strict reasoning" enables us to "see clearly what the facts are" and thereby enables a rhetor to confute someone who "argues unfairly" (*Rhetoric* 1355a). For the rhetor, the consideration of the opposite point of view enriches one's understanding of the truth of the matter and of one's rhetorical situation. It enables a rhetor to discover what is true, predict opposition arguments, and create the strongest argument for one's own case. In short, this recursive approach to invention and disposition has cognitive, rhetorical, and stylistic consequences.

Humanist rhetoric not only emphasizes invention and reinvention *per se* more than, for instance, Ramistic rhetoric, but also particularly values methods useful for extemporaneous speaking. Controversia has long been especially vital when the public sphere is a place of multiple voices—quite literally. The relationship of multivocality and controversia are mutually reinforcing. If the sorts of places in which one might speak are ones in which the opposition can also speak, then both the rhetor and the audience have just heard the opposition voices. In such a place, the rhetor can and should respond to the arguments just made; whereas a prepared speech is likely to be at least slightly off the point. The methods of invention under these circumstances need to be highly practical, easily remembered, and appropriate to very disparate rhetorical situations. Rhetoricians who try to teach how to include an unpredictable opposition will suggest a variety of methods of invention, including using the places (Aristotle's *Rhetoric*), or playing with language itself (Erasmus's *De Copia*), or drawing on all of the fields of learning (Cicero's *De Oratore*). These methods are disorderly in two senses: used in a recursive and slightly chaotic manner, they are also drawn from a lack of respect of strict disciplinary boundaries. The places that Aristotle uses in *Rhetoric* overlap with his discussion of the same topic in *Dialectic*; Erasmus's amplification draws from the field of grammar; Cicero famously argues that the rhetor should know a little bit about several areas. This cavalier attitude toward disciplinary boundaries, as well as the assumption that the composing process is recursive and dynamic, are the characteristics that make the processes of production in humanist rhetoric necessarily so chaotic.

Defenders of rhetoric praise this eclecticism—as when Brian Vickers refers to Aristotle's "remarkably open-minded spirit of inquiry into everything that depends on language" (23)—but it was precisely this disorderliness that so frustrated the Ramists, and that caused them to insist upon clearer and cleaner categories of the arts, ones that concurrently premised a strictly linear and nonrecursive composing process. Charles Taylor neatly catches the Puritan horror of disorder of any kind, and their tendency to see disorder as sinful, when he describes why Puritans became so interested in enforcing a detailed social order: "The reconciled person feels the imperative need to repair the disorder of things, to put them right again in God's plan. . . . To the Calvinist, it seemed self-evident that the properly regenerate person would above all be appalled at the offence done to God in a sinful, disordered world; and that therefore one of his foremost aims would be to put this right, to clean up the human mess or at least to mitigate the tremendous continuing insult done to God" (228). And in this regard the Puritan ontology becomes important. Because Creation is perfectly ordered, and because everything was created by God, there is a true order to *everything,* from the right sort of clothing to the true arrangement of the liberal arts. Disorder, dynamic taxonomies, changes in order, variation due to context (in any realm) are all forms of turning from God's manifest will. Thus, for the Puritans, a disorderly method of invention is a sinful one.

Ramists called following the order and procedure placed in Creation the "natural method." That natural method presumes that everything begins with what Richardson calls "simples": "The world is one . . . it is made of many simples" (8). The single correct method in all arts is to use analysis and genesis to break down something into its simples or build something up from simples (24). To understand anything is to be able to name all of the simples that compose the whole. Logic, because it is the art that best identifies those simples and their various possible true arrangements, is the highest and first art (Richardson, 14, 17).

Sloane, Ong, and others have pointed out that Ramists make logic the primary art because they believe that this discipline deals with the universally valid premises that constitute true knowledge: "For I see everything by my Logicke, and that sees nothing but arguments, axioms, syllogismes, and method: *ergo,* I can see nothing but that that it doth thus dictate to my reason" (Richardson, 9). Logic is not a human-created art, nor merely a mental faculty that exists only in the mind; Richardson complains that "the Schooles runne into many absurdities, whilst they have thought that Art is in a mans head, and not in the thing" (15). Logic is *in* Creation. And the mind is logical when and only when it submits to the form of the universe. This form must then be replicated in the human arts: logic must be seen as the universal foundation, so that epistemologically, pedagogically, and curricularly, it is the first discipline; second, all arts are taught and defined as the two skills that enable a person to map Creation correctly (analysis and genesis). Genesis is the accretion of simples into its true arrangement; analysis is the "unwinding" or dividing of a subject back to its simples (24).[2]

What can get lost in this discussion is that it is more than narrowing all forms of knowledge to species of logic—it is also a very narrow view of logic itself. As previously argued, Puritan ontology describes Creation as static, so logic is the art of mapping something that remains still. This map, this analysis and genesis, is simply the addition or subtraction of pieces that are hooked one onto another.[3] The "logical" analysis of any topic will always be a list. It should be no surprise, hence, that Puritan sermons are always list structures.

In addition, because these simples reside in Creation, there is only one true analysis of any subject—the one that accurately distinguishes and names the arrangement of simples as God has arranged them. There is, consequently, not "invention" in the humanist rhetoric sense of the term (where the same subject might be handled dozens of ways), but "discovery" of the true construction of God's manifest will. One discovers such construction by observing the world "with this act of his eye of reason" (Richardson 43), that is, Logic, not with any form of introspection "for they are not written in him" (43). The process of writing an argument begins with the submitting of one's mind to what one perceives in the arrangement of the world. Hence, no discipline—neither logic nor rhetoric—can teach *invention* (meaning a possibly idiosyncratic or contextually specific approach to a topic). The interpretation of God's will is a function of Logic alone; thus, the discipline of rhetoric cannot teach methods of *discovery* without engaging in a disorderly duplication of what is "naturally" a part of the discipline of Logic. This was the argument Ramists made for expurgating invention from rhetoric, substituting the word "discovery" for the word "invention," reducing arrangement to a single structure (thesis with supporting reasons), and restricting rhetoric to embellishment.

Although there has been much discussion of the Ramistic view of invention, little attention has been paid to the implications for arrangement. But Ramists' rigidity in that regard is fascinating. Ramists insisted that humanist rhetoric violates natural boundaries of God's Creation by teaching arrangement, for the "true" or "natural" arrangement of any subject is to follow out the branching dichotomies created by the correct perception of the simples. The rhetor should break every subject into its parts, then discuss each part in the way in which one "naturally" perceives it. This is not some proto-Romantic form of expressivism in which the rhetoric follows his or her own way of seeing things, but a method whereby one follows the order in which God has placed pieces of knowledge in Creation.

In the rhetorical tradition, the conventional recommendation is to begin with some kind of common ground shared with one's audience. As one's audience changes, so would that common ground. Humanist rhetoric assumes that there is no arrangement that would work with all audiences, and it demands that one pay careful attention to the needs of one's audience in considering the disposition of the topic. Ramistic arrangement, on the contrary, recommends that one pay attention to the topic rather than the needs of the audience. There is one way to handle any topic, and the speaker should find that way through analysis of the topic, not through consideration of audience.[4]

Puritan theories of rhetoric suggest that any two good ministers (that is, ministers with grace and perception) would handle the same topic in exactly the same way, and this way would be arranged in a list. Ramists use terms like "addition" or "sum" to describe Creation as the *accretion* of simples. If one follows Creation, then one has an arrangement that is itself an *accretion* of points. Thus, lists seem like the "natural" arrangement for any piece of discourse, and the other kinds of arrangements available to rhetors (from chiasmus to enthymeme) come to seem "artificial."

It was this obsession with following a clear and perfect order that caused Ramists to condemn Aristotle for including invention, arrangement, and memory in the art of rhetoric—such inclusion is "contrary to both art and reason" (Rainolds 175). More accurately, Ramus tried to redefine classical rhetoric, projecting his own precision with categories back onto the classical tradition. It seems that Ramus was, to a large extent, successful at promoting his own view of classical rhetoric. Recent and influential scholars of the history of American rhetoric, for instance, posit an unintentionally Ramistic reading of Aristotle. Berlin's text on nineteenth-century rhetoric asserts that rhetoric was classical prior to that era (thus equating Ramism and classicism). Similarly, a frequently anthologized essay by Berlin promotes the characterization of classical rhetoric as current-traditional: "In the Aristotelian scheme of things, the material world exists independently of the observer and is knowable through sense impressions. Since sense impressions in themselves reveal nothing, however, to arrive at true knowledge it is necessary for the mind to perform an operation upon sense data. This operation is a function of reason and amounts to the appropriate use of syllogistic reasoning. . . . The strictures imposed by logic, more- over, naturally arise out of the very structure of the mind and of the universe" ("Contemporary Composition" 49). This is not an accurate description of Aristotelian epistemology; on the contrary, current- traditional is *opposed* to the classical tradition by being essentially Ramistic. It is, however, an apt way of identifying the presumptions behind Puritan and Ramistic rhetoric. Ramistic "discovery" is a ques- tion of perception, and as indicated above, syllogisms are *the* method of checking one's perception.

John Gage has written an eloquent investigation into the epistemol- ogy of enthymemes; proponents of rhetoric would do well if an equally well-done investigation of the epistemology of the syllogism existed. I do not have the necessary background in logic to pursue such a course, but I can remark on some obvious qualities in the theories of logic that so influenced American Puritans. The major premise of an enthymeme is something that the rhetor predicts the community will accept, but the major premise of a syllogism is something that the logician be- lieves is True and *must* be accepted. It is, in Puritan logics, a univer- sal statement, both ontologically and epistemologically. The major premise is true under all conditions, and it appears true to all people.

I want to digress briefly here to discuss the connection between how reasoning works and the notion that discourse is always a form of force. In logic, as opposed to rhetoric, the major premise is a statement that one *must* accept. One hears in discussions of this point of a kind of language of coercion—that logic forces its points home, that a lis- tener is forced to acknowledge the truth of an assertion, and so on.

This force operates in different ways in rhetoric versus logic in that this distinction has implications for how one thinks about relative re- sponsibilities in the rhetor-audience relationship. If the audience does not accept the major premise of an enthymeme, rhetoric puts the re- sponsibility on the rhetor to find a different enthymeme; the rhetor *must* change or give up. Puritan logic puts the responsibility on the audience for being wrong; the audience *must* submit to the speaker.

In addition to having fairly obvious consequences for handling dis- sent, this displacement of responsibility indicates one source of the prophet ethos. If the minister's duty is to speak the truth in the single way that God intends, and to punish those who refuse assent to what is manifestly true, then he simply announces what is true.

Putting together a true syllogism is largely a question of getting the categories right—not the categories of syllogisms (an obsession for which Ramus criticized the Scholastics), but the categories of Being described by a syllogism. The distinction is subtle, but important. The Scholastic categories are explicitly mental categories, but Ramism claims that the parts of a syllogism each name an entity in God's Creation. Perkins explains this point:

> The sum of the scripture is contained in such a syllogism or form of reasoning as this is which followeth.
>
> The true Messiah shall be both God and man of the seed of David; he shall be born of a virgin; he shall bring the gospel forth of his Father's bosom; he shall satisfy the law; he shall offer up himself a sacrifice for the sins of the faithful; he shall conquer death by dying and rising again; he shall ascend into heaven; and in his due time he shall return unto judgment. (Major)
>
> But Jesus of Nazareth, the son of Mary, is such a one. (Minor)
>
> He therefore is the true Messiah.   (*Works* 335)

He goes on to explain that the major premise is the Old Testament, and the minor premise is the New Testament. Scripture does not simply contain or convey the premises, but *is* them.

Knowing the world means naming the place of everything in God's hierarchies; the syllogism enables one to check one's naming of things. Or, the other metaphor sometimes used was that of counting: a syllogism enables one to add up ideas properly. As Richardson says, "*Syllogismus* signifies properly the summe of an account in the *species* of numeration" (emphasis in original, 287). Whether the metaphor is naming or adding, for the Puritans, knowing and perceiving were essentially identical. That is, knowledge is *in* the discrete objects in the world, and it is carried to one's mind in the same way that scent is carried to the nose. The major work in knowing is not in cognition but in perception. Arnauld, for instance, makes perception the first (and most important) ability, and he describes what we might see as additional processes as adding premises.

Ames's discussion of the processes of conscience is particularly illustrative of the status that Puritans gave to perception. Ames maps the judgment of conscience onto the syllogism: the Major Premise is synderesis—the perception of God's Law; the minor premise is the operation of the will—essentially the application of that law; the conclusion is the final judgment of one's own actions.[5] The example that Ames uses is: He that lives in sin shall die; I live in sin; I shall die. The Major Premise is "naturally written in the hearts of al men" (*Of Conscience* 5), so there cannot be error in regard to such premises: "No mans Conscience can erre in such like things as these, or doe them against Conscience" (10). Where a person might err is in the second stage of conscience in which one must apply the general principles, a process that depends upon the functioning of the will, and the will is quite capable of misleading a person: "The *Will* can turn away the understanding fro[m] the *consideration* of any object, which at present it apprehendeth and judgeth to be good, to the consideration that it hath formerly apprehended and judged to be so. By reason of this commanding power, the *Will* is the first cause of unadvisednesse, and blame-worthy error in the Understanding" (emphasis in the original, 23–24). Inasmuch as synderesis, that ability to perceive God's law, is reliable, what one can do to promote true knowledge is to strip away the things that one's mind has created in order to try to get back to basic perceptions.

This metaphor—that the correct procedure in anything is to strip away human-created excess to get back to what is simple, pure, and true—recurs throughout Puritanism, invoked in the various realms of religious dogma, religious practice, religious organization, political organization, clothing, sermon style, the arrangement of the disciplines, the content of courses, and the organization of material. The assumption is that direct contact with God's Creation is both possible and necessary. Anything (including one's own process of cognition) that has the ability to get between God's creation and one's perception is dangerous.[6] I will return to this point later, but here I want to emphasize that unlike humanist rhetoric, Puritan epistemology makes perception reliable and cognition unreliable, so that the work of learning does not rest in cognition. The only purpose of internal reflection is to test one's ideas against one's perceptions.

Puritan epistemology, then, conflates knowing and perceiving, and perceiving means submitting oneself to the knowledge that God has placed *in* Creation. It is no accident that Ames sometimes refers to synderesis as existing in the mind and sometimes in the objects the mind perceives: "*Synteresis* is the object apprehended, or the apprehension of the object" (*Of Conscience* 5). Whereas the understanding was damaged in the fall, perception was not; so the understanding may be redeemed by submitting to perception: "Neither do we need any other marks to distinguish Truth, then the brightness of the Evidence which surrounds it and subdues and convinces the Understanding" (Arnauld 1: 10).

One consequence of this epistemology is that it demonizes difference. Interpreting Scripture is nothing more than a question of submitting one's mind to what is obviously in the text: "Any point of doctrine collected by just consequence is simply of itself to be believed and doth demonstrate" (Perkins, *Work* 341). I would suggest that it is precisely because Puritan logic is essentially a question of naming that it is a system of thought that cares more about what things are than what they are not. For much of the rhetorical tradition, as Farrell notes, there is a sense that rhetoric is inherently relational and that the goods of rhetoric "require some *other* in order to be practiced" (94). In contrast to this rhetorical sense that one learns by contrast, a sense that tends to make a diverse and active audience a necessity for public discourse, Puritanism dismisses the study of contrasts (such as when the Puritan logician Richardson is extremely dismissive of heterologia but emphasizes the importance of homologia).

Puritanism precludes the ability to explain differences in words or perceptions as the result of equally valid but different perspectives. The argument that different ideas might be equally valid imagines a world larger and more dynamic than the human mind is capable of perceiving at any single moment (such as a house that one cannot see on the inside and on the outside at the same time). But Puritan ontology and epistemology presume a flat and static world that can be known. If two people claim to know different things, then one or the other has permitted a fallen understanding to corrupt perception or, more likely, is simply denying what s/he knows to be manifestly true. Winthrop attributes the idea that the same thing might be expressed in different words to the scheming, Satan-worshipping Antinomians who would say, when contradicted or refuted by someone they were trying to seduce, "*Nay, mistake me not, for I doe meane even as you doe, you and I are both of one minde in substance, and differ onely in words*" (emphasis in original, "Short Story" 207). Because knowledge is an object that resides in Creation and that the properly cleared mind receives, disagreement is a sign that someone is doing the devil's work.

For instance, when Hooker discusses the objection that a "naturall man" might make (a "naturall man" being one who is filled with sin), according to Hooker's interpretation, "the world knowes, and you know that you are a naturall man" ("No Man" 89). The sinner may object to the doctrine but secretly knows him/herself to be filled with sin. Similarly, "Day of Doom" includes a section that is a direct refutation of the argument that sin is a result of innocent ignorance. A group of sinners argue to Jesus that since far better educated people than they often disagree about theological issues, how can the uneducated be expected to have the correct answers to such questions? All they could do, they argued, was to rely on authorities to tell them what to believe, and they happened to have relied on the wrong authorities.

> We had thy Word, say some, O Lord,
>   but wiser men than we
> Could never yet interpret it,
>   but always disagree.
> How could we fools be led by Rules,
>   so far beyond our ken,
> Which to explain did so much pain,
>   and puzzle wisest men?   (121)

The sinners try to argue that because of the disagreements of experts they were misled into believing the wrong things, that they had incorrect ideas in their heads (and, therefore, disagreed with the interpretations of Puritan authorities). Jesus responds by first rejecting the possibility of anyone actually disagreeing—the sinners knew all along what the true rules were: "You understood that what was good, / was to be followed" (119). He then rejects that Scripture is so difficult that people might actually disagree as to what it means:

> Was all my word abstruse and hard?
>   the Judge then answered:
> It did contain much truth so plain,
>   you might have run and read,
> But what was hard you never car'd
>   to know nor studied,
> And things that were most plain and clear
>   you never practised.   (122)

Calvin's argument that the world is a mirror of God's wisdom enables him to say that all humans are at fault for failing to follow God's will:

"It follows, then, that mankind do not err thus far through mere ignorance, so as not to be chargeable with contempt, negligence, and in-
gratitude" (Calvin, *Corinthians* 1: 85–86). Cotton Mather also argues
that it is fairly simple for anyone to determine the right side, even in
very complicated controversies. First, everyone (including women) is
given reason (*Ornaments* 45–46). Second, anyone can use the following
procedure to keep "from going out of the way" when authorities appear to disagree:

> Mind what has the most obvious Tendency to advance the *fear of God*,
> in your Hearts and Lives; mind what most magnifies *Christ* and villi-
> fies Man, and recommends *practical Godliness*; 'tis the *Doctrine accord-
> ing to Godliness*, which is the *true Doctrine*. Or if thou can't penetrate so
> far, then mind how those Men which are most eminent for the *fear of
> God*, are most generally inclined; mind what is most generally grateful
> to the *sober*, gracious, patient, heavenly, mortify'd Part of Mankind;
> and on the other Side, what the most *loose*, proud, carnal, railing, pro-
> fane, Party chuse to fall in withal.
>
> (emphasis in original, *Ornaments* 53–54)

There is something almost breathtaking in the Puritan tendency to assert that a particular interpretation is indisputable, as they often did so
in the midst of a dispute over it. In the face of a long history of differ-
ing interpretations, Calvinists asserted that theological truth is easy
and obvious.[7]

There is a famous story to that end. Winthrop's outrage at the obvious errors of Antinomians inspired him to write a response. He was
dissuaded from publishing this response by Hooker and other ministers, because they felt that he fell into error in his own treatise. This
incident should have demonstrated that there might be different interpretations or different methods of expressing doctrine (or, at the very
least, that doctrine is not obvious), but it failed to do so. It is likely that
incidents like the above failed to inspire skepticism because Puritans
could not imagine anything other than two kinds of people—sinful
people who deride but do not disagree with doctrine and godly people
whose agreement with doctrine should be confirmed. Any kind of
skepticism would have complicated this neat division. The rigidity of
Puritan ontology and epistemology is necessarily connected to a rigid
and limited set of roles when it comes to discourse.

This limitation of audience roles is a significant departure from

classical rhetoric. For Aristotle, Cicero, Quintilian, and other classical rhetoricians, there are as many potential audiences as there are social roles. The Christian tradition is somewhat more limited, but still
presents at least three possibilities. In his *On Christian Doctrine*, Augustine, adapting Cicero to the needs of Christian proselytizing, articu-
lates three different kinds of audience (see especially 136–37). With
people who have never heard or understood Christian doctrine, one in-
forms them of it. With people who have heard and understood such
doctrine but still disagree with it, one tries to persuade them that it is
true. With people who agree with doctrine but do not act like Christians, one must convince them to change their behavior. Augustine
may be particularly aware of that second kind of audience (those who
have heard Christian doctrine but disagree with it) because he describes himself as having spent much time in that state. In his autobiography he describes his intellectual objections to Christianity, especially problems with various passages in the Old Testament and a
misunderstanding of the nature of God. He had heard correct doctrine
(including sermons by such priests as Ambrose), but simply being told
correct doctrine did not resolve his intellectual objections. Nor does he
ever say that those objections were mere cavils. Ultimately, his conversion was not a purely intellectual experience, but the resolution of his
intellectual objections was a necessary stage in his conversion process.
He did not always know the truth, even though he had heard correct
doctrine.

The Puritans, however, did not include such a person (or people in
such a state) in the possible kinds of audiences that a rhetor might face.
Perkins lists seven kinds of audiences, which loosely fall into four
categories: people who have not heard correct doctrine, people who
have heard it but are not sufficiently humbled, people who need com-
forting, and people who are fallen (*Work* 342 and "Arte" 665–68). No
category exists for people who have heard correct doctrine and have
reasons (as opposed to motives) for disagreeing.

This is not only a rigid theory of audience, but a very direct hermeneutic. The Puritans presented their interpretations as certain and undeniable; as Samuel Mather says, "There is nothing so clear, and sure,
and certain, as the Gospel" (*The Figures or Types* 12). Perkins too insists
upon the ease with which one can know right from wrong: "We must
further know that every article and doctrine concerning faith and
manners, which is necessary unto salvation, is very plainly delivered
in the Scriptures" (*Work* 239). Hooker, in the midst of an explication of

predestination, says that the doctrine is "here plainely set open in the text, and therein manifestly expressed" ("No Man" 85). Higginson insists that the minister's interpretation is nothing "but what might be more abundantly made out by Scripture light, and what the generality of all the People of God (not engaged unto parties) will readily subscribe unto" ("Cause of God" 1: 9–10). Hooker refers to his argument having "beene prooved by reason plaine and undeniable arguments" ("No Man" 105). Hubbard begins his explication of a text by saying that his interpretation is "very obvious to the view of the observant reader" (2). Calvin, in regard to a particular difficult passage, says, "I know that some give a different explanation; but all the sound-minded, as I expect, will assent to this view" (Calvin, *Hebrews* 104). This same sense that the correct interpretation is easy appears in Puritans' interpretation of events. Winthrop prefaces his defence of the irregular proceedings against Hutchinson's ally Wheelwright by saying, "But the answer to this is easie, it being wel known to all such as have understanding of matters of this nature" ("Short Story" 297). Because Scripture is so clear, there is no genuine disagreement about it. Clearly, this hermeneutic mutually reinforces the Puritan inability to admit difference. The Puritans granted that certain kinds of spiritual knowledge might be beyond human capability (unless aided by grace), but like most Calvinists, they always assumed that any standards for ethical behavior are perfectly clear.

How then did the Puritans explain disagreement? They generally denied that it existed. They continually asserted that people, even sinners, do see the correct interpretation in Scripture, but they refuse to submit to it. That is, there is no disagreement, only disobedience.

Hooker's sermon "No Man By Nature Can Will Christ and Grace," is about this subject. Hooker uses Matthew 19.16–22 to typify people who disagree with what they know to be true. In that passage, a young man comes to Jesus to ask what he should do to inherit the Kingdom of Heaven. When Jesus tells him to sell everything he has and follow him, the young man goes away sorrowful, "for he had great possessions" (13). Hooker interprets the young man's reaction as proof that he actually recognizes the truth of what Jesus says but rejects the teaching because he is unwilling to give up his wealth. Hooker uses this man as typical of all people who disagree with Puritan doctrine: they recognize the obvious truth of what Puritan authorities say, but they are too attached to their sins to do what they know is right. This characterization of disagreement is reiterated throughout the sermon:

disagreement is cavilling motivated by carnal lusts; it is "swellings and bublings of heart against the word" ("No Man" 20–21); desire to silence or ostracize a minister is motivated by a hardened heart that does not want to have its conscience pricked. Disagreement with Hooker (which is treated as identical with disagreement with God's word) is never motivated by goodwilled disbelief or benevolent ignorance or Hooker's being in error. If someone disagrees with Hooker, s/he is disagreeing with God, and, obviously, that disagreement with God is proof that s/he is a "naturall man"—that is, someone who is completely fleshly and has nothing spiritual. So, any attempt to dispute the sermon is itself proof of the dissenter's sinfulness. This results in the circular logic that is typical of closed systems: any disagreement is itself proof that one does not have the intellectual or moral authority to participate in the discourse. Consequently, one's disagreement can be dismissed as irrational.

II

Charles Taylor's point that Puritanism connects disorder and sin can be taken even further: even lack of certainty suggests sin. Because of the Puritan ontology, inability to perceive correctly and immediately is an unwillingness to submit to God's knowledge; it is distance from and insubordination to God. Because God's will extends to everything, correctness on any matter is submission to God's will, and any lack of correctness (including, by implication, lack of perfect certainty) is sinful. Changing one's position means acknowledging not only that one made an error but also that one had been in a state of sin. Although Puritan conversion narratives presume that one would narrate one's life as having had such a state, the structure and importance of those narratives also put pressure on a person to limit the instances in which one made incorrect pronouncements as a result of sin. This tension was simply impossible to resolve for a minister, who could not admit to having ever said something sinful in a sermon without throwing doubt upon ministers as prophets of God.

This is not to say that Puritan ministers preached an easy certainty about whether or not one was in a state of sin. In fact, as will be discussed in the fourth chapter, this was a topic on which they preached a kind of skepticism. That skepticism, however, was never self-reflexive to the ministers, nor did it apply to Puritan authorities or institutions. It was never applied to the means of discourse (the minister, his interpretation of Scripture, his words, or the ability of the congregation to interpret his sermon). Again, it is a system that allows only two possible positions. A person is correct or not, is certain or not, is in a state of grace or not. The presumptions of this system reveal an important difference compared with the presumptions that underlie humanist rhetoric.

An interesting way to think about this problem is by contrasting Puritan notions of sin, hell, redemption, and knowledge to traditional Catholic doctrine. In Catholicism, there were conventionally degrees of sin; for instance, a distinction was made between venial and mortal sins. The different sins had different degrees of punishment (not only layers of hell, but a distinction between those who went to hell and those who went to Purgatory) and different degrees of work for redemption (the greater the sin, the more Masses that must be said or the greater the penance). Similarly, the Church hierarchy was a hierarchy of knowledge. The parishioner was assumed to know less about doctrine than the priest, who himself was assumed to know less than those people higher in the institution; the Pope was the one whose knowledge was perfect. All of these distinctions on the basis of degree were rejected by Calvinism: To Calvinists, the idea of degrees of sin and redemption were seen as the scandal of indulgences or the heresy of Arminianism (that an individual might work his/her way to grace). The idea of degrees of knowledge was rejected in the Protestant move to make each individual the locus of interpretive authority. Every individual, they insisted, could know as much as any other, so there is no need for a hierarchy of more and less complete knowledge.

Thus, instead of seeing the world as degrees, Renaissance humanism is more similar to Catholicism than Calvinism in this regard; one selects an argument that seems stronger, that provides more reliable evidence about which one can feel more certain, while always acknowledging the possibility of a later answer that will be still stronger, and so on. Puritanism is dependent upon choosing between logically opposed binaries. Of any two conflicting propositions, at least one must be false. The incompatibility of these two ways of thinking—rhetorical versus Puritan—can be seen in the question of interpretive certainty. As will be discussed in a later chapter, this interpretive certainty and clarity assumes a particular model of linguistic reference, as is indicated in Ames's argument that Scripture is clear in all "necessary" matters: "Hence there is only one meaning for every place in Scripture. Otherwise the meaning of Scripture would not only be unclear and uncertain, but there would be no meaning at all—for anything which does not mean one thing surely means nothing" (*The Marrow of Theology* 188). There are neither degrees or shades of meaning nor multiple perspectives. Either there is one meaning or none at all. Since God would not have given human beings a meaningless document, there must be one meaning. In a system that presumes no degrees of certainty and assumes a beneficent God, this is a perfectly logical argument—but the crux of the argument is in the premises.

Perhaps due to Ramistic dichotomies, many Puritan theories assume a binary opposition in terms of the positions available. There are two kinds of audiences (the elect and the damned); there are only two positions in a rhetorical situation (the speaker who demonstrates and the listener who immediately recognizes the truth of the demonstration). On one side are certainty, order, and clarity of purpose; on the other side is sin. One is either on God's (the minister's) side, or one is attempting to fight God. There is the "natural" way to arrange a sermon, present a body of knowledge, or arrange a curriculum, and there is human-imposed artifice.

These binary oppositions contribute to occluding the role of the individual minister in interpretation or persuasion. Hooker, for instance, apostrophizes someone who would argue that an individual can will grace: "The Text saith, God saith, the truth saith, you doe not, nay you cannot [will grace], you say you doe, whom shall wee beleeve in this case, God or you?" ("No Man" 11). Hooker never mentions himself in that list. It is not that *he* says the person cannot will grace, nor that *he* interprets Scripture in such a way, but that a disagreement with his interpretation is a dispute with Scripture itself and, thereby, with God. This is a common move in Calvinist writings; Calvin, for example, says: "The subject, indeed, does not require a long discussion. For we are not singular in our doctrine, but have Christ and all his apostles with us. Let our opponents, then, consider how they are to come off victorious in a contest which they wage with such antagonists" (*Institutes* 1: 275–76). Richard Mather is careful to make clear that his argument regarding church discipline is not his cause, nor that of the New England congregations: "Nay, it is Christs Cause" ("Church Government" 9). When Anne Hutchinson argued that the ministers examining her were acting as judges and prosecutors of their own cause, John Winthrop responded, "It is not their cause but the cause of the whole country" (Hall, *Worlds*, "Examination" 327). John Cotton said that he was not fighting Roger Williams, but that Jesus was "with the sword of his mouth (as himselfe speaketh, Rev. 2.16) in the mouthes and testimonies of the Churches and Brethren" (Williams 2: 298), thereby equating himself and Jesus. When Williams responded that this was arrogance and spiritual pride on the part of Cotton, Cotton countered that he was not taking pride in himself, but glorying in Jesus (Williams 2: 88). In Puritanism specifically and the rhetoric of the voice in the wilderness generally, the ideal rhetor has no personal stake in the issue, does not speak from a particular point of view, and is completely free of any self-interest. As laudable as such a stance may be in principle, in practice it means that the speaker tends simply to deny his/her rather obvious personal investment.

There is a kind of circle here: Authorities saw themselves as vessels of God's power; they therefore denied the role of the minister in interpretation; this denial supported the faith in interpretive certainty and binary oppositions; that view encouraged authorities to see themselves as nothing more than vessels of God's power.

Any dispute with a minister was seen as a battle with God himself. John Cotton continually talks in terms of battling with God when he refers to disagreeing with a minister or the church: "If therefore any shall set themselves against God and his servants, and make battle against him . . . " ("Gods Mercie" 61); "God hath promised that hee will march through with his worke, if God give us an heart to submit to his colours . . . he will march an end, not only in his owne providence . . . so hee will march an end in his servants . . . they will march in his strength, and he will keep them that they shall not retire disorderly" (64). Salvation comes from submitting not only to God, but to the ministers of the established church: "First, If you would lay hold on Gods strength then lay downe all your owne weapons, all weapons of hostility against God, doe not onely lay aside opposition against Gods Church, but what ever sinnefull frame of heart or life thou hast" ("Gods Mercie" 69)

Yet another factor plays into this ability to equate God's will and the ministers; it comes partially from the Puritan hermeneutic (the belief that the individual minister could absent his will, his perceptions, and his desires from the process of interpretation) and also from the Puritan sense of communal destiny. The American Puritans believed they had a covenant with God "by virtue of which Covenant the Lord was their God and they were his people; and the cause of God was theirs, and their cause was his; the cause of God & his People Israel was one and the same, and that was the cause of Religion according to the word of God" (Higginson 1: 4). The result is an antithesis: the minister's way (which is God's) or the sinful way of the person who disagrees with him.

III

In conjunction with the theory of power discussed in the previous chapter (that any source of authority other than the official government is necessarily an attack on the government's power), this antithesis between God (minister) and evil contributed to the Puritans' inability to recognize any value in disparate points of view. One consequence and sign of this attitude is that Puritan discussions of discourse do not mention the possibility that a person in authority would engage in a disagreement with a member of the congregation in order to learn. Reasoning with others means telling them logically and clearly how they are wrong. Listening to others is for the purpose of being instructed (if they have more authority) or learning things that might enable one to instruct them. Perkins describes how to prepare an audience for the receiving of grace: "This preparation is to bee made partly by disputing or reasoning with them, that thou mayest thorowly discerne their manners and disposition" ("Arte" 665). One looks for signs of how "teachable" they are, by which Perkins means, "the doctrine of Gods word is to bee declared to them generally in some common termes, or ordinarie points" ("Arte" 665). If they approve, they are teachable, and if they disagree, they are unreachable. Godly discourse is the godly minister *demonstrating* correct doctrine.

If, however, all Puritan discourse was purely demonstrative and could not itself change the will of others, what was the purpose in engaging in so much of it? There can be no doubt that scholars who characterize Puritanism as fundamentally discursive are largely right. But what if they did not expect to change sinners into saints, what did they think would happen? What place does Calvinism leave for discourse? The short answer is that there are two kinds of audiences, and discourse affects them in different ways.

The elect are confirmed in their goodness; the reprobate are essentially given a writ. As Calvin argues, the sinner will not be persuaded but will be further condemned; the elect will not be saved, but they may be confirmed:

What purpose, then, is served by exhortations? It is this: As the wicked, with obstinate heart, despise them, they will be a testimony against them when they stand at the judgment-seat of God; nay, they even now strike and lash their consciences. For, however they may petulantly deride, they cannot disapprove them. . . . Had exhortations and reprimands no other profit with the godly than to convince them of sin, they could not be deemed altogether useless. Now, when, by the Spirit of God acting within, they have the effect of inflaming their desire of good, of arousing them from lethargy, of destroying the pleasure and honeyed sweetness of sin, making it hateful and loathsome, who will presume to cavil at them as superfluous?

(Calvin, *Institutes* 1: 276–77)

Thus, by ensuring that a sinner has heard correct doctrine, correct sermons add weight to the just condemnation on Judgment Day; they remove the possibility that a sinner might plead ignorance of the law. Further, God might choose to use the moment of the sermon as an opportunity to confirm the goodness of the good, to work within them to arouse them from lethargy. These two purposes of sermons—condemning sinners and confirming the already present good feelings of the good people—are important but do not effect any change in the listeners; Calvin does not mention as one of the possible functions of sermons that a bad person might become good.

Telling correct doctrine to sinners, as long as one has been clear and correct, enables one to consider oneself absolved of responsibility for them. It is not necessary to try to understand why they disagree, or to listen carefully to their objections, arguments, or interpretations. This notion of the limited functions of discourse is exemplified in *Pilgrim's Progress*, in which there are two kinds of discussions: wasteful and unproductive discussions with sinners; and potentially productive discussions with like-minded (i.e., godly) persons. In the book, Christian wastes his time trying to persuade his family (especially since he does so before he has reached the Celestial City), and Faithful's discourse with Talkative does not change the perceptions of either person. No one is persuaded of anything during the trial at Vanity Fair. In such cases, the only possible benefit is to exculpate the godly speaker from responsibility because, as Calvin says, it ensures that the sinner has heard correct doctrine. It thereby enables the godly person to say, "I have dealt plainly with him; and so am clear of his blood if he perisheth" (Bunyan 133). Similarly, Charity says that Christian is justified in not having tried harder to persuade his family to come with him because, "if thy wife and children have been offended with thee for this they thereby show themselves to be implacable to good; and thou hast delivered thy soul from their blood" (97). One has an obligation only to speak the truth, not to persuade, and certainly not to listen.

There is some, albeit limited, profit to godly speakers discoursing with one another: It keeps them alert; it helps them understand their experiences; it helps them understand what will happen to them on the road. So, the dreamer in *Pilgrim's Progress* notes: "When saints do sleepy grow, let them come hither, / And hear how these two pilgrims talk together: / Yea, let them learn of them, in any wise / Thus to keep ope their drowsy slumbering eyes. / Saints' fellowship, if it be managed well, / Keeps them awake, and that in spite of Hell" (188). Hopeful proceeds to narrate his conversion experience, and Christian listens carefully, posing questions from time to time. If Hopeful's narrative has any effect on Christian at all, it is no more than to confirm Christian in his interpretation of his own experience, because he relates almost exactly the same kind of experience that Christian has been undergoing. They do not argue about theology; they do not disagree with each other; they do not pursue challenging questions or competing interpretations; and they do not engage in any forms of discourse that involve difference.

In *The Soules Implantation into the Naturall Olive*, Hooker echoes this two-part division of the audience when he says that the two consequences of Peter's preaching were that "he made men either yeeld to his doctrine, and be humbled, or else he made them know, that they should be condemned by his word for ever" (81). Thus, the opposition is included only in the sense of being an object of abuse. There is a rhetorical consequence of this form of inclusion. Given the sense that humans cannot change a sinner into a saint, it is most likely that the direct addresses serve the rhetorical function of apostrophe: appearing to speak to someone who is not actually the intended audience. The function of such a figure of speech is to encourage the intended audience to join with the speaker in his condemnation of the absent. That is, the saintly are confirmed in their godliness by participating in the minister's abuse and rejection of the opposition.

The implications for the public sphere of this two-part division of audience are obvious in the authorities' handling of the Hutchinson controversy. Once they had identified her as the "root" of all the disagreement, "they resorted to her many times, labouring to convince her, but in vaine; yet they resorted to her still, *to the end they might either reclaime her from her errours, or that they might beare witnesse against them if occasion were"* (emphasis added, Winthrop, "Short Story" 300–301). They told her she was wrong. They went to her with two possible outcomes in mind: she would agree (and be confirmed in righteousness), or she would disagree (and be convicted). The interesting word in the passage is "convince," for the rest of the passage demonstrates just what "convince" meant to the American Puritans. They did not enter the conversation with Hutchinson to see if they were in error or if she was right, or even if there was some merit to her interpretations. It does not seem to have been a possibility to view the discourse with Hutchinson as a dialogue with reciprocally binding obligations. The discourse would be successful only if they convinced her, and to convince her meant to get her to submit.

It is an understatement to say that this view of rhetoric is a self-fulfilling prophecy. Going to someone with the view of forcing them to submit has narrow rhetorical consequences, and being certain that one cannot get sinners to change generally ensures that one will not approach the discourse in ways that might actually persuade them. But self-fulfilling prophecies are not particularly bad in a world of determinism.

There is another set of rhetorical problems created by the Calvinist formulation of predestination, especially when linked to the doctrine of total human depravity, which creates serious rhetorical problems. Thomas Hooker's sermon "No Man By Nature Can Will Christ and Grace" is a good example of the paradox of Puritan rhetoric given this sense of predestination and human depravity. This sermon was the fourth in a series of five on the subject of "The Unbeleevers Preparing for Christ," in which he deals with the rocky issue of how much (and what) a sinner can do to effect redemption. To argue that a sinner has any power to choose grace would be to undermine the logic of predestination, the innate depravity of humans, and God's complete omnipotence; but to argue that a sinner has no power at all in the process of conversion would be to invite fatalistic hedonism. That is, if I have some power to bring grace upon myself, then my fate has not been predetermined, I cannot be completely depraved (since the ability to will good must itself be a good), and God's power is somewhat reduced (since he is sharing it with me). If, however, my fate is predetermined and I am depraved and powerless, I may as well not worry about the fate of my soul and have a good time while I can. The rhetorical problem for a minister like Hooker was that he had to prevent anyone from drawing either of these conclusions.

The American Puritans believed that the stories of Sodom and Gomorrah demonstrate God's policy of condemning and punishing entire communities for the sins of some of the people in them so that one family's sanctity can neither prevent nor exempt them from drought, famine, or war. To prevent communal disasters, ministers had to keep the sinful from behaving so sinfully that they might disrupt or endanger the saints.

This problem, as one can see in Hooker's sermon "No Man By Nature Can Will Christ and Grace," is not a logical dilemma, but a rhetorical one. Developing from the text of 1 Corinthians 2.14, Hooker argues that a human in the unredeemed state (called a "naturall man" because he is completely fleshly and has nothing spiritual in him) cannot choose to be saved or move himself toward salvation because grace is effected by the spirit, which is good, and the "naturall man" has nothing good in him; therefore, he cannot have the spirit within him; therefore, spirit (and grace) comes from outside man: it comes from God, at God's will. All a human being can do is to try to prepare the way for God's conversion, first, by admitting his abject, depraved, and powerless state, and, second, by engaging in moral actions.[8] Humble carriage and moral behavior do not cause, earn, or ensure salvation; grace is completely at God's will.[9]

The attitude toward the audience is almost oxymoronic: the sermon seems to attempt to convince them that the only power they have is the ability to admit that they have no power. It is hard to imagine, therefore, that the last portion of the sermon (in which Hooker tries to prove that the audience must do everything they can to prepare the way for Christ's grace) would do anything other than ring hollow. And herein lies the odd relationship that Hooker establishes with his audience: he is demanding good from people he says he knows to be "naturall men" and who, therefore, have no capacity for good. Thus, Hooker was presenting undeniable facts to those who, by their very nature, must refuse assent.

It would be perfectly logical for Hooker to have left off the last part of the sermon, to argue that the "naturall man" cannot will grace and let the sinners be damned. If some people choose fatalistic hedonism, let them go to hell—he would not be responsible. But there would have been serious rhetorical problems with such a stance. As a theologian, Hooker may be able to tell some people to sin and be damned, but as a minister with a responsibility to keep the community from becoming a Sodom he had to present predestination in such a way that it encouraged moral behavior in the majority of the community. Yet he could not promote incorrect dogma. At one and the same time, he had to be clear that very few people would be saved and yet argue that everyone should act morally in the hope that he or she will be among the elect. His paradoxical conclusion is that the individual cannot choose grace and that everyone should try to do so.

As previously discussed, strict predestination is a perfectly logical doctrine, especially given Calvinist premises about power. The paradoxes result from unacceptable rhetorical consequences. The very structure of Wigglesworth's "Day of Doom" typifies this paradox. Jesus sends the saints to heaven (which includes their getting to participate in judging others) and then proceeds to judge those who have already been identified as damned. He announces that he has no obligation to explain or defend predestination, but the majority of his part in the poem is a series of defenses. One such defence follows:

> If upon one what's due to none
>   I frankly shall bestow,
> And on the rest shall not think best,
>   compassions skirts to throw,
> Whom injure I? will you envy,
>   and grudge at others weal?
> Or me accuse, who do refuse
>   your selves to help and heal?
>
> Am I alone of what's my own,
>   no Master or no Lord?
> Or if I am, how can you claim
>   what I to some afford?
> Will you demand Grace at my hand,
>   and challenge what is mine?
> Will you teach me whom to set free,
>   and thus my Grace confine?   (101–2)

This argument is typically Calvinist. Because God is God, he has no obligation to act by human standards; whatever he does is, by definition, just: "Because His will is the most certain rule of perfect equity, whatever He does must be perfectly right; and therefore He is free from all laws, because He is a law to himself, and to all" (Calvin, *Four Last Books of Moses* 1: 82). Norton explains the same point in the same way: "God doth not will things because they are just, but they are just because God willeth them" (*Orthodox Evangelist* 42). Human beings have no right to instruct God or demand that grace be subject to human rules: "The mercy of God, because it is free, is not tied, but he may show it where he lists" (Calvin, *Romans* 261).[10] Yet, Jesus makes this argument after having spent 127 stanzas justifying predestination and defending his decisions to send various kinds of sinners to hell (stanzas 51–177). The poem takes a strict reading of predestination, proceeds to spend a considerable amount of time defending the justice of that doctrine (even in regard to people who have never heard of Christ, people too ignorant to understand doctrine, and infants too young to have undergone the conversion experience), *and* argues that such justification is unnecessary. One can only wonder why Wigglesworth wrote the poem if he thought justification was really unnecessary.

This paradoxical attitude toward engaging in discourse continually recurs in early Puritan writings. In the voluminous correspondence between Williams and Cotton, for example, they reiterate that the other is persisting in obvious error because of a hardened heart caused by Satan. Thus, the other person simply cannot be persuaded. Yet, they express this rhetorical fatalism in the midst of rhetorical excess. Roger Williams explains his inability to persuade John Cotton by quoting Scripture: "*There is a Proud refusall of the mind of God*"; Cotton attributes Williams's intransigence to Christ *and* Satan: "And thus the good hand of Christ that should have humbled you, to see and turne from the errour of your way, hath rather hardened you therein, and quickned you onely to see failings (yea intolerable errours) in all the Churches and brethren, rather then in your selfe. . . . it is no new thing with Satan to transforme himselfe into an Angell of light, and to cheare the soule with false peace, and with flashes of counterfeit consolation" (Williams 1: 317, 298–99). Because Cotton can move Williams only "if it were the holy will of God" (Cotton, in Williams 1: 298), he does not express much hope that anything will come of the correspondence: "Though I have little hope (when I consider the uncircumcision of mine owne lips, *Exod.* 6.12) that you will hearken to my voyce, who hath not hearkened to the body of the whole Church of Christ with you, and the testimony, and judgement of so many Elders and Brethren of other Churches, yet I trust my labour will be accepted of the

Lord; and who can tell but that he may blesse it to you also" (Cotton, in Williams 1: 297). Such a statement makes the entire correspondence deeply puzzling, especially considering the sheer amount of time that writing the response must have taken Cotton. The apparent absurdity of this situation—that he proceeds to write twenty-seven pages to someone whom he says he is inadequate to persuade—poses the same problem as Hooker's speaking directly to those who cannot be moved by human discourse.

The question posed by these situations seems to be whether Puritan divines were genuinely interested in converting sinners or whether they actually intended simply to provide a logic for their persecution (and were therefore willing to use any verbal tricks necessary). My argument is that this question relies on a false dichotomy of hoping for persuasion or expecting rhetorical failure when, in many senses, Puritan rhetors simultaneously did both. Puritan notions of discourse put severe limits on how much a human being can do. Given those notions, as much as a minister might like sinners to repent, that event is out of his control; it is neither more nor less likely to happen as a result of how he shapes his text. He cannot move a sinner; he can only make the condemnation as clear as possible. Like Cotton, he writes the text because he has a duty to God to do so, not because he has deluded himself into thinking that one human being has power over a sinner's soul. If asked, chances are that Puritan rhetors would have described themselves as engaging in a kind of performance. At the most fundamental level, they may well have had God as the intended audience, an audience whom they perceived as deeply internal. And, obviously, the minister is not trying to change God's mind. Instead, the minister's responsibility is to perform in a way that would please God—to announce God's will in unequivocal terms. Worrying about the means of such discourse is not as important as whether or not one has taken the correct stance. If any sinners will be saved, they will be saved by God's will, not by the rhetorical skill of a minister.

It is crucial to understand that this attitude toward the impossibility of persuasion is closely attached to assumptions about what people already know. The sermon does not change the thinking of the sinners or the saved, since it reminds them of things they already know, and it thereby confirms their place in God's creation. Calvin indicates that the sinful already agree with the argument of any sermon—"however they may petulantly deride, they cannot disapprove them" (*Institutes* 1: 276–77)—so the sermon does not change their understanding. That sin is hateful is hardly news to the godly (they are, after all, unlikely to think that they should love sin). The sermon inflames the desires they already possess. This sense of what audiences know means that sermons have an almost ritualistic function, which cannot be described as superfluous, but like all other forms of human discourse, cannot be attributed causality. They might confirm but cannot cause a change in anyone's thinking. Eugene White has said that the Puritans believed that "the sermon provided the means by which the function of the church would be realized: to foster saving grace through enlightened understanding" (14), but this is projecting enlightenment theories of rhetoric back onto the Calvinists. The fallen understanding is not regenerated by anything a minister says, but by God; therefore, if one has been prepared by God, then one can be appropriately affected by the sermon; if one has not, then one cannot.

I am arguing that three concepts are mutually supportive: Puritan ontology; Puritan epistemology; and Puritan rhetoric. Having one concept did not cause the Puritans to construct the others, but the three were mutually reinforcing and mutually dependent. The static ontology and the perception-based epistemology are clearly intertwined with a theory of public discourse that makes all language use a form of demonstration. This theory of rhetoric reinforces the perception-based epistemology, a theory of knowledge that denies that people genuinely disagree. With such mutually reinforcing concepts, Puritanism severely limited the responses available to communities in disagreement. Since they continually argued that spiritual dogma are logically demonstrable, and since dialectic had long held that its first principles are undeniable to any who understood them, it was logical for the Puritans to conclude that a true statement is logically indisputable. If one is confronted with someone who does dispute the statement, the discursive options are seriously limited. One can either decide that the recalcitrant listener is sincere and that one is not in the realm of dialectic, or one can decide that the listener is lying—that s/he secretly agrees. Because the first option was virtually unthinkable—the Puritans believed that the world is controlled by logic—they continually (and I think sincerely) asserted the second. This is not to say that the Puritans believed a person who had never heard a sermon could read the Bible correctly, or that someone completely ignorant would articulate correct doctrine. Rather, as the Puritans narrated the process of conversion, no possibility existed of a person understanding but not agreeing with Puritan dogma. A Puritan, confronted with persistent disagreement, could not imagine it as anything other than lying.

IV

The same sense of putting on a performance for God affects the Puritan conception of communal behavior. The Puritan ethic insists that part of one's worldly responsibilities is to participate in the realm of governmental activity, especially if one is a full member of the church. The Puritans hoped to found a public sphere that would be free to reach its own decisions, that is, decisions grounded in rationality and truth, not merely authority, *and* that would perfectly replicate the public sphere as they saw it operating in the pious communities of the Old Testament.

The members of the public sphere were required constantly to remember New England's special place in history, the godly community in which piety and public activity would be perfectly melded. It was to be a community on display, a city on a hill whose performance was watched by God. Their actions are performances in two senses—an ambiguity that Winthrop manipulates in "A Model of Christian Charity." God expects, he says, "a strict performance" of the articles of their covenant (40). It is also a performance in the sense of a dramatic and highly public display. In a famous passage, Winthrop says, "For we must consider that we shall be as a city upon a hill. The eyes of all people are upon us, so that if we shall deal falsely with our God in this work we have undertaken, and so cause Him to withdraw His present help from us, we shall be made a story and a by-word through the world" ("Model of Christian Charity" 41). Consequently, their laws must regulate religious as well as civil behavior: "to countenance and encourage those that fear God and work righteousness, but sharply to rebuke and timely to repress whatever is contrary to sound doctrine, or apparently tends to hinder the power of Godliness, and progress of true Religion, with all other profaneness or unrighteousness, that under the shadow of your Government we may lead quiet lives in all godliness and honesty" (Hubbard, *Happiness*, "Epistle" 3). The Puritan laws would be an expression of the Puritan communal identity.

The public sphere would be typified by perfect obedience in that the people would perfectly obey the authorities: Hubbard praises the godly tribes of Israel because "when the heads of the Tribe had counselled and determined what was needful to be done, the Brethren were ready to put their resolves in Execution" (2). The underlying meta-phor—the body politic—is also used by Bradford, John Cotton, Cotton Mather, and, especially, Winthrop. The metaphor is commonplace in Renaissance and Reformation political theory, and it is a clear indica-tion of the Humanist influence on Puritan thought. But as was typical of the Puritans' use of some commonplace, they manipulated the meta-phor in a particular and almost literalized manner—to insist upon the need for perfect agreement in a community, even among parts with greater and lesser status: "Hereby is noted the unamity and sweet agreement between the Heads and the People of this Tribe, as if one Spirit had run through the whole body thereof . . . This Spirit of unity and obedience" (Hubbard 7). Here the sense of power implied within Calvinist theories of predestination weaves back in. Puritan discus-sions of the government assume a hierarchy, with power beginning at the top and moving downward onto the people. Each place in the hier-archy is the object of power being wielded by the place immediately above; any other site of power is a threat upward. Hence, multiple sites of power (and interpretation is an important sort of power) are also sites of rebellion, discord, and sin.

The desire for uniformity was repeatedly expressed. Higginson in-terprets 1 Corinthians 1.2 to support perfect uniformity, telling his audience that there should be "no divisions amongst you but that you be perfectly joyned together in the same Judgments, and the same mind, and that you speak the same thing" (Higginson 1: 15). Calvin's interpretation of the same passage is typical of the Puritans: "Let us then observe, that nothing is more inconsistent on the part of Chris-tians than to be at variance among themselves, for it is the main article of our religion that we be in harmony among ourselves; and farther, on such agreement the safety of the Church rests and is dependent" (Calvin, *Corinthians* 1: 62). Increase Mather interprets "divided coun-sels" as a sign that days of trouble are near, and he insists that people in New England try to avert God's imminent wrath by ending all of their disagreements with one another ("Day of Trouble"). It is interest-ing to point out that these various writers—all of whom equate any kind of public disagreement with discord, factions, and instability— do not explain how to resolve any disagreement; they simply insist that the ideal community is in perfect agreement.

They did occasionally acknowledge that disagreement exists, as when Increase Mather admits that sometimes even a majority of the people will have "their unreasonable Dissatisfactions" ("Primitive

Counselors" 13). Nevertheless, as indicated by Mather's use of the word "unreasonable," the Puritans never admitted the possibility that disagreement in the public sphere could have anything but Satanic origin: "Such divisions, especially in the Church of God, are in a great measure to be ascribed to the policy of Satan, who endeavors by all wayes and meanes to foment divisions, amongst those of the Church, by that course to ruine them" (Hubbard 17–18). Even when the authorities recanted on the Salem witchcraft horror, they continued to attribute the disaster to Satan, rather than to their own inability to acknowledge sincere and well-founded difference of opinion.

This denial of difference both resulted from and reinforced the Puritan stance on religious toleration. The most famous articulation of that stance was made by John Cotton during his exchange of letters and pamphlets with Roger Williams. As the debate progressed, it came to focus on the issue of whether the New England authorities had an obligation to permit people to disagree about religious matters. In the pamphlet "The Bloody Tenent of Persecution," Williams argues that civil authorities have neither right nor reason to dictate conscience. The gist of Cotton's reply is indicated in the title of his pamphlet: "The Bloody Tenent, Washed and Made White in the Blood of the Lamb." Although Cotton grants that certain actions would be persecution if done by human agency, he goes on to argue that these actions are purified if done in the service of Christ.

This argument is somewhat complicated. He argues that a government that forced people to do things that everyone knows are wrong would be causing people to violate their consciences, but one that forces people to do what is right is merely causing people to follow their consciences. There are several important assumptions in this argument; the most obvious is that it is easy for a person to determine what is right. As is clear in the following interpretation of Titus 3.10, the crucial assumption in this argument regarding religious toleration is that no genuine disagreement regarding religion exists because Scripture is so clear: "For an Erroneous and blind Conscience, (even in fundamentall and weighty Points) it is not lawfull to persecute any, till after Admonition once or twice . . . That so such a man being convinced of the dangerous error of his way; if he still persist (being condemned of himselfe, ver. 11.) it may appeare, he is not persecuted for Cause of Conscience, but for sinning against his own Conscience" (emphasis removed, in Williams 2: 30). Williams has taken this argument and concluded that Cotton is in favor of persecuting for Cause of Conscience, a move that Cotton attributes to Williams's "extreme prejudice" on the issue. Williams's argument seems so absurd to Cotton that he poses the rhetorical question: "I that doe expressly, professedly deny Persecution of any, even of Hereticks, unlesse it be when they come to persist in heresie, after conviction, against conscience; how can I be said to maintaine Persecution for Cause of Conscience?" (Williams 2: 31). For Cotton, it is not considered persecution for cause of conscience if someone has first told the heretic s/he is wrong.

Because Scripture is so clear, everyone knows what it says. Hence a good Christian ruler enforces the rules that everyone already recognizes as good and true; he "shall encourage the good in a Christian course, and discourage such as have evil will to Sin, and punish none for matter of religion, but such as subvert the principles of saving truth (which no good Christian, much less good magistrate, can be ignorant of) or at least such as disturb the order of the gospel in a turbulent way" (Cotton, "Bloody Tenant" 206).

The assumption that everyone knows what is right and wrong is also reflected in Ames's famous treatise on conscience: "This *Synteresis* may for a time be hindred from acting, but canot be utterly extinguished or lost. Hence it is that no man is so desperately wicked as to be void of all Conscience" (*Of Conscience* 5). Not only do all men have consciences, but these consciences all tell us the same thing so clearly that one need never rely on probability in regard to ethical matters. One must reject skepticism in favor of certainty: "First, in all those *doubts* which doe any way belong to our practice, diligent enquiry is to be made, that we may clearly perceive the truth and not *doubt;* because while the minde remains in *doubt,* the action must of necessity want that perfection which it would have, if it were done with Knowledge, and certainty of judgement" (*Of Conscience* 16).

Cotton says that it would be impossible for Roger Williams to find a single Scriptural citation to support his obviously heretical argument (Williams 2: 36). When Williams proceeds to do exactly that, Cotton responds that he is astonished that someone could so obviously distort evidence. Like the examiners of Anne Hutchinson, Cotton insists that there is *no* logic behind the dissenting point of view, no reason whatsoever to support it, and no innocent motive that someone might hold it. Religious or ethical toleration amounts to permitting people to engage in behavior that everyone (including those people who are behaving badly) knows is wrong.

To American Puritans, any government that allows religious toleration is blasphemous because "would not such a state be guilty of having *other Gods,* where such a toleration is?" (Higginson 1: 12). Because everyone knows what Scripture says, allowing someone to preach a heretical view is encouraging the work of the devil. Nathaniel Ward insisted that "true Religion" "strictly binds every conscience to contend earnestly for the Truth; to preserve unity of spirit, Faith and Ordinances, to be all like minded, of one accord; every man to take his brother into his Christian care: to stand fast with one spirit, with one mind, striving together for the faith of the Gospel: and by no means to permit Heresies or erroneous opinions" (Ward 7). Since "God doth no where in his word tolerate Christian States, to give Tolerations to such adversaries of his Truth, if they have power in their hands to suppresse them" (6), to allow religious toleration would be to forsake Christian duty. To allow people to act upon a different interpretation of Scripture is to encourage people to sin. The only liberty that a government should permit is the Liberty "to Serve God in the way and after the manner which Himself in His Holy Word has Appointed" (I. Mather, *Primitive Counsellours* 17). The ideal community is a group of individuals who believe exactly the same thing and therefore behave in exactly the same way. It is contrasted to the kind of place founded by Roger Williams, where people full of errors live "in great strife and contention in the civill estate and otherwise, hatching and multiplying new Opinions, and cannot agree, but are miserably divided into sundry sects and factions" (Winthrop, "Short Story" 218), in other words, where difference of opinion is permitted.

The person who disagrees with the minister knows he is wrong because spiritual truths are, as Puritan ministers continually say, undeniable and indisputable. One might reject them, put them away, walk away from them sorrowfully, but one cannot deny their truth. To permit someone to disobey such clear dictates is to encourage them to do what their own conscience tells them is wrong.

It is ironic that ministers insisted that Scripture is clear, indisputable, and undeniable in the midst of disputes arising because someone has denied an interpretation, but the Puritan controversialists never took seriously the possibility that both disputants might be sincere. Instead, they refer to all counter-arguments as foundless cavils and regularly assert that their oppositions know that the doctrine is correct but pretend to disagree with it because they are unwilling to give up their sinful ways. The opponents do not have reasons for disagreeing, but evil motives, and one moment of reflection would prove that even to them. Nathaniel Ward, for example, says that anyone who assents to the notion of religious toleration, "if he examines his heart by day-light, his conscience will tell him, he is either an Atheist, or an Heretique, or an Hypocrite, or at best a captive to some Lust" (7–8).

It is an understatement to say that this is a circular argument, incapable of proof or disproof. It is also clear that such emphasis on the motives of the participants is extremely destructive to the community of discourse. It shifts the locus of discussion from what reasons a dissenter may have to whether or not s/he has the right to participate in the discussion at all. By making the very act of dissent proof that a person has no right to speak (and that others have no reason to listen), this move (which Wayne Booth has called "motivism") precludes the possibility of genuine discussion of different opinions.

By denying that someone may have legitimate reasons for dissent, the rhetorical strategy of motivism frees the speaker(s) from any responsibility of incorporating (let alone understanding) what those reasons might be, why someone might find them persuasive, or what merit they might have. Reciprocity—the notion that all points of view have equal rights and obligations in discourse—is entirely denied. Only the righteous have rights; dissent and evil are synonymous. When Hooker says that all sinners who try to argue their point are of "that wayward and pettish disposition, that it will not be satisfied though all his reasons be answered, and all objections taken away" (*Implantation* 95–96), he makes clear that including such people in discourse is a waste of time. It may even be worse than pointless; it may indicate a lack of piety on the part of both participants. Nathaniel Ward says that a person who would rather argue with other religions than "try the Truth of his own by valuable Arguments, and peaceable Sufferings; either his Religion, or himself is irreligous" (11). One can be slightly more patient with a heretic—admonish him once or twice before giving up on him (17). But as quoted earlier, Ward insists that everyone should be cautious about discoursing with people who hold heretical opinions; discussion with people who disagree causes one to come into contact with things that are wrong.

The recurrent metaphor to describe this danger is that of disease, that the heretics carry something that might be transferred to the healthy body politic. The 1648 Synod's defence of refusing to permit "ignorant and erroneous persons" to be members of church depends upon likening such people to victims of the plague: "We conceive the receiving of them into our churches, would rather loose and corrupt our churches, than gain and heal them" (Synod 14). Winthrop explains that the authorities felt that they must send Williams to England because Williams's plan to settle in Naragansett Bay would provide a site "from whence the infection would easily spread into these churches" (*Winthrop's Journals* 1: 168). John Cotton uses the same contagion metaphor in defending the policy of banishing or executing dissenters: "Yea what if a child of God were infected with a plague-sore, or some other contagious disease, may not their Brethren exclude them the common ayre, both of their religious, and Civill Assemblies, and yet hope to live eternally with them in the Heavens? Truely there be some unsound, and corrupt opinions, and practices, (and that of him too) which are more infectious, and contagious, then any plague-sore" (Williams 2: 27). It was fear that Williams's ideas might "breed a winters spirituall plague in the Countrey" that justified their forcing him to leave in winter (Cotton, in Williams 2: 93). John Winthrop entitled his version of the Antinomian controversy *A Short Story of the Rise, reign, and ruine of the Antinomians, Familists & Libertines, that infected the Churches of New England.*

This stance is a near literalizing of the body politic metaphor. It results from the Puritan ontology, specifically the assumption that ideas are things, because the contagion metaphor is consistent with the objectification of knowledge. Just as knowledge can be carried from one thing to another, so can sin. Just as a good sermon carries the good thing to a receptive audience, so bad discourse carries something evil. If one is forced by one's station in life to have contact with such evil (such as, if one is a minister) then one should handle the situation in the same way that a doctor would treat a plague patient—with as little contact as possible, administering the cure, but certainly not partaking of the disease. One can see an interesting example of this sense of the corrupting influence of heresy in various contemporary discussions of Hutchinson's case. She was regularly referred to as a "poyson" (see Hall, *The Antinomian Controversy* 307–8, 371).

Even those few Puritans who argued for some kind of religious toleration had essentially the same view of the ideal community and ideal public discourse. Cotton Mather's argument against executing heretics, for instance, does not suggest that people might learn from an open discussion of competing views, but that since heretics like Quakers are all insane anyway, they cannot learn from being killed: " 'Tis true, these Quakers did manifest an intolerable contempt of authority, and needlessly put upon themselves a vengeance, for which the authority would have gladly released them, if they would have accepted of a release; but it is also true that they were madmen—a sort of lunatics, demoniacs and energumens" (quoted in Erikson 133). One should not attempt to engage heretics in discourse; rather, tell them how and why they are wrong and banish them. By telling them that they are wrong, one has freed oneself of obligation toward them. By banishing them, one has prevented their corrupting the community. If they refuse to be banished, then they must be fought with words or deeds.

Because one can be certain that the other person is wrong and that one is right, any theological disagreement is a battle between what is demonstrably right and what is obviously false, and any method of compromise or negotiation in such a situation would be a mixing of good and evil. Ward was, in a sense, accurate when he said that there is "no reconciliation, without atonement" in religious matters (9). Given Puritan ideas about Scriptural certainty and conscience, two disparate parties can reconcile only when one of them admits to having been wrong. Otherwise they will, like Cotton and Williams, continue accusing the other of being in the service of the devil until one of them dies.

This attitude toward difference makes participation in genuine public deliberation positively dangerous. One cannot disagree with the authorities unless one is willing to be a martyr to the argument one proposes, to say, like Williams, "I shall be ready for the same grounds, not only to be bound and banished, but to die also, in New England, as for most holy Truths of God in Christ Jesus" (Williams 1: 325). Thus, public "deliberation" is, in the ideal, the godly beating the sinful with discourse and telling them what to do; in practice, it is everyone telling each other what to do (since very few people define themselves as sinful). One can see how this view of public discourse continually creates the ethos so popular in American rhetoric: the voice(s) crying in the wilderness. If one has the power of government behind one, then one tortures, banishes, and/or hangs one's opponents. If one does not have such power, then one dies a martyr to the cause. One can also see how these views would lead to an essentially coercive public sphere.

I began with the theory of controversia, and here I want to suggest a partial answer to the question of why the Puritan inclusion of dissenting arguments does not constitute rhetorical controversia. Controversia presumes that the most important work is done in contemplation; Puritanism makes cognition faulty and relies on perception. The "meaning" of the discourse is a statement that the listener is forced to accept because its very accuracy acts as a kind of force. So, this meaning is stated at the beginning and restated throughout, whereas rhetorical thinking presumes a flickering relationship between any given proposition and the "meaning" of the discourse. The meaning might actually be the ineffable position that the listener reaches at the end, the moment of balancing oppositions. As Sloane has argued, rhetoric presents oppositions as heuristics: the assumption is that one learns from intellectually and affectively experiencing the tensions between two or more terms that are each equally important. In Puritanism, on the contrary, the oppositions are presented so that one can be confirmed in one's clear choice between them.

Puritan rhetoric presents the opposition argument as an object to be rejected in favor of the truth, which is itself an object already in some sense possessed by the regenerate. The opposition argument is presented in such a way that a listener or reader could only identify with it by also accepting the argument's identification with Satan and sin. The arguments against predestination in "Day of Doom," for example, are made by sinners about to go to hell who are daring to argue with Jesus; ministers like Hooker characterize objections as cavils even as they present them. The method of presentation of these counterarguments is, of course, perfectly consistent with the epistemology previously discussed, and it runs directly counter to the epistemology behind rhetoric. This method of including counter-arguments—of the thesis and antithesis as two items between which the audience immediately selects the self-evidently correct one—is distinctly different from the use of oppositions in dialogic rhetoric. Dialogic rhetorics generally describe the oppositions as necessary to reaching fuller understanding—typically because it is assumed that the truth is ineffable, so one must settle for various approximations.

This difference in rhetorics is, as mentioned earlier, largely a question of epistemology—proponents of dialogic rhetoric presume a model of the mind that puts the work of understanding in cognition, whereas Puritanism (and, I would suggest, other forms of monologic discourse) puts the work in perception. In other words, Berlin's previously quoted characterization of Aristotelian rhetoric ("The strictures imposed by logic, moreover, naturally arise out of the very structure of the mind and of the universe" ["Contemporary Composition" 49]) is true of that form of classical rhetoric that was filtered through Ramism, but only of that form. For Puritanism, correct understanding is primarily a question of making the mind match the universe. For humanist rhetoric, however, it is a question of investigating the mind itself. This difference in epistemology is reflected in the different metaphors for understanding: dialogic rhetoric frequently relies on metaphors of tension, balance, and simultaneity (thereby tending to describe discourse as a process), whereas Puritanism relies on metaphors that presume sudden revelation (ones that it is interesting to note often suggest undressing, unveiling, or stripping) and submission. The arguments of the opposition are included in Puritan discourse in order to make that undressing and submitting more stylish.

At the simplest level, then, the answer to the question with which this chapter began is that Puritanism precludes controversia because Puritan ontology and epistemology reject that one might learn by contemplating the opposition. One can not learn by considering what must be patently false; one learns by returning to perception. The oppositions do not move the listener to a new cognitive understanding; they might make the discourse more moving, but they do not change (nor convey) the meaning of the discourse. That meaning is the thesis. Whereas a humanist like Donne seems to try to hover between opposing positions and thereby reaches some nearly ineffable understanding, a Puritan like Ames asserts that "No man can at the same time have two *contrary probable opinions,* concerning the same thing" (*Of Conscience* 17). For Puritanism, the presence of contraries requires that the person with integrity use the skills of perception to choose the one that is obviously true and reject the other that is equally obviously false.

4

Sugaring of Rhetoric

[E]loquence is not at all at variance with the simplicity of the gospel,
when it does not merely not disdain to give way to it, and be in subjec-
tion to it, but also yields service to it, as a handmaid to her mistress.
—Calvin, *Corinthians* 1: 77

In the previous chapter I argued that although Puritan discourse
includes statements from the opposition, it is not controversia. Such opposing points of view are not part of the composing process because
they are neither taken nor presented as legitimate interpretations or
viewpoints. The place of the opposition in specific instances of Puritanism thereby neatly epitomizes the place of difference in the Puritan
public sphere. And noting what work is actually done by that opposition helps to resolve the paradox with which the first chapter begins.
Defenders of Puritanism have pointed to the apparent freedom of the
Puritan public sphere: It did include oppositional voices in the sense
that people like Hutchinson had the opportunity to make a statement
in front of the meeting (just as a Puritan sermon includes a statement
of the opposition). This is a very limited notion of participation, however, for Hutchinson was presented to the congregation as a sinner already condemned by the authorities, just as the opposition argument is
defined as cavilling at the moment that it is introduced. It permits the
opposition to participate as a separate and fixed object that must either
submit or resist the equally separate and fixed object of authority. The
question here is: what is the point of the rhetor bringing up opposition
arguments? The answer is that such inclusion functioned as a figure of
speech rather than as a substantive point of view to be seriously considered.

This answer is deceptively simple, for it presumes the very dichotomy that should be questioned: Why is style necessarily opposed to
cognition? That is, what is the process of interpretation assumed in a
model that makes a figure of speech something different from the substance of an argument? To include points of the opposition in order to

reinforce how strongly one feels about rejecting them but then not to consider them as genuine alternatives that might change one's basic thesis, presumes that the elements of style are items that should be considered separate from the processes of inventing an argument (if they are considered in argumentation at all). These points are taken into consideration as the last step in the composing process, the stage at which one deletes excessive, incorrect, or infelicitous language and adds figures of speech like ribbons on a dress. The goal of this stage of composing is to create a perfect instance of the plain style, a piece of discourse in which each word nicely conveys the correct information.

Underlying this attitude toward style is an implicit model for the very way that style, rhetoric, and metaphor function, a model that is presumed throughout Calvinist discussions of language use. It is, for instance, behind Calvin's previously quoted explanation of the function of exhortation: that it enables the meaning (the confirming or convicting) to be conveyed with more force.[1] In this model, there is an object (the meaning) that is carried in the discourse, and style is something added on that makes the delivery of that package more effective. As Richardson says, in addition to needing Logic, which enables us to utter the truth, the effective promulgation of correct ideas is enhanced by "also a fine sugaring of them with Rhetoricke, for the more easie receiving of them" (9). The same metaphor is used for both the function of counter-arguments and the function of exhortation generally: there is something superficial in the discourse that affects something shallow in the human mind, and there is something deep in the discourse that is directed at something deep in human nature. Or, another way to describe this concept is that there is something (meaning, reasoning) over which something else (emotional force, metaphor, or rhetoric) is placed. This same antithesis—emotions being possibly placed in such a way as to cover logic—is reflected in models of human understanding. What may not be so obvious is that this antithesis of surface/depth in regard to style and meaning is concurrently a theory of metaphor and a metaphor for communication.

The inclusion of opposition argument, for instance, is clearly a rhetorical strategy that does not affect the meaning of the sermon or argument: Because recognition of truth is more or less immediate (the regenerate and reprobate equally quickly recognize the truth of a sermon, but the latter choose to push it away) the audience can be counted upon to recognize immediately the speciousness of counter-arguments. This view of audience reaction assumes that neither the counter-arguments nor their presentation could possibly change the listeners' intellectual understanding of the issues at hand, although it may add a certain stylistic attractiveness or emotional force to the speech. As Arnauld says, "Figures express the Passions of the Soul" (1: 156); they "signifie the Motion and Gesture of him that speaks ... whereas simple expressions sets forth only the naked Truth" (1: 155). Perkins's analysis of Scriptural figures always describes their emotional significance: "The Pleonasme of the Verbe doth either make the speech more emphaticall and significant; or else signifieth and sheweth vehemency, or certainty, or speedinesse" ("Arte" 658). He explains repetition: "Figures of a word in the repetition of a word or sound, have for the most part an emphasis in them" ("Arte" 659). Dialogic rhetoric simply assumes that a piece of discourse is itself a process, the "meaning" of which is the experience, but monologic rhetorics describe it as an object, the "meaning" of which is a logical proposition that can be stated in one sentence. The discourse demonstrates that proposition, and the speaker uses rhetoric to dress it up to make it more attractive or vivid to the audience.[2]

In addition to being a theory of audience reception, this is, as Sloane has pointed out, a theory about the relationship between emotions and reason, which posits that there are two separable mental and verbal processes. The assumption is that the two operate separately by being conveyed through different parts of a piece of discourse *and* by appealing to different parts of the mind. The logic of the argument is conveyed to reason through the thesis of the discourse, and the emotional appeal is conveyed to the emotions through the stylistic elegance (meaning, for the most part, metaphor). Whereas the will—that is, the part of the mind that enables someone to behave a particular way—may be more or less influenced by how strongly one feels about the proposition, emotions have nothing to do with one's intellectual understanding of the proposition under consideration. This will is not quite the same as free will. It is the ability to choose, but not the existential capacity to choose freely (see Fiering 144–46). Although it is easy to overstate this hierarchy (the Puritans did not utterly reject the emotions or emotional appeals), logic is always given a more valued position than emotions; it is not only more reliable, but ultimately the place of meaning.

To discuss this as a Puritan theory is not to say that it is only a Puritan theory. This idea about the relationship between emotional force (conveyed by metaphor) and meaning (which can be stated literally) still has its adherents. Donald Davidson is perhaps the most recent proponent of such a view. He has argued that "metaphors mean what the words, in their most literal interpretation, mean, and nothing more" (245). The metaphor qua metaphor has no cognitive content other than that also present in a paraphrase using literal language: "What I deny is that metaphor does its work by having a special meaning, a specific cognitive content" (262). One does not learn something from the metaphor that one could not have learned from the paraphrase; hence, the only difference between a metaphorical statement and its literalized paraphrase is the effect it might have on the audience. That is, it might strengthen certain *feelings* about some proposition, but it does not teach us anything or convey the meaning. It can "make us appreciate some fact—but not by standing for, or expressing, the fact" (262). This limitation of the work that metaphor does is woven into the idea that metaphorical language use is the exception to the rule of literal language: it is "marked" language use.

In this chapter, I will suggest that an argument about Puritan rhetoric (both the academic discipline of rhetoric and the practice of Puritan public discourse) is an argument about metaphor—not simply about the Puritans' use of a particular metaphor, nor even about their theory of metaphor, but about the role of metaphor in cognition. Because the various issues I have raised in previous chapters (about ontology, epistemology, religious tolerance, and the assumption of linearity in the process of composing) are woven into Puritan theories and use of metaphor, it is very easy for this argument to get tangled. To try to put it very simply, my argument is that the Puritan insistence that metaphors have no cognitive content is part and parcel of the desire for monologic discourse: Puritan theories of metaphor presume a model of linguistic references that makes all difference a form of dissent, whereas the limited power positions in discourse contribute to seeing all dissent as a violent attack upon God himself. Thus, simply using different words can be perceived as an attack; having a different view is a kind of war. I will here mention that the implicit theory of linguistic reference, meaning, and metaphor is actually internally contradictory, in that it also appeals to a set of assumptions that are incompatible with other aspects of Puritanism; but that is a point that will be pursued in the next chapter.

As said before, this theory of the function of metaphor in language itself relies on a metaphor, one that is used throughout other issues in Puritan discourse (such as the relationship of reason and emotion, and the above discussion of meaning and affect). The true and most valued thing (reason, meaning) is separable from some outer covering of problematic value (emotion, rhetoric). This outer covering is necessary because of the cupidity of audiences, but in a perfect world, or at the right moment, it is removed to unveil the body of knowledge. There are, then, several binary oppositions that line up rather neatly: surface/depth; appearance/reality; meaning/effect; body/clothing; reason/emotion; logic/rhetoric. The metaphor of rhetoric (and metaphor) as ornamentation on a body of meaning is, I will argue, profoundly meaningful, both reflecting and reinforcing the model of composing as a strictly linear process. Again, I will emphasize that this issue regarding the aptness of the Puritan metaphor for metaphor is more than a pedantic issue about language use: This theory of metaphor also reflects and reinforces the Puritans' inability to include oppositions in discursively productive ways.

I

The discipline of rhetoric, although a part of a gentleman's education since the sophists, has been wildly variant in terms of just what is taught in courses called rhetoric. For some theorists (such as Aristotle and Cicero) it is a discipline of *inquiry* that enables one to pose the kinds of questions that would help resolve conflict, understand a situation better, even move toward the truth (if not the Truth). In such a tradition (typically called the classical or humanist tradition), eloquence, always a part of rhetoric, is assumed to be necessarily connected to morality and truth.[3]

For others, especially in the Augustinian tradition, rhetoric is a discipline that teaches the eloquence helpful for effectively presenting the knowledge that one has gained through some other form of inquiry (such as logic or theology). Calvinism was essentially within that latter category, and it was especially important for the death of rhetoric as a discipline of *inquiry*. When Calvin explains the place of eloquence in Christian preaching, the most that he can grant it is the place of a handmaid:

> Eloquence is not at all at variance with the simplicity of the gospel, when it does not merely not disdain to give way to it, and be in subjection to it, but also yields service to it, as a handmaid to her mistress. . . . That eloquence, therefore, is neither to be condemned nor despised,

> which . . . tends to call us back to the native simplicity of the gospel, tends to exalt the simple preaching of the cross by voluntarily abasing itself, and, in fine, acts the part of a herald to procure a hearing for those fishermen and illiterate persons, who have nothing to recommend them but the energy of the Spirit.   (Calvin, *Corinthians* 1: 77)

In other words, Calvinist eloquence should be nothing more than a transparent and immaterial container encapsulating and conveying the word of God.

As soon as style itself has any kind of presence, it has usurped the place of its mistress, attempting to draw attention and power to itself. So, the perfect use of rhetoric is one that effaces itself: "the minister may, yea and must, privately use at his liberty the arts, philosophy and variety of reading while he is framing his sermon, but he ought in public to conceal all these from the people and not to make the least ostentation" (Perkins, *Work* 345). His use of the traditional Ciceronian recommendation that "it is also a point of art to conceal art" (345) is non-Ciceronian in an important way. When he says that "Human wisdom must be concealed," he is not worried about alienating the audience by pomposity but about retaining the proper power relationship. He warns that excellence in style could cause people to attribute grace to human agency, and "hearers ought not to ascribe their faith to the gifts of man, but to the power of God's word" (345).

In a world that cannot imagine human agency in grace, the role of a humanist discipline like rhetoric becomes extremely complicated, if not confused. Rhetoric should teach ministers to exercise certain skills, but in such a way that the skills themselves (and the ministers' excellence at them) should disappear. This is simultaneously a theory of language use and the composing process. I want to set aside the second theory, although it is important, in order to talk about what it means to think of eloquence as something superficial that results from adding style (meaning, more or less, metaphor) onto a piece of discourse.

Having limited rhetoric to the study of embellishment, the Puritans limited the amount and kind of embellishment, since they recommended (almost exclusively) the plain style. The difficulty of describing exactly what Puritans meant by plain style indicates the unhappy fit between classical terms and Christian literature. In classical rhetoric, it is conventional to list three levels of style, indicating the degree and complexity of the figures of speech (primarily metaphors). In the classical era, the high style, with the greatest number of complicated figures, was considered the most learned, sophisticated, and elegant. This association of the high style and sophistication made it difficult for some early Christians trained in rhetoric to see any elegance in Christian literature. As Augustine observed, some were repelled by the apparent crudeness of New Testament Greek (and classical culture had never viewed Hebrew as a learned language). Christian apologists responded in two ways: they argued that Scripture actually contains a mixture of styles, and they valorized the plain style.

Prior to the Reformation, the former defense was probably more common, but Puritans reasserted the importance of the second. It has been suggested that Puritans objected to Anglican preaching on the grounds that it was often too high for the general public who made up the congregation—that the style was inaccessible to the populace.[4] But this interpretation ignores that Puritan sermons discussed complicated points of doctrinal controversy and that the structure associated with the plain style "with its myriad of points and sub-points" is difficult for anyone to follow (Stout 95). The problem with high preaching, according to the Puritans, was not that it was too intellectually demanding, nor that it excluded any section of the audience, but that it presented the wrong relationship among rhetoric, text, and audience. Puritans argued that preachers who used the Anglican method were too concerned with sweetening or dressing up doctrine, and they were thereby ignoring their primary duty: humiliating the listeners by logically demonstrating humanity's inherent unworthiness to receive grace. In addition, as Calvin said of the Corinthians, too much ornamentation (or inappropriate ornamentation) draws attention to itself and the speaker rather than the body of Scripture beneath. It thereby constitutes a mixing of the sacred and the profane, while making the minister and texts objects of contemplation rather than transparent vessels of God's word. Sermons, they said, should be plain. As early Christian apologists had pointed out, however, Scripture itself is not purely plain in the rhetorical sense, so any sermon that relies heavily on Scriptural language will necessarily involve all three styles.[5] The Puritans' use of the term "plain style" is somewhat complicated, then, sometimes being used in ways compatible with the classical rhetorical tradition and sometimes not.

There is an ever deeper problem with the vagueness of the concept of "style" in regard to the Puritans. John Wilson, in his very influential book *The Pulpit in Parliament*, has defined the plain style as the structure that Puritan sermons used (see especially chapter 5), but such a definition of style would have violated Ramist rhetoric. Ramus (and Ramists) put arrangement (i.e., structure) under the heading of logic, not rhetoric. And style was in the discipline of rhetoric. In other words, the term "plain style" should not refer to the structure of the sermon but the degree of figuration at the sentence and paragraph level. But in practice the "plain style" is as much identified by structure and intention as by anything that might fit classical conceptions regarding stylistic complexity. The term is, in other words, a synechdoche. The synecdoche was and is never explicitly discussed as such, probably because acknowledging the term "plain style" to be a kind of figure of speech that cannot be literally and thoroughly paraphrased raises the fundamental irony that Paul Ricoeur has noted. Discussions of metaphor, even (or especially) those that insist that metaphor is purely ornamental, are always highly metaphorical. One wonders why people who insist that metaphor is a meaningless ornament do not discuss the point in literal language.

The term "plain style" typically evokes a style of preaching that consists of a four-part sermon structure, with Ramistic outlining structuring each of those parts. It is, in some vague sense, language that is not intended to draw attention to itself or to the eloquence of the minister. Figures of speech, therefore, might be appropriate, as long as they have Scriptural origin, effectively explicate doctrine, and do not draw attention to themselves. If, on the contrary, one is using such ornamentation with an eye to displaying one's skill, then such use is neither plain nor godly. Thus, one determines whether or not something is the plain style partially by inferring motive—is the speaker trying to draw attention to himself or to God—and through some unspecified notion about how much ornamentation is too much.[7]

Here we have returned to the discussion of speaker motive from the first chapter. Such a reliance on speaker motive makes limited sense in Puritanism because it fits with the general viewpoint that the morality of an action is determined entirely by motive. No action is inherently good, they said, because anything can be done for the wrong motives: "In fact, there is no action so perfect as to be absolutely free from stain; though it may appear more evidently in some than in others" (Calvin, *Four Last Books of Moses* 1: 35). As Milton says: "So little knows / Any, but God alone, to value right / The good before him, but perverts best things / To worst abuse, or to their meanest use" (bk. 4, 201–4). Desiring to please God is not necessarily good, if one is motivated purely out of fear of his wrath; one might live a fully virtuous life and still go to hell, if one behaved merely out of habit or out of some desire to get along with one's friends. In this sense, the Puritans' attitude toward rhetoric is like their attitude toward everything else: human use of it is good insofar as that use is as God intends; it is bad when we use it to our own ends. What distinguishes good from bad is the motive that we have in our actions.

The Puritans, then, categorize style in the same way that many modern rhetoricians categorize discourse: by the motives of the speaker. And as was discussed earlier, such a strategy for distinguishing types of discourse is problematic. That is not to say that other methods of distinguishing levels of style—such as saying that metaphorical language use is marked—are more simple or clear. For instance, there is a famous story generally repeated about the change in Cotton's style when he converted to Puritanism. He was a preacher famous for his effective use of high style until he was converted to Puritanism. That conversion was made public when one Sunday he preached a sermon free from the flights of verbal fancy and literary conceits that his audience expected. This story is typically repeated as a synecdoche for the importance of the plain style to Puritanism, and it points to what I earlier referred to as the muddled notion of what distinguishes metaphorical from literal language. If plain style is determined by its lack of marked-ness in regard to language use (that is, if "literal" language is opposed to "metaphorical" language by the former being the norm), then Cotton's strikingly plain sermon was not plain style. After all, he was drawing attention to his use of language; the only reason that we know of this incident is that his audience was so stunned that at least one listener wrote about it, and the story has become famous. They were not stunned by the doctrine he preached, but by his linguistic style, by what was conveyed about him and his new relationship to religion through his use (or lack thereof) of metaphor.[8] I am arguing, in short, that at least in that era, "un-marked" and non-metaphorical language use were not synonymous. In fact, Puritans were "marked" by their lack of ornamentation and figural complexity.

As vague and even contradictory as this notion was (and is) it is extremely important for the status of rhetoric. The sort of playfulness that Sloane and others have noted in a rhetorician's use of language results from the sense that catachresis, not simile, stands as the prototypical use of language. Catachresis is a metaphor for which there is no literal translation, such as Aristotle's own use of the word "metaphor." George Lakoff and Mark Johnson are the most recent representatives of this view, but it has a long tradition in rhetoric. If there is always a slip between the lip and cup when it comes to language and representation, then rhetoric (as the study of figures) is necessary for thinking carefully about the world. If, however, the world can easily be represented in literal language, then rhetoric is nothing but a trivial art of adding glitter onto a preexisting piece of discourse.

Cmiel has noted that valorizing the plain style is connected to a certain sense of how language works: "The plain style also creates the illusion that language can be like glass, a medium without the infusion of a self" (260). The Puritan tendency to absent themselves and their own thinking from the process of communication (especially by universalizing the process of interpretation) relies on just such an illusion. More specifically, Puritan discussion of linguistic meaning connects truth in language with a word-to-thing reference. This assumption as to what makes a statement true can be seen in, for instance, Cotton Mather's recommendation to virtuous women as to how they should speak: "As your *Speech* ought always to be *true,* and there should be no less an Agreement between your *Hearts* and *Words,* than between your *Words* and *Things*" (emphasis in original, *Ornaments* 55). For this, as for other Puritan theories of linguistic references, language functions to communicate only when each word clearly refers to a thing that exists in God's Creation. Thus, clarity of language and specificity of reference are one and the same: "Nevertheless we may call every *Idea* clear, so far as it is distinct. . . . Now because *Clearness* and Distinction are one and the same in *Ideas*" (emphasis in original, Arnauld 1: 97). This equation of clarity and specific reference is a theory of language appropriate to the role of objects in Puritan ontology; Arnauld says that words are clear "when they represent to us as much as suffices to apprehend the object clearly and distinctly" (1: 99). This idea about linguistic reference is not unique to the Puritans. Sallie McFague has referred to it as "the myth that in order for images to be true they must be literal" (32); that is, they must exist in the ontic world created by God.

Puritans were not univocally hostile to metaphor, but they were troubled by the rupture in linguistic reference that metaphor continually threatens. Like Aristotle, Puritan rhetoric categorizes metaphor as a form of substitution, or translation, a "borrowing" from one category to another. Smith's handbook of rhetorical terms (which Cotton Mather recommended to his son) defines metaphor as "Metaphor: it is a Translation of words from one species to another: It is a trope when we expresse ourselves by a word of a like signification to that which we mean" (9), and "a Trope which notes out comparison, and is when one like is put for another like unto it" (10). A trope (a term he uses interchangeably with metaphor) is "when words are used for elegancy in a changed signification; or when a word is drawn from its proper and genuine signification to another" (2). These definitions have the various assumptions that one generally finds in definitions of metaphors: metaphors (and tropes) operate at the level of a word; they function through the substitution or exchange of one word for another thing with which it shares some quality or qualities.

With this model of metaphor, there is always something wrong or deviant about metaphor, since one is not using a word in its "proper" reference. Calvin, for example, points out that Christ is regularly referred to with "words borrowed from nature" and that "We must allow that there is a degree of impropriety in the language when what is borrowed from created things is transferred to the hidden majesty of God" (Calvin, *Hebrews* 35). Such "impropriety" is not inherently wrong, as elsewhere he notes that "this impropriety of language is so far from having anything harsh in it, that on account of the contrast it adds beauty to the sentence" (Calvin, *Hebrews*, 167–68). Metaphor is dangerous in that it threatens to mix together things that should be separate, but this mixing is a kind of superficial application of something inappropriate onto something else—it does not change deep meaning but superficial appearance.

This theory that style is nothing more than ornament added on to a body of discourse involves several problematic assumptions about the nature of language. I want to emphasize three: first, that figures of speech function by substituting one word for another; second, that simile is the typical figure (so that a theory can explain all figurative language by explaining how simile works); third, that language itself works by a word-to-thing reference. Belief in the plain style (and the attendant denigration of rhetoric) is dependent on these three assumptions.[9] And they are deeply problematic, if not obviously false.

The notion that figures of speech work by substitution has a long history in the discipline of rhetoric, beginning with Aristotle's use of that metaphor in order to describe how metaphor works. As with Aristotle, discussion of style quickly becomes a discussion of metaphor. Although books on rhetoric always list other figures, they explain how figurative language in general works by discussing metaphor.

That discussion is itself limited to the sorts of metaphors that can themselves be explained by substitution; catachresis is treated, if at all, as an anomaly to be ignored. Paul Ricoeur has aptly summarized the typical explanation of metaphor that results from this series of moves: "Instead of giving their proper names to certain things, or facts, or experiences, the writer chooses to use the name of something else by extending the meaning of this foreign name" ("Word, Polysemy, Metaphor" 76). So, for example, when what I mean is "John is brave" I say, "John is a lion." I have thereby substituted the metaphor (lion) for the correct name (brave). As Ricoeur says, this explanation of the function (and effect) of metaphor makes figures of speech nothing more than an ornament added on to the real meaning: "[M]etaphor offers no new information. It teaches nothing. For the same reason, metaphor is a mere decorative device. It has no informative value; it merely adorns language in order to please. It gives colour to speech, it provides a garment to cover the nudity of common usage" ("Word, Polysemy, Metaphor" 77).[10]

As indicated in its very definition (that a metaphor substitutes one word for another) this explanation for figures of speech assumes that the word is the basic unit of meaning, and as Ricoeur and others have argued, it is not. One even sees the problems with this assumption in the same handbooks that define metaphor in such a way, such as Smith's 1657 handbook. Some figures function by rearrangement of elements of a sentence, not substitution of one word for another. "Epistrophe," for example, is defined as "a repetition of the same word or sound in the ends of divers members of a sentence" (Smith 98). The effect of the example ("When I was a childe, I spake as a childe, I understood as a childe, I thought as a childe") is not a result of individual words, but the sentence as a whole (Smith 99). More important, many figures do not function at the sentence level but at the level of paragraph, section, or entire discourse. "Symploce" is defined by the same handbook as "when severall sentences or clauses of sentences have the same beginning, and the same ending; or when all our beginnings and all our endings are alike" (100). The description of rhetoric, therefore, as the skill of ornamentation through substitution of individual words for other words is simply inaccurate, or accurate only for the kinds of metaphors that are clearly compressed similes.

But in addition, this assumption that metaphor is a question of stylistic addition that does not change the underlying meaning is itself belied by analysis of Puritan metaphor. As will be discussed later,

Puritan metaphors for metaphor are deeply meaningful, for they sig-nify (and probably reinforced) profoundly held cultural assumptions about gender, servitude, and truth. If metaphors merely added to emo-tional force, then analysis of recurrent metaphors would not uncover *beliefs.*

The second assumption about ornamentation is that a statement is true when each word in it corresponds to some external state of affairs. Such a theory of linguistic reference (that places the locus of meaning in the word) is what Paul Ricoeur has called "the tyranny of the word in the theory of meaning" (*Rule of Metaphor* 45) and his objection is that it is inaccurate. My objection is that it contributed to the Puritan con-ception of the ideal speech situation that made any difference a dis-agreement and any disagreement a sign of Satanic presence. For the Puritans, a godly community would be a group of individuals who be-lieve the same thing and articulate it in exactly the same words. Here is most clearly where one sees how the Puritan theories of ontology, epistemology, linguistic reference, and the public sphere are entan-gled. The assumption is that everyone actually has the same ideas in their heads because those ideas have been placed in Creation by God and are perceived by Logic. The godly will naturally use the right words for those correct ideas, thereby communicating correct ideas to one another. Any slippage at any point was threatening to the Puri-tans—such as Quakers who appeared to have different ideas, episte-mologies that suggested human perception might be unreliable, theo-ries of persuasion that made rhetoric more important than logic, or theories of language that suggested that words might not literally re-present things that exist in the ontic logos.[11]

The third problem with seeing use of metaphor as a kind of super-ficial and easily decoded substitution is that it makes all figurative lan-guage a subset of simile. It is to say, as the Puritans did, that the only difference between a simile and a metaphor is whether the "like" is explicit or implicit ("John is like a lion" or "John is a lion"). This equa-tion of simile and metaphor, although made by rhetoricians like Aris-totle and Quintilian, is deeply problematic in regard to metaphors. It is completely untenable when one recognizes that metaphors are not the archetypal figure of speech, that the figures that cannot be explained through substitution of individual words (e.g., symploce) are far more common than metaphors.

In addition, as McFague and others have argued, simile and meta-phor actually function in different ways. Metaphor insists upon "two active thoughts which remain in permanent tension or interaction with each other" (emphasis removed, 37) so that it "is and is not" in the interpreter's mind. This tension enables us to reflect on both parts of the metaphor, so that we are surprised into seeing the similarities and dissimilarities *at the same time* between, for example, God and someone who loans us money: "By retaining the interaction of *two* thoughts active in the mind, one recalls, as one does not with a simile, that the two are dissimilar as well as similar. One difficulty with simile in contrast to metaphor is that simile softens the shock of the linkage through its 'like,' reducing an awareness of the dissimilarity, and hence allowing us to slip into literalistic thinking. A metaphor that works is sufficiently unconventional and shocking so that we instinctively say no as well as yes to it, thus avoiding absolutism." (emphasis in original, McFague 38). One of the absolutisms that we avoid when we are reminded of the dissimilarities is an equation of identity. As McFague says, "if all of our knowing is seeing one thing in terms of something else, those terms can never be collapsed" (54). Kenneth Burke has argued that an attentiveness to the metaphorical nature of language itself reminds one that "the word's 'meaning' is not identical with its sheer materiality. There is a qualitative difference between the symbol and the symbolized" (*Rhetoric of Religion* 16), thus keeping one mildly skeptical about the ability of words to convey exactly what one means. This skepticism about language is, as I have argued in an earlier chapter, a recurrent theme in the history of rhetoric, and Sloane has claimed that it is one of the defining characteristics of the rhetorical mind. In contrast to Ramistic theories of language, rhetorical humanism points to the paucity of literal language and presents metaphor as a necessary and effective method of enriching that situation, because it highlights (rather than denies) the inherent imperfection of linguistic reference. Hence, for rhetoricians, language is essentially metaphorical, and not only can metaphor teach, it inevitably does so.

Ramists, too, sometimes point to the paucity of language, but the problem is not that language necessarily points in two directions at once, as much as there cannot be enough words to have a single word for every thing. So, we find the plaint later repeated in Locke: "The best way to avoid the confusion of Words, which we find in different Languages is to make a new Language, and to coyn new Words, to belong only to those *Ideas,* which they are assign'd to signifie" (Arnauld 1: 126). Arnauld does not doubt the ability of words to represent everything that would need to be expressed in language. His only objection is to the sheer number of words that would then be necessary. The Ramistic solution to the problem of poverty of language is that one must use abstractions, but one can and should define them clearly and distinctly. And, of course, abstractions are explained not as metaphors (as they are for people like Lakoff, Burke, or McFague) but as aggregates of specific words (1: 126–56).

II

Having discussed the general explanation of metaphor, I now want to look more closely at the Puritan metaphors for metaphor: superficial glitter or ornamentation, clothing, and handmaid. To begin with the last, it was nearly a cliché even by the time that Calvin used it. But this metaphor would have considerably different meaning in Calvinist New England both because of the complicated status of handmaids in Scripture and because of New England's servant problems.

In regard to the first, the most famous handmaid in Scripture is Hagar, whom Abraham (at the urging of Sarah) impregnates when Sarah appears infertile. The Calvinist reading of this text emphasizes that Hagar responds to her pregnancy by becoming contemptuous of Sarah, is punished by Sarah for her insubordination, and bears Ishmael who is himself insubordinate. Ishmael, according to Calvin, later expresses contempt for Isaac, and Sarah "usurps the government of the house" by demanding that he be expelled (Calvin, *Genesis* 1: 542–43). The Calvinist reading of the story, then, is one of real and threatened usurping of rightful power, of the lower trying to become the higher, the true seed of Abraham being supplanted through the apparent heir, divine will obscured by a human arrangement, and the appropriate social order harassed by feminine sexuality and desire for power.

Calvin uses many of the same images in his discussion of this human arrangement as he does in his discussion of bad eloquence: it is an over-reliance on the fruits of human wisdom and ingenuity rather than a simple faith in God's will (Calvin, *Genesis* 1: 425). It is also a deviation from the word of God in which Abraham has permitted himself "to be borne away by the persuasion of his wife" (1: 426) and the result of clever "contrivance" and "an exceedingly common disease of the mind" (1: 427). The various threatened usurpations—of a human plan for divine will, of the true wife for the false one, of the true son for the apparent one—are the result of Abraham's "mixing his own and his wife's imagination with the word of God" (1: 429). Just as the Corinthians' eloquence involved a mixing of the pure with the impure, so does Sarah's sin.

Hagar's sin was to assume that she was given power by being made the vessel of Abraham's seed and to think that her changed state (that is, communicating Abraham's seed) should have resulted in a change in her worldly situation. But as Calvin says, "her condition was not changed in the sight of God" (Calvin, *Genesis* 1: 431); she remained a servant who owed complete obedience to her mistress. This is the same accusation that Calvin (and Calvinists) makes against rhetoric: that it mistakes its role as the communicator of knowledge for having some share in that knowledge itself. It is the warning that Perkins makes about human eloquence—that we will credit the container for the thing contained. And this is the part of the metaphor that we are likely to miss by thinking of it as a conventional cliché: to say that eloquence is a handmaid carries the accusation of potential usurpation. Rhetoric, as the discipline of eloquence, should not think of itself as powerful, even if it helps to carry the seed of grace. In short, to call eloquence a handmaid would have been a deeply meaningful metaphor for New England Calvinists, suggesting the vices that any human discipline might exhibit; it is potentially dangerous because it may misunderstand its own power and attempt to usurp the place of the truth.

There are other implications about power involved in describing eloquence as the handmaid considering Calvinist ideas about servants. For instance, Calvin says that even if Sarah's punishment of her had been completely unjust, any rebellion on the part of Hagar was forbidden: "By the same argument it is proved, that if masters at any time deal too hardly with their servants, or if rulers treat their subjects with unjust asperity, their rigour is still to be endured, nor is there just cause for shaking off the yoke, although they may exercise their power too imperiously. . . . They who have proudly and tyrannically governed shall one day render their account to God; meanwhile, their asperity is to be borne by their subjects, till God, whose prerogative it is to raise the abject and to relieve the oppressed, shall give them succour" (Calvin, *Genesis* 1: 431). This emphasis on endurance was continued by the New England Calvinists: "The Puritan ministers never tired of inculcating obedience. It made no difference, they said, whether the master was kind or unkind, harsh, or lenient; his servants must obey every command" (Morgan, *The Puritan Family* 112).[12]

Servants were not always obedient, however, and court records and sermons indicate a near obsession with the problems that servants presented. Laurel Ulrich quotes from a woman's letter to her daughter recommending against opening a dairy because she would have to hire servants, "and you may be sencible by your own experience how unsteady servants are" (74). It was not simply that they were insufficiently pious (although they were) or insubordinate, nor that they sometimes stole, but that they were often quite shrewd at finding sources of power for themselves. As Edmund Morgan says, "by the threat of minor annoyances, an unscrupulous servant could win concessions from his master," and "a master who wished to save his house from fire and his goods from theft had to make some effort to win the goodwill of his servants" (*The Puritan Family* 123, 124). Like the worldly art of rhetoric, the worldly servants continually threatened not to stay in their correct places.

Servants, like Hagar, also threatened to usurp the position of their betters, and unlike Hagar, they often succeeded. Winthrop's "Model of Christian Charity" describes a perfectly static society with its social hierarchy divinely dictated and preserved. But his *Journals* describe a chaotic situation in which someone who had been a servant might someday hire someone who had been his master. Ulrich interprets the legal conflicts between Patience Denison and her one time servant Sarah Roper as revealing "the difficulties experienced by the New England gentry in maintaining a system of deference inherited from the Old World" (63). The insubordination of servants (and inferiors in general) was a nearly constant plaint in Puritan Jeremiads. This insubordination was generally attributed to the servants being what Puritans called "strangers," that is, they were not professing members of the church, so, like the impropriety of metaphor, they added a profane element to a godly community. Like rhetoric, they thereby threatened the stability of the community by potentially seducing others (as when Granger taught another servant to engage in sodomy). Also like rhetoric, they threatened to conceal the good by sinning so much that God's wrath would be vented on the entire community.

Finally, and perhaps most interesting, is the issue of sexual transgression. Morgan has suggested that the particular practices of indentured servitude, slavery, and apprenticeship provided no sanctioned method of expression of adult sexuality, so that servants continually posed the threat of sexual instability of various sorts. Forbidden from marrying, indentured servants and slaves, according to Morgan, conspired to meet lovers (*The Puritan Family* 128–31), sometimes stealing food from the masters to feed the secret family. David Konig has pointed to the "great deal of uneasiness" that existed about servant sexuality and the ways that issues about sexuality were woven into court cases. Courts were often asked to determine whether a servant had seduced a master (with the implication that it was done in order to improve her situation), or if she had been raped, or if any contact had in fact taken place (152). The sexual danger of servants is most famously indicated in Bradford's discussion of Thomas Granger's buggery of a mare, two goats, five sheep, two calves, and a turkey. The moral of this sad episode is, according to Bradford, "what care all ought to have what servants they bring into their families" (356).

Much of this tension is in Calvinist reading of the Hagar story, as the sexual relation between her and Abraham threatens the legitimate social order by introducing a foreign element. To say, then, that eloquence is the handmaid of the gospel is a very complicated metaphor that effectively conveys Puritan ambivalence about rhetoric—that rhetoric threatens to usurp the real, that it can confuse the mind by appealing to one's emotions and desires too effectively, that it potentially mixes the foreign with the true, and that it can change the appropriate authority relations by seduction. In other words, the Puritan metaphor of eloquence as a handmaid is meaningful.

I want to emphasize this point, as it is actually an important counter-argument to the assertion that metaphor is ornamentation, or that it merely adds emotional thrust to a proposition. If metaphors did not have cognitive content, were they only indicative of the emotional force that an author adds to the proposition, then one could not analyze metaphors in order to understand systems of thought. Puritans used the metaphor of rhetoric as a handmaid because it accurately expressed their ambivalence about rhetoric and servants.

Many of these same tensions are indicated in the metaphor that rhetoric is the clothing on the idea. I do want to emphasize that it is a mistake to think that Calvinism is simplistically hostile to rhetoric. In his commentaries on the Bible, Calvin presents Paul as the model for the Christian preacher (including in terms of his relationship to rhetoric), yet the very nature of his praise shows Calvinism's deep ambivalence toward rhetoric. The issues in determining moral versus immoral use of rhetoric involve self-consciousness and motive, not arranged skill at persuasion per se. Calvin uses rhetorical terms to identify Paul's strategies (such as prolepsis and concession) at the same time that he contrasts Paul's "rude, coarse and unpolished style" with the

love of vain words, which he attributes to the Corinthians. Calvin
thereby points to a striking paradox in Paul's discussion of preaching: although Paul claims not to be a rhetorician, he uses rhetorical
strategies. Calvin identifies such figures as circumlocution, antithesis,
prolepsis, synecdoche, hypallage, anastrophe, (Calvin, *Acts* 2: 30, 47,
69; *Corinthians* 1: 83, 100, 126). In fact, "rhetoricien" is the word that
Calvin uses in his French translation.[13] He says that Paul rejects the
kind of eloquence that "consists in skilful contrivance of subjects, ingenious arrangement, and elegance of expression. He declares that
he had nothing of this: nay more, that it was neither suitable to his
preaching nor advantageous" (Calvin, *Corinthians* 1: 73–74). But Calvin
also analyzes how carefully (even ingeniously) Paul arranges his discourses: "So that we see that Paul did not utter all things at one time,
but he tempered his doctrine as occasion did serve." He recommends
such a method to all preachers: "And because like moderation is
profitable at this day, it is convenient for faithful teachers wisely to consider where to begin, lest a preposterous and confused order do hinder
the proceeding of doctrine" (Calvin, *Acts* 2: 182). Calvin praises Paul
because his sermon "surmounted so many hindrances, while deriving
no assistance from the world" (Calvin, *Corinthians* 1: 101); yet, Calvin
uses rhetorical terms to identify Paul's strategies (thereby suggesting
that Paul did receive assistance from the worldly skill of rhetoric). Paul
is not a "rhetoricien" but he does use rhetoric.

What seems to make Paul's use of rhetoric moral is that he does not
use it in order to draw attention to himself, his skill, or his learning,
but as a means to bring the Word of God to his listeners; his motives
are pure. This difference in motive is made manifest in clothing, that
is, the ornamentation that the Corinthians used signified their spiritual state.[14] What was wrong with the Corinthians, Calvin says, was
that they used "human wisdom" to disguise the word of God. The result was that "by these disguises (so to speak) the simplicity of the gospel was disfigured, and Christ was, as it were, clothed in a new and
foreign garb, so that the pure and unadulterated knowledge of him
was not to be found. Farther, as men's minds were turned aside to neat-
ness and elegance of expression, to ingenious speculations, and to
an empty show of superior sublimity of doctrine, the efficacy of the
Spirit vanished, and nothing remained but the dead letter" (Calvin,
Corinthians 1: 73). The metaphor with which Calvin is working was a
cliché in medieval and Renaissance handbooks on rhetoric: style is the
clothing on the idea. One gets the idea (or content) from some other

discipline (such as theology), which one dresses in the fashion one has learned in the discipline of rhetoric. Calvin's objection was that they have put the wrong clothes on Christ.

As with the handmaid metaphor, this is a deeply significant way of thinking about language use and a metaphor, which would have conveyed a considerable amount of information in the Puritan era. The Puritans were in the midst of the transition that took place elsewhere in the eighteenth century and that Sennett has discussed in *The Fall of Public Man*. Sennett argues that authenticity came to be a social and moral value because "What makes an action good (that is, authentic) is the character of those who engage in it, not the action itself" (11).[15] Sennett aptly describes the Puritan obsession with social display when he points out that "when a society mobilizes these feelings, when it deflates the objective character of action and inflates the importance of subjective states of feeling of the actors, these questions of self-justification in action, via a 'symbolic act,' will come systematically to the fore" (11–12). In Puritanism, these questions came to the fore via one's public confession of faith, one's business dealings, and one's clothing.

The extensive sumptuary laws of New England demonstrate this near obsession with the possibility that people could appear to be different from what they were. Whereas some of the laws forbad certain kinds of clothing for everyone (such as bodices that exposed breasts), most involved questions of people wearing clothing that would convey the wrong message about their true identity in the community. The laws were especially concerned with someone wearing clothing above one's station. In other words, what made clothing "showy" was that it was a false sign, a metaphor with a dishonest reference. Sennett has described this issue in regard to European clothing in the late eighteenth century when discussing the considerable anxiety created by clothing that did not clearly communicate the class and profession of the wearer. In Puritan New England and late-eighteenth-century Europe, people who wore such meaningless (or, more accurately, misleading) clothing did so out of pleasure with the ornamentation itself, thereby implicitly or explicitly threatening two forms of usurpation. First, they were reversing the proper order of depth and surface by taking pleasure in the superficial. Second, this misrepresentation of their true social rank was considered threatening to the proper social order because it was seen as flaunting, as social inferiors expressing envy and contempt for their betters. Like Hagar, maidservants who wore petticoats and lace were seen as attempting to draw for themselves the privileges that properly belonged to their mistresses. Cotton Mather's condemnation of such misrepresentation is typical: "The *Ranks* of People should be discerned by their *Cloaths;* nor should we go in any Things but what may be called *Suits.* The Woman which will go as none but those who are *above* her, do or can, she shows her self to be as much out of her *Wits* as out of her *Place*" (emphasis in original, *Ornaments* 61).

Also like Hagar, they were seen as threatening to social order because they were mixing—not just signs of wealth with humble persons (and thereby the false with the true) but also foreign and native. Ward's rant about religious toleration naturally leads into a rant about clothing styles: both religious toleration and what he objects to about contemporary clothing involve mixing of foreign and native, false and true. Nathaniel Ward's criticism of contemporary clothing fashions involves many of the same metaphors of disguise, mixing the true and the foreign and mixing the genders. He complains of "goodly English-women imprisoned in French Cages" (27), and women who "disfigure themselves with such exotick garbes, as not only dismantles their native lovely lustre, but transclouts them into gantbar-geese, ill-shapen-shotten-shell-fish, Egyptian Hyeroglyphicks, or at the best into French flurts of the pastery" (26). His attack on men wearing long hair is that it disguises who they really are, and it is a mark of femininity (31). The association between ornamentation of women and ornamentation of a piece of discourse is quite explicit: "I honour the woman that can honour her selfe with her attire: a good Text alwayes deserves a fair Margent" (26). In all the cases of clothing use that should be forbidden, the problem is that there is a false implication between the sign and the signified—the ornamentation misrepresents the body underneath.

Michael Wigglesworth's "Praise of Eloquence" is an almost perfect instance of the Puritans damning rhetoric through the faint praise of the clothing metaphor. Eloquence's main virtue is that "by the power of eloquence ould truth receivs a new habit; though its essence be the same, yet its visage is so altered that it may currently pass and be accepted as a novelty" (from "Praise," quoted in P. Miller, *The American Puritans* 2: 674). The very effect that he attributes to eloquence is problematic in several ways: the Calvinists were ambivalent about any innovations or novelties in religion or doctrine; they generally equated such re-dressing of truth with pandering. In addition, this defense of eloquence conveys the arguments that rhetoric is nothing more than the study of selecting the form for a content that one gets from else-where. The choice of form is severely limited by convention; the clothes one should wear were usually determined by one's class and gender.[16] Finally, since the requirement for clothes is a result of the fall, in a per-fectly regenerated world we would need no clothes at all, so the meta-phor of clothing for rhetoric communicates that rhetoric is (at best) a kind of necessary evil.

These are precisely the same ambivalences conveyed through the metaphor of ornamentation for eloquence or rhetoric. In Cotton's dis-cussion of the Song of Solomon (*A Brief Exposition*), he differentiates good ornamentation from bad (as does Cotton Mather in *Ornaments*): glittery surface ornamentation is useless at best and misleading at worst, but beauty that glows from within is true beauty. Eloquence that comes from things that are simply added on to the outside is vastly in-ferior to eloquence that truly communicates the grace of the minister. As with handmaids and clothes, ornamentation that involves a mix-ing, a false representation, or a foreignness is wicked.

There are two points that are particularly important to the orna-mentation metaphor, which I want to emphasize. First, this is where one most clearly sees the composing process implied in Puritan theo-ries of eloquence. As I will discuss below, Puritans were actually con-tradictory on the role of calculated ornamentation versus inspired elo-quence. But when they do talk about ornamentation, it is as something that one adds on to a more or less finished piece of discourse. That is, as one can infer from the very metaphor, there is the assumption of a strictly linear composing process: one learns the truth from theology, one arranges the sermon according to Ramistic principles of organiza-tion, and one adds eloquence on to the finished product. Selecting the appropriate metaphors will not cause the author to reconsider the ar-gument, nor to refine one's sense of audience. This is, as I have said be-fore, very different from the recursive and somewhat chaotic method of composing recommended by humanist rhetoricians.

Second, any kind of surface beauty has the same limitations and potential dangers that the Calvinists attributed to rhetoric. When Cotton Mather describes the kind of beauty appropriate to a good woman he says: "By *Beauty* is meant a good Proportion and Symmetry of the Parts, and a Skin well varnished, or that which *Chrysostom* calls, *a good mixture of Blood and Flegm shining through a good Skin;* With all that harmonious Air of the Countenance which recommends it self, as a *Beauty* to the Eye of the Spectator. The *virtuous Woman* is not unthankful for this *Beauty*, when the God of Nature has bestow'd any of it on her; and yet she counts it no *Virtue* for her to be very sensible of her being illustrated with such a *Beauty*" (emphasis in original, *Ornaments* 11–12). Symmetry, proportion, modesty, a natural arrangement, and a glow that comes from one's inner state are the same qualities that distinguish good rhetoric from bad. And as with rhetoric, a beautiful woman should count herself lucky, but not powerful, for her beauty.

This raises the final meaning that I want to draw out of Puritan metaphors for rhetoric and eloquence: that rhetoric is continually put into a feminized position. There has been considerable, and utterly inconclusive, debate regarding the place of women in American Puritanism—whether they were more or less powerful than women from a similar economic class in England—but it is certainly established that Puritans were ambivalent about the social value of femininity. And the vices ascribed to rhetoric are ones conventionally associated with the most socially troubling parts of effeminacy: seductiveness, vanity, superficiality, excessive ornamentation, manipulativeness, and potential insubordination.[17] Therefore, this too is a profoundly meaningful metaphor that enables one to understand the role of rhetoric in Puritanism. Like women, it is not inherently evil, but it is potentially dangerous when not held to its proper role. And as when it dresses Christ in the wrong clothes, it is most dangerous when it attempts to usurp power by feminizing the true rulers.[18]

The anxiety over the femininizing quality of rhetoric arises also in discussions of relations with the audience. Puritan ministers periodically found themselves defending their own somewhat aggressive rhetorical posture, and they generally did so through the presumption of an antithesis: either the minister engaged in the (obviously male) militaristic and violent attack on the listeners (which was, interestingly enough, a metaphor used interchangeably with logical demonstration) or he engaged in the (implicitly female) pandering to the audience. The metaphors that ministers use for describing the ideal sermons are not only disturbingly violent but also almost absurdly phallic; as Hooker says, "The words of a faithfull Minister are like arrowes, which if they be shot a cock height, they fall downe againe and doe nothing; but when a man levels at a mark, then, if ever, hee will hit it" (*Preparation* 63).

Edwards compares a minister with a sermon to a surgeon with a lance, and it is difficult not to see the metaphors as sexual: "When he has begun to thrust in his lance, whereby he has already put his patient to great pain, and he shrieks and cries out with anguish, he is so cruel that he will not stay his hand, but goes on to thrust it in further, until he comes to the core of the wound" ("Preaching the Terrors" 101–2). In addition to being male rhetoric (in that this sense of rhetoric assumes that the minister thrusts a phallus into the passive listener), rhetoric with such an intention is explicitly violent: "When the truth of God is delivered with a holy violence, and hearty affection by Gods servants, evermore it makes way, it beats downe, and breaks all before it, it wets more and sinkes more and farre deeper, then any kind of other teaching" (Hooker, *Implantation* 79).

This is to say that in several ways Puritan sermonizing is a question of dominating the audience, and the audience submitting to the minister in the same way that the minister should submit to God: "God hath promised that hee will march through with his worke, if God give us an heart to submit to his colours . . . he will march an end, not only in his owne providence . . . so hee will march an end in his servants . . . they will march in his strength, and he will keep them that they shall not retire disorderly" (Cotton, "Gods Mercie" 64). Salvation comes from submitting not only to God but to the ministers of the established church. Calvin describes how thoroughly submissive a sinner should be upon hearing the word of God: "and then we must not be slightly pricked or torn, but be thoroughly wounded, that being prostrate under a sense of eternal death, we may be taught to die ourselves" (Calvin, *Hebrews* 101). Or, as Cotton says, "First, If you would lay hold on Gods strength then lay downe all your owne weapons, all weapons of hostility against God, doe not onely lay aside opposition against Gods Church, but what ever sinnefull frame of heart or life thou hast" ("Gods Mercie" 69). Of course, this is the same way that the wife is to submit to the husband, or the servant to the master, and the husband and master to God. As discussed in the first chapter, power operates downward in a hierarchy, and any failure to submit to one's place in that hierarchy (such as by criticizing those above one) constitutes an attack on the supposed source of the power structure itself.

Other scholars have remarked on the Puritan tendency toward militaristic metaphors, as people who were, as Stout has said, "an embattled people of the Word who were commissioned to uphold a sacred and exclusive covenant between themselves and God" (7). Indeed, people on *both* sides of controversies invoked the sense of warfare that was so much a part of Calvinism. The Antinomian John Wheelwright, for instance, uses Ephesians 6.11 to argue that his congregation must "all of us prepare for battell and come out against the enimyes of the Lord" (Hall, *The Antinomian Controversy* 158). This sense of oneself as the righteous individual battling against self-evident evil is at the heart of the Puritan sense that the "Church shall be engaged in uninterrupted war in this world" (Calvin, *Harmony of the Evangelists* 1: 362).

My point, however, is not simply that militaristic metaphors were important for the self-definition of the Puritan community, but that they were not entirely metaphorical. These metaphors of discourse as a form of violence, of God's business as a kind of continual warfare, were literalized by Puritanism. As Boyd Berry has said, "The Puritans who fought with guns acted in precisely the same style as the Puritans who spun out theological doctrines, each functioning in a different sphere yet functioning in the same way" (170). Every aspect of the religious life—including engaging in discourse—is like the soldier's life, and "God is on our side, so long as we go on warfare under the kingdom of Christ" (Calvin, *Acts* 1: 184).

There are two ways in which this metaphor of the righteous battle for God was literalized. Obviously, this equation of discourse and violence figured in the New England Puritan tendency to engage in violence when discourse might have sufficed and to glorify violent engagements with indigenous peoples. After all, if there is no difference between someone saying something against the state and someone attacking the state, then all verbal dissent is open rebellion. Winthrop uses this argument to say that he was not persecuting people for difference of opinion or matters of conscience, but for sedition. Any criticism of the New England elders, he argues, is the same as a call to arms against them because it might undermine their authority (Winthrop, "Short Story" 299). In his *Journals*, Winthrop tells the story of an anabaptist who refused to let his child be baptized. "Being presented for this, and enjoind to suffer the child to be baptized, he still refusing, and disturbing the church, he was again brought to the court not only for his former contempt, but also for saying that our baptism was antichristian. . . . he was ordered to be whipped, not for his opinion, but for reproaching the Lord's ordinance" (2: 177). The distinction in the last sentence is extremely subtle; he was not punished for his opinion, but for what the opinion was. Similarly, Cotton insists that Williams was banished, not for holding different ideas about church membership, but for "his violent and tumultuous carriage against the Patent" (Cotton, in Williams 2: 44)—a carriage that consisted of Williams *saying* that he disagreed.

In other words, like Kibbey, I agree that the Puritan tendency to identify only one possible locus of meaning (which was, not coincidentally, that possessed by the New England authorities) was important both for their maintenance of social power and for justifying the threat or fact of violence (148). This identification of minister and God is what Kibbey points to as the hegemonic discourse of Puritanism. And, certainly, she is right that the practical consequence of such identification is that it presents not only a single meaning but a single source of meaning for all discourse—a problem in Christianity that McFague attributes to ignoring the distinction between simile and metaphor. That source of meaning is, in practice, Puritan authorities' consensus. But in theory, the single source of meaning is in Scripture, not in any individual, and true meaning is transmitted to anyone with basic perceptive abilities.

The sense of one meaning is implicit in Puritan theories of metaphor and discourse. Also implicit is the second consequence of literalizing the battle metaphor for discourse. This is a theory of rhetoric, of words as things that one uses to pummel one's opponent. Discourse is not a journey that one takes with someone else, words are not imperfect pointers to ideas, and language is not an exploration of self-discovery. As both Wheelwright and Hooker say, the word of God is a sword that should be used to cut our listeners to the heart (Hall, *The Antinomian Controversy* 163). The righteous individual fights for God by expressing the truth in such a manner that it dominates the audience and leaves the audience two possibilities: to be killed or to join the righteous side. Such a view of discourse means that resistance, disagreement, even hesitance to submit, are all indistinguishable from attacks that must be met with further verbal (and, if necessary, physical) coercion.

As will be discussed in the next chapter, this view of discourse is especially problematic in a culture that emphasized personal conviction and a self that is revealed through dissent and conflict. My point here is that Puritan theories of discourse did not provide discursive methods of productively resolving conflict, partially because the presumption is that there are two possible power positions in discourse—an essentially masculine position of announcing one's stance and thrusting one's point into the audience's mind or an essentially feminine position of manipulating one's audience through pandering, indirection, and seductive beauty. With such limited options, it can seem that to change one's argument in substantial ways is to adopt the feminine position.[19] Worse, it is to adopt the position of a unsubmissive feminine, trying to usurp the power of the appropriate authorities.

III

These metaphors for eloquence limit the discipline and practice of rhetoric in unintended ways. Just as their complicated attitude toward personal authority and hermeneutic certainty planted the seeds of Antinomianism and anti-intellectualism (both of which the Puritans loathed), so did their paradoxical attitude toward rhetoric set the stage for the ranters who kept appearing in New England and enraging the authorities. In other words, the emotionalism of the Great Awakening was not simply a reaction *against* Puritan assumptions about the function of sermons, but a natural outgrowth of them. In addition, the denigration of rhetoric was part of the plain-style movement, which was, I have argued, as much about referentiality as it was about style.

The clothing metaphor comes from the argument that rhetoric is moral only as long as it is used to propagate the truth. Although this view has been attributed to Aristotle—Perry Miller, for example, says that Aristotle "dedicated [rhetoric] solely to embellishing and popularizing that which was demonstrably right" (*Seventeenth Century* 308)—it is actually derived from Augustine's reading of Plato's *Phaedrus*. For Aristotle (and Cicero), rhetoric may be used to promulgate notions that one has learned in other disciplines (such as dialectic), but it also can be a means to discover the truth. That is, some of the skills that one learns in rhetoric (such as considering opposite sides of a question or using the argumentative figures outlined in book 2 of *Rhetoric*) enable a person to "see clearly what the facts are" (Aristotle, *Rhetoric* 1355a). For Augustine, however, one does not discover ideas in the study of rhetoric, but merely effective ways to present them. To simplify: for Aristotle, one discovers the content *and* form through rhetoric; for Augustine, one can only discover the form, whereas the "content" comes from a different discipline.[20]

This content, an "argument" or thesis that appeals to the logical faculty in the mind, is then dressed in the clothing that will appeal best to the faculty of imagination. That is, the images one might add on to a piece of discourse make certain arguments more vivid to the mind and thereby appeal to the affections.[21] Yet in this regard, Puritan theories of communication led to fundamental contradictions about the role of the minister's emotion in a sermon. One sees one of these contradictions in the discussions of the part played by a calculated consideration of style and delivery in the preparation of a sermon. Perkins, for example, in his foundational "Arte of Prophecying," makes three different arguments about the role of self-consciousness in preaching: although the discourse should be carefully constructed, it should look spontaneous; although the preacher should be inspired by the Holy Ghost, he should maintain a grave manner; although the preacher should think carefully about how to make his sermon effective, he should understand that a sermon is never demonstration or persuasion, but only a testimony. In short, he should and should not rely on rhetoric, be self-conscious, and try to move his audience.

This difficult balance is quite typical in Puritanism, and in this case it results from the Puritan desire to be intellectually rigorous and divinely inspired at the same time, to be sincere and calculated. The New England authorities wanted to distinguish themselves from the ranters on one side—whose spontaneous outbursts were clearly "enthusiasm" that lacked all reason—and overly learned preachers on the other—whose complicated discourses failed to inspire audiences to greater piety. They did not want to revert to the Catholic argument that the person who delivered the object of grace need not contain it, and they did not want to attribute grace to human agency, but they did want to insist upon the importance of a morally upright clergy. The Puritans condemned the Anglican practice of delivering written sermons and depended instead on brief notes or outlines. Yet they also condemned the ranters whose speeches were seen as spontaneous outbursts.[22]

The Puritan compromise (be prepared and spontaneous) balances on the problematic place of emotion in Puritan religion. It is conventional to say that the plain style forbad emotional appeals, that Puritans mistrusted the emotions, and that incidents such as the Great Awakening (the religious revival of the 1730s and 40s) were reactions against the cold rationalism of Puritan sermons that are supposed to have been "dull and abstruse exercises in old dogmatic controversies" (Hofstadter 65; see also White, *Puritan Rhetoric*). But Calvinist divines had always emphasized the importance of affections. As Pettit has said, "Seventeenth-century New Englanders examined their hearts with an intensity now quite alien to the American mind. The image of the heart, the biblical metonym for the inner man, held a central position in their total conception of the spiritual life" (Pettit 1). Wigglesworth praises eloquence because it transports the listener's mind "with a kind of rapture" and inspires it "with a certain oratoric fury, as if the oratour together with his words had breathed his soul and spirit into those that hear him" ("Praise of Eloquence" 329). Thomas Hooker generally talks in terms of the effect that sermons should have on the heart, and "broken-heartedness" is a crucial stage in the process of conversion. He says that the ideal minister is one who "particularly and soundly applies the word of God to mens hearts and consciences, that evidently by Scriptures and strong arguments convinceth others with an holy and hearty affection" (*Implantation* 79).[23] That is, for Hooker, the minister considers the particular sins of his audience, uses plain arguments soundly based in Scripture, and communicates emotions that he himself feels.

In regard to the place of emotions in religion, Puritans were in agreement with Ramist rhetoricians like John Rainolds who, in his lectures on Aristotle's *Rhetoric*, explains that although emotions are inferior to reason (in that they are part of the appetitive aspect of the soul), they are necessary for leading a virtuous life: "For true knowledge of good and evil things depends upon the intellect, but once these are known, the desire for good things—and the aversion to evil things— lies in the appetite" (141). Rainolds defines emotion as "a natural commotion of the soul, imparted by God for following good and fleeing evil" (143). He is clear that even "strong" emotions are seemly (145) and that they contribute to justice: "A judge will decide the case more justly, the more vehemently he is aroused to hatred of the guilty, the more burningly aroused to pity for the innocent, swept away by the artifice of the orator" (147). Emotional appeals are not entirely disregarded nor entirely unimportant—but what they do is to make one engage in the action with more emotion.

A conventional criticism of the emotions and emotional appeals in the history of rhetoric is that they can be false. Aristotle lists affected indignant language as one of the fallacies, and Milton attributes to Satan the ability to pretend to create the appearance of certain affections through artifice. The Puritans tried to downplay the traditional mingling of artifice and pathos. In his discussions of style, for instance, Rainolds acknowledges the role that artifice may play in eloquence, but he insists that artifice is only one part of that skill: "Eloquence has two parts; the first belongs to life, the second to the tongue" (389). That second kind of eloquence is of almost negligible import, whereas the first is absolutely necessary: "The life of a speaker persuades, not his speaking" (389). As Perkins says, "The speech is gracious wherein the grace of the heart is expressed" (*Work* 346). Hooker says: "The foundations and pillars of a mans speech are not in the tongue, but they proceed out of the heart. . . . When the heart of a minister goeth home with his words, then he delivers the word powerfully and profitably to the hearers . . . And observe that when a man speakes from the heart, he speaks to the heart: and when a man speaks from the head onely, and from the teeth outward (as wee use to say) hee speakes to the eare onely, he speaks to the conceit only" (*Implantation* 77). This concept of eloquence nearly literalizes the metaphor of communication as carrying (as will be discussed below). It also serves to denigrate traditional rhetoric even further by making one of few things that Ramism left to rhetoric (eloquence) a function of conditions outside the discipline of rhetoric (grace).

Since eloquence comes from piety, and rhetoric does not teach piety, genuine eloquence does not come from anything rhetoric has to teach, but from some other field. For Ramus, virtue, which is part of eloquence, is taught by moral philosophy rather than rhetoric (83–86). For most other Puritans (like Cotton Mather or Thomas Hooker) eloquence comes from the minister having grace. Therefore, although the Calvinists attributed the study of style to rhetoric, what one learned in that discipline would never make one truly eloquent. Here again the Puritan ontology must be woven back into the discussion. As I said earlier, for the Puritans, whatever God has created is a thing placed in Creation that is communicated to the mind through perception. The rhetor communicates this thing to the audience—the meaning of an event (a death or providence or election), and the correct way to understand Scripture. If, then, grace is to be communicated to the audience during a sermon, it is carried through the minister. It is not carried through the metaphors.

Here one sees the cultural and political significance of the Puritans' metaphors for the minister as the carrier of grace. Hooker says that "you must conceive" of God's ministers as Prophets ("No Man" 93), thereby making any disagreement with a minister tantamount to rejecting one of God's prophets. Although, as will be discussed in the next chapter, Puritan theology insisted upon skepticism regarding the state of election of any individual, this theory of the location and communication of grace presumes that ministers have grace. Thus, the minister is doubly privileged as the vessel of God's grace and as the being standing in for God. With such a view, it is almost impossible to envision a criticism of a minister as anything other than an attack on God or a rejection of what the minister is transporting. Indeed, that is how Puritan authorities described (and probably genuinely saw) any criticism of doctrine—not as a criticism of them, but as attack on God. The metaphor for communication contributes to the reification of grace, which then contributes to the Puritan inability to distinguish between the person and God, and that failure to distinguish fuels the tendency to respond with violent repression to discursive acts.

Finally, by putting so much emphasis on the need for the minister to be in the correct frame of spirit, to have the right relation to God, Puritan theories of rhetoric risk losing the place of the community in a piece of discourse. Classical rhetoric teaches a speaker to focus on the audience and context in order to prepare an argument. It recommends that one consider the frame of mind of the listeners, the objections they might have, the conflicting arguments they might have heard, the kind of evidence they might find effective, and the style most suited to their natures, not simply in order to put one's ideas into their heads, but because such a consideration might actually cause one to reconsider one's position. In other words, the classical tradition in rhetoric— at least as it was understood prior to Ramism—insists that one engage in a dialogue with one's opponents, in which one's own position could be changed by what one hears from the other participants.

With the Puritan limitations of rhetoric, however, such a consideration of the opposition amounts to permitting sinners to communicate their sin to their listeners. Any audience-oriented preparation is logically indistinguishable from pandering, which is a form of submission to evil. Therefore, unlike the classical rhetor who prepares for a speech by considering the best means for reaching and persuading his particular audience (by himself arguing both sides of the issue, by studying the characters of the people in his audience, or by listening carefully to what others have argued), the Puritan rhetor focuses on his personal relationship to God. Perkins's description of how to prepare a sermon is noticeably lacking in discussions of audience: "Preparation hath two parts: interpretation and right division or cutting" (*Work* 337), and "right cutting" is done by attention to the material itself and not to the needs of the audience (*Work* 340–41).

Puritan theories of communication—especially that grace can only be communicated through a sermon if the minister possesses it—contributed to making the minister's major rhetorical duty attention to the state of his own soul. Puritan theories of arrangement contributed to making his second duty attention to the divisions inherent in the material. In other words, it is extremely significant (in the Puritan sense) that, for example, Edward Taylor prepared for his sermons by writing meditative poetry that investigated the state of his own soul, and he made to no attempt to make that poetry public.

IV

Ultimately, the danger of this vision of the composing process is that one says what one knows to be true, and one uses rhetoric to find ways to make it attractive. Similar to the apparent inclusion of counter-arguments, one appears to include metaphor, but the metaphors are used to appeal to the shallow parts of a human soul, whereas the real work of the discourse is being done through the argument that is self-evidently true. As Thomas Conley has said: "If it is nothing else, rhetoric is an alternative to the use of force, as it is the art *par excellence* of persuasion in place of coercion, of deliberation by examination of alternatives in place of autocracy" (110). As defined by the early American Calvinists, however, it was nothing else. In Puritanism, analysis, critical thinking, and explication are not part of rhetoric (but are part of theology or logic); mediation is a sin; all that is left to rhetoric is a set of intellectually vapid tricks for the display of various static propositions.

In previous chapters I argued that monologic and dialogic rhetoric assume different ontologies and different epistemologies; here I am arguing that they assume different theories of linguistic reference. These differences, especially regarding linguistic reference, both cause and result from the denigration of the discipline of rhetoric. At its best (by which I mean the dialogic forms), the discipline of rhetoric teaches the art of genuine public deliberation. It enables rhetors to determine what they think about a particular issue, to understand the positions that others have taken (or might take) on that issue, to identify the reasons for the competing proposals, to understand the interrelations of various points of view, and to present their own arguments effectively. It is far more than the study of eloquence, but the study of the skills of analysis, critical thinking, explication, and mediation that are necessary for people with conflicting views to converse. This denigration of rhetoric was often strongest in those writers whose own rhetoric is rich and significant, whose style is deeply meaningful. Cotton Mather typifies this paradoxical relationship with rhetoric: He was a constant controversialist whose own rhetoric was considerably helped by his playful and subtle use of style. He tells his son that the discipline of rhetoric is not worth very much attention, and states that

> Instead of Squandering away your Time, on the RHETORIC, whereof no doubt, you tho't, your *Dugard* gave you enough at School; and upon all the *Tropes* and *Schemes* whereof a just Censurer well observes *Possunt una atq; altera Hora ita no ari, ut eorum Notitia per omnem AEtatem sufficiat;* And the very Profession whereof usually is little more than to furnish out a *Stage-Player;* My Advice to you, is, That you observe the Flowres and Airs of such *Writings* as are most in Reputation for their *Elegancy.* Yet I am willing that you should attentively Read over *Smith,* his, *Mystery of Rhetoric Unveiled,* that you may not be Ignorant of what *Figures* they pretend unto.   (emphasis in original, *Manuductio* 34)

Arnauld's logic makes a similar point about the limited utility of the discipline of rhetoric: "As to what concerns Rhetorick, we consider'd that there is little advantage to be drawn from that Art, for the finding out of thoughts, expressions, and embellishments. Our wit furnishes us with thoughts; use affords us Expression, and for figures and ornaments they are many times superfluous; so that all the Benefit from thence consists in avoiding certain evil habits of writing and speaking" (1: 27). The Calvinist restriction of rhetoric was closely tied to crucial assumptions about the limits of human learning, the nature of truth, and the relation of truth and language, all of which are most evident in the privileging of the plain style.

Because the world and all things in it were created by God, language that uses words that perfectly correspond to things in the world will be true. Any breakdown in such reference, however, introduces two equally objectionable possibilities: first, that a speaker might use words that have no referent in God's world but that are purely created by the human mind; second, that a speaker might introduce false ideas through false linguistic reference, that is, through referring to one thing with the word for a different thing. If one perceives metaphor as functioning through substitution or translation, as Puritan explanations of metaphor did, then metaphor necessarily contains the possibility of both.

The first possibility represents the Puritan mistrust of the imagination, which was that it could create ideas with no true referents in God's world, such as centaurs, and it can thereby serve as the means of entry for the Devil. When the guardians of Eden find Satan attempting to seduce Eve, they find him "Squat like a toad, close at the ear of Eve, / Assaying by his devilish art to reach / The organs of her fancy, and with them forge / Illusions, as he list, phantasms and dreams" (Milton, bk. 4, 800–803). Perkins's mistrust of mental images is indicated in his rejection of the method of memory often taught in rhetoric (vivid images for one's speech): "The animation of the image, which is the key of memory, is impious, because it requireth absurd, insolent and prodigious cogitations, and those especially which set an edge upon and kindle the most corrupt affections of the flesh" (*Work* 344). He recommends instead the use of "axiomatical, or syllogistical, or methodical" methods—that is, things that are *in* the material rather than in the human mind. Samuel Mather says that the Puritan use of a type is distinguished from the Popish use of allegory because the type clearly refers to something "of the Mind of God" (53), whereas the latter is merely an invention of the human mind. Similarly, Calvin interprets the Epistle to the Hebrews as enforcing the same distinction between what is created by God and what is invented by human beings: "We are here taught that all those modes of worship are false and spurious, which men allow themselves by their own wit to invent" (Calvin, *Hebrews* 184). To avoid being like the Papists, "surely it is not lawful for us to allege anything of Christ from our own thoughts" (158).

This hermeneutic is also interdependent with the Puritan ontology. Interpretations are right or wrong depending upon where they reside: the correct interpretation is in the text, and the wrong interpretation is in the human mind. Hutchinson's interpretations are, according to her examiners, imposed upon the text, "for nothing but a word comes to her mind and then an application is made which is nothing to purpose" (Hall, *The Antinomian Controversy* 342). The conventional accusation to make against people with dissenting interpretations—such as Anne Hutchinson or Roger Williams—was that they were imposing ideas from their own minds onto the text. As discussed earlier, the authorities' interpretations, on the contrary, reside purely in the text, so that any reasonable reader must come to the same conclusion. The correct interpretation is one that submits the mind to the text, and the false interpretation creates something in the human mind—the former is eternal, and the second changes.

The role of the Christian minister is to express the truth as God has communicated it to him. To modify one's proposition in any but the most superficial ways is to adorn the truth too much, or to place oneself in a feminized position of pandering to the audience, or in the (also feminized) position of attempting to usurp the place of the divine with human invention. Thus, if one is faced with an audience who is already in agreement, a sermon that simply displays correct doctrine in a pleasing garb might serve to make vivid the propositions previously shared. But what this vision of composition cannot do is to provide a method for people who genuinely disagree to understand one another, let alone to reach some kind of agreement. If the display of truth does not work, and this limitation of rhetoric exhausts the possibilities of discourse, then one is left nothing but violence.

5

Prophets in a Howling Wilderness

It will behoove Mr. *Williams* in Conscience to understand, that himselfe
is the Persecutor, as of other servants of God, so of my selfe especially.
—Cotton, in Williams 2: 26

Andrew Delbanco has bemoaned the current scholarly tendency
to demonize the Puritans: "We seem to be returning to an older, hostile view of the Puritans, as expressed in the 1920s by William Carlos
Williams and recently summarized with sympathy by a sitting president of the Modern Language Association: the Puritans were the
people, *tout court*, 'who massacred the Indians and established the self-
righteous religion and politics that determined American ideology' "
(7). Thus far it may seem that I have contributed to this hostile view—
that by typifying Puritan theories of discourse as promoting monologism, I have branded them as among those who engage in hegemonic
discourse; however, the situation is much more complicated.

Like a good Puritan sermon, this chapter will take Delbanco's
quote as its text, beginning with a clear statement of the proposition to
be argued and a list of supporting reasons. My argument is that although Puritan discourse was (in theory and self-description) monologic, it is neither useful nor accurate to criticize the practice of Puritan
discourse on the grounds that it was hegemonic, nor to claim that it
was never dialogic. First, such a criticism would have been incoherent
to the Puritans themselves, a point that is itself a significant criticism
of the concept of hegemonic discourse. Second, this criticism assumes
that the Puritan descriptions of practice were accurate. Third, this argument requires a hegemonic view of Puritan discourse (one that I
have thus far presented), relying only on public discourse and ignoring the theories of self and language involved in more private uses of
language. Fourth, as will be explored in the conclusion, the rhetorical position of historical critique can be disturbingly close to that of a
Puritan minister speaking to one group of people about how wrong-

headed, hard-hearted, and hell-bound some *other* group is. It becomes monologic discourse about how wrong others are to be so monologic.

I

Histories of the public sphere are fundamentally rhetorical. Not only are they histories of rhetoric—that is, of deliberative argument as a form of communal inquiry—but they are useful only insofar as they are persuasive. Ideally, studying instances of more and less inclusive public spheres enables us to identify the qualities of a liberatory discourse that might foster rational critique of the conditions of oppression. The promise of such scholarship (that it will effect change in discursive practice) is based on the reasonable assumption that dominant forms of public discourse do not permit such critiques.[1] Such a promise thus assumes that articulating these qualities would result in persuading people to change their discursive practices, and this is what I mean by the project being rhetorical. For it to have the intended consequences, the argument for dialogic discourse must persuade people who currently engage in monologic discourse (or who refuse to engage in public discourse altogether) to adopt a more inclusive form of argument.

And as currently stated, the critique of monologic discourse is not rhetorically effective. Any definition that might actually contribute to changing a coercive system into a noncoercive system (or that might persuade people to abandon the former in favor of the latter) must contribute to self-reflection and self-criticism. It must enable a person to recognize that s/he is relying on coercion to promote and preserve hegemonic discourse, at the same time that it must persuade him/her to see such reliance as undesirable. This is the problem with my criticism of Puritans up to this point. I have discussed the numerous epistemological, ontological, hermeneutic, and linguistic models that contributed to the Puritan inability to have a public sphere with difference of opinion. But such a criticism presumes that a multivocal public sphere is a good thing. On the contrary, Puritans strove for a univocal public sphere that would force compliance to a single reading of Scripture. For them, that was a godly community.

In addition to their epistemology, ontology, and hermeneutics, the Puritan theory of typology ensured that they would see a hegemonic public sphere as an ideal for which one should strive. Especially since

Ursula Brumm's work on the significance of Puritan typology for American literature, scholars have pointed to the importance of Puritan hermeneutics for early American culture.² There has not been, however, much work on how this typology affected the practice of dissent. The effects were twofold: While ensuring that such dissent would exist, typology made such dissent a squabble over roles; yet, typology also suggests a different view of meaning, one that would have permitted dissent.

Typology was not new to the Puritans. A fairly traditional reading of the Old Testament was to see it as filled with types (such as Adam) who prefigure their anti-types that appear in the New Testament (such as Jesus). Less traditional was the Puritans' placing equal emphasis on three other levels of meaning that they read in Old Testament types. They believed that Old Testament types not only prefigure events in the life of Christ but also the events in the life of each member of the elect, in the history of the true church, and in the secular history of a community of Saints. This method of reading Scripture makes it a palimpsest, with types synchronously prefiguring a multiplicity of persons, histories, and incidents, for there might be multiple references even on the same level. For instance, the Egyptian captivity of the Israelites was typically read as prefiguring on the levels of church, communal, and personal history. It prefigures the era of the Christian Church being held in papal captivity *and* the captivity of the Puritans under Charles I *and* the captivity of each individual in sin. Mary Rowlandson evoked the type in her Indian captivity narrative; the authorities and Antinomians each invoked it with the other side in the role of Egyptian persecutors; John Cotton compared Williams's publishing pamphlets about him to Egyptian captivity; and so on.

Bercovitch has discussed some of the implications of this use of typology in regard to Puritan histories, especially the conflation of the sacred and secular. By signifying in three ways at the same time—christologically, typologically, and historically—all Christian history exemplifies and culminates in both the temporal history of New England's New Jerusalem and the lives of the specific members of that community. That is, each representative individual (as well as the community) signifies the life of Christ, the recurrence of a Scriptural type, *and* the particulars of that historical individual or community. Bercovitch has argued that this conflation of the sacred and secular contributes to (if not causes) the American tendency to deny difference

and has "subsumed the facts of social pluralism (ethnic, economic, religious, even personal) in a comprehensive national ideal" (*Self,* 186).

The special place in history that the New England plantation typologically claimed for itself—"the holy people in covenant with God,
separated and distinguished thereby, from the rest of the people of the
world" required a specific governmental purpose (Hubbard 6). The
plantation's "end must be far different also, as neither flowing from the
same fountain, nor resting on the same Principles or Foundation, but
altogether Eccentrick thereunto" (Hubbard 6). Specifically, New England's special status as a plantation of God's Chosen People requires
that the authorities refuse to permit any difference of behavior in civil
or religious matters; it is required "to countenance and encourage
those that fear God and work righteousness, but sharply to rebuke and
timely to repress whatever is contrary to sound doctrine, or apparently
tends to hinder the power of Godliness, and progress of true Religion,
with all other profaneness or unrighteousness, that under the shadow
of your Government we may lead quiet lives in all godliness and honesty" (Hubbard 3). Hubbard presents the godly tribes of Israel as typifying the ideal public sphere, one that would consist of authorities
speaking what is true and of a public piously obeying: "when the
heads of the Tribe had counselled and determined what was needful to
be done, the Brethren were ready to put their resolves in Execution" (2).
In a longer passage, he again emphasizes the willingness that a godly
people have to submit to the authorities in all their affairs:

> At this time it seems there were two hundred Heads of the chief Fami-
> lies of the Tribe of Issachar, in whose wisdom and integrity the rest of
> the Tribe had such confidence, that they were willing to refer the man-
> aging of all their civil Affairs, and great concernments to their pru-
> dence and discretion, engaging themselves to be ready to put in execu-
> tion whatever should by their joynt consent be determined and agreed
> upon. So sweet was the accord between those Heads, and their Breth-
> ren, that they seemed like one intire body, animated and directed by
> one and the same Spirit and Principle of life and Wisdom.
>
> (Hubbard 4)

Thus, as Hubbard describes it, the Heads of the Tribe determine the
true course and all others follow.

Unanimity of a community is a sign of a godly one, and such unanimity requires that everyone think the same thing: unity cannot happen "where the whole multitude is not of one heart, and of one mind. . . . Thus in the body politick, where it is animated with one entire spirit of love and unity, and setled upon lasting and sure foundations of quietness and peace, all the several members, must and will conspire together to deny, or forbear the exercise of their own proper inclinations, to preserve the union of the whole; that there be no Schisme in the body" (Hubbard 16). Although each person in this unified community has come to the same truth(s), s/he has done so independently, through listening to sermons; reading the Bible; being isolated, chastened, and humbled, resisting some larger entity; undergoing a conversion. Once one has had these particular and often isolated experiences, one joins a group of people who have experienced the same things, have come to the same conversion, have reached the same understanding of Scripture, have the desire to live by the same rules, and express their thoughts in exactly the same words. The ideal Puritan community is a group of individuals who think, speak, and behave exactly the same way, whose individuated self is most signified by precisely those characteristics that mark that self as part of a group.

Thus, for early American Puritans, there is no virtue in a public sphere that permits difference of opinion, and there is no vice in one that promotes only one way of thinking. Therefore, many criticisms of Puritanism (for instance, my criticism that it promotes hegemonic discourse through an equation of the personal authority of the minister and the divine authority of God) do not enable such recognition and self-reflection. Similarly unpersuasive is the argument that I have thus far made—that Puritan ontology, epistemology, theories of linguistic reference, and denigration of rhetoric weave together to make monologic discourse seem the only ethical option. To say that Puritanism is unethical because it is hegemonic or monologic is persuasive only for people for whom the concept of an authoritarian public sphere is unethical. And such was not the case with Puritanism.

This incommensurability of arguments typifies the larger problems with the argument between monologism and dialogism: each ideology presumes as a desirable end something that the other perceives as a consequence to be avoided. For instance, modern theorists of dialogism praise inclusive models of public discourse because such models (and such theorists) presume and protect a skeptical epistemology. Inclusion of different points of view is a virtue only if one thinks that such other views might be right. In the ways previously discussed—

in terms of ontology, epistemology, theories of linguistic reference, and theories of textual meaning—Puritanism assumes that certainty is possible and necessary and that any uncertainty on substantive issues is a sin. Skepticism is a sin to be avoided, not a good to be embraced.

In a very important sense, then, current arguments for dialogic rhetoric are themselves insufficiently dialogic, in that they have failed to account for the worldview that makes monologic rhetoric so attractive. It may be that this failure to include those who argue or assume that argumentation must be monologic accounts for the continued marginal status of dialogic argumentation even in current composition practices. As with Kibbey's critique of the Puritans, many arguments assume premises not shared with adherents of monologic discourse. We fail to persuade people who find monologic forms of argument attractive because the "goods" for our arguments seem undesirable and unnecessary to the very people whom we most need to persuade.

There is another problem with criticizing Puritan public discourse for being hegemonic. Monologic discourse—by which I mean a form of public argumentation that purports to get audiences to adopt the right course of action through clearly stating and logically demonstrating true propositions—is not absolutely hegemonic in that although the opposition is not genuinely included, it is stylistically included. I have heretofore considered Puritan public discourse regarding Puritan public discourse—the things that Puritans said in public regarding what public discourse should be. In such arguments, monologic discourse is presented as the ideal, and the Puritan public sphere is described as one in which all rational people are in agreement with the self-evident propositions that authorities state. But the practice of Puritan public and private discourse was not effectively monologic, nor truly hegemonic, in several important ways. For instance, a fundamental precept of monologism is that one can and should state one's thesis—a proposition that encapsulates one's intentions—at the beginning of the discourse. But Puritan sermons, while not dialogic rhetoric, testify to multiple intentions not capable of being stated in a thesis at the beginning of the discourse.

Thomas Hooker's *Soules Preparation for Christ* exemplifies this nearly palimpsest quality that sermons often had. Given as part of a series of sermons on preparation and predestination, it was published in London in 1632. The thesis is stated at the beginning: Hooker is defining the "fourth circumstance" of preparation: "which is that no man by nature can will Christ and grace" (81). For this point, Hooker begins with a text from Paul's sermon to the Corinthians (1 Corinthians 2.14), and he follows the traditional Puritan structure that can easily be outlined in Ramistic fashion:

I. Textual explication
   A. Plainness of Paul's preaching (speaks as though Paul speaking to the Corinthians)
   B. Objections to Paul's doctrine
      1. How can some people know the mysteries?
      2. Why doesn't everyone know them?
   C. Answers
      1. We have received the spirit of God
      2. The "naturall" man cannot know them
         a. Definition of "naturall man"
         b. Definition of "things of the Spirit"
II. Restatement of thesis ("A man hath not power to will to receive grace and salvation by Christ")
   A. Praeteritio about Papists
   B. "A man hath not power to will to receive grace" because:
      1. A "naturall" man turns from things of God when explained by a minister
      2. A "naturall" man resists God
      3. A "naturall" man cannot behave with grace
      4. A "naturall" man will not be subject to God or God's word
   C. Three reasons that a "naturall" man resists the things of God
      1. Scripture: They are spiritual things
      2. Definition: The things of God are spiritual things, which the "naturall" man does not have
      3. Analogy: A dead man cannot will himself alive
III. Four applications/uses of doctrine
   A. Enables one to recognize foolish objections
      1. Objection: That they were born with grace
      2. Objection: That grace is close and available for the asking
   B. That you may read your own estates
   C. [There is no third use in the printed version.]
   D. Use of terror
IV. Exhortation

Although the thesis is clear and is restated nearly verbatim five times during the sermon, in another sense it is not clear exactly what the sermon is about. This is a published text that will reach one set of readers, a set who may or may not include the people who heard the original sermon on which the published version is based. The discourse takes as its text a different sermon given to another set of people, which itself mostly concerns the problem of preaching the words of Christ, words that were themselves spoken to listeners not present. The consequence of this palimpsest of rhetorical situations is that when Hooker discusses how a sinner reacts to hearing the Word of God, there is a superfluity of referents for each role—Christ and his listeners, the Corinthians and Paul, ministers and congregations in general, Hooker and the people who heard the original sermon, and Hooker and the reader of the published version.

The audience is thereby continually made aware of the shifting similitudes and dissimilitudes implied in the multiply analogous situations. Such awareness would be heightened by Hooker's rhetorical strategies, such as his use of praeteritio and his frequent apostrophizing. Early in the sermon, when explaining the text itself, he amplifies the Scriptural text by talking as if he were Paul talking to the Corinthians, "as if he had said, though you thinke (O yee *Corinthians*)" (83). In discussing the first use of the doctrine, he begins by speaking to those who may know people who cavill at the doctrine, "if any of you know such" and then shifts to saying what those people to whom he began by speaking would say to the people who would make the foolish objection, "aske them when did you receive grace" before apparently simply speaking to such reprobate sinners himself (107–9). There are passages in the sermon in which he speaks for an extended time in the voice of such sinners, saying what they should be saying to themselves, "I have been deluded, I thought if I would have grace at any time, I might have grace when I would" (109). In a praeteritio, he even introduces the voice of the Papists who themselves admit a point that he discusses in the course of explaining that he will not discuss it. He begins the point by saying, "First to omit that which the Papists themselves confesse in this case," explains the doctrine, and then says, "I will omit this" (90).

Identity is a crucial question in the sermon. The use portion of the sermon is largely about this doctrine being used in the course of an individual figuring out who s/he is. Certain answers to the questions he poses, he says, demonstrate that one is a naturall man, whereas other answers indicate that one might have the right relation to Christ. The rhetorical strategies (especially of apostrophe and praeteritio) echo this question of identity—as each analogous situation invites the listener to become aware of how close or how far s/he is from the rhetorical situation being played out. The reader of the published version is even more aware of the shifting similitudes and dissimilitudes by the printer's error of leaving out the third use. At that moment, one is reminded that this is a printed version and that one is experiencing something very different from the congregation who heard it.

This is precisely the situation of language that Mikhail Bakhtin has pointed to—that as much as we might like to think that we have created a piece of monologic discourse that states and demonstrates a single thesis, that represents a single and unified voice, in actual practice, any instance of discourse has multiple voices and polysemous reference. Hooker is, in many ways, performing for his audience—himself taking on various roles and inviting them to adopt various roles. In that very specific sense, then, Hooker's sermon is not monologic, but dialogic. If, however, Puritan discourse—although aspiring to be monologic—is in practice dialogic, this raises the possibility that the very distinction with which I began the book—between dialogic and monologic discourse—is nonexistent.

In effect, Puritan discourse aspired to be monologic but continually failed because Puritan rhetors could not preclude a multiplicity of voice and intention. I have tried to weave together the various threads that together explain what seems so attractive about monologic discourse (the static ontology, perception-based epistemology, faith in hermeneutic certainty, the notion that language can and should function as an invisible receptacle of ideas, the desire for one-to-one linguistic reference, and the attendant denigration of the discipline of rhetoric), but for the sake of making a clear and clean argument, I have left out those parts of Puritanism that cut across that neat tapestry. Among those parts are: the importance of suffering in the revelation of the true self; the significance of dualities in conversion; and the polysemous reference implied in typological hermeneutics. In addition, Puritan descriptions of their community emphasize their unity and bemoan any difference as a sign of backsliding, but there were continually differences of opinion. The resulting public sphere therefore included differences of opinion, and the authorities alternated between denying the existence of these differences or pointing to them as signs of a fallen community.

The Puritan use of Scriptural types figures into this tension of denial and despair in complicated ways, simultaneously presenting perfect uniformity as the goal and requiring dissension. That is, Puritan ethics and theology require a sense of self separate from (and often in conflict with) a community, and they require the dissolution of the self into the community of the elect. It is a culture that as Lang has noted, "simultaneously celebrates and fears the authority of the individual" (3). Joseph Alkana has remarked on this same paradox, arguing that "the logic of the American Jeremiad demands that the centrality of the community routinely be reconceived by the marginalized individual consciousness. And the individual consciousness, authorized by the community, no longer appears as a detached and free point of origin for ethical action" (xii). Independent from human society yet completely dependent upon God, relying upon one's own conscience yet in perfect agreement with other members of the elect, the Puritan self is simultaneously the bedrock of religious experience and dissolved into it. Bercovitch has emphasized the first part of this paradox, arguing that Puritan "self-examination serves not to liberate but to constrict; selfhood appears as a state to be overcome, obliterated; and identity is asserted through an act of submission to a transcendent absolute" (*Self* 13). But Bercovitch's argument, although an important correction of the tendency to represent Puritans as unabashedly individualistic, discounts the other and equally important part of that paradox: whereas Puritanism puts a tremendous emphasis on uniformity and submission, it also demands conflict and dissent. This chapter explores the nature of that dissent.

II

There is a productive ambiguity in the word "self" in the notion that an effective critique enables people to recognize their self. They must see themselves and their self—that is, not only behavior that is like theirs, but the identity critiqued must resemble the sense of self that the people have. Criticizing Puritan authorities as powerful oppressors who force their views on dissenters would have made no sense to the seventeenth-century Puritans (as it often makes no sense to similar people today) because they could not see themselves or their self in that description. One of the problems of describing Puritan discourse as hegemonic and oppressive is that it tends to put the authorities in the roles of authoritarian and powerful persecutors. Although they used the narrative of persecutor/victim, they never put themselves in the role of persecutor.

How and why they adopted the role of innocent victim is complicated, and it raises a fundamental contradiction in Puritan descriptions of the self. As was emphasized earlier, Calvinist discussions of public discourse posit a static self, who may be confirmed but never changed. The self is not only internally static but also socially static, remaining in a specific place in a hierarchy of power. At the same time, however, a substantial body of Puritan writings describe a self who is changed by becoming victimized—by being the object of persecution by a powerful entity. Hence, although we tend to describe people like John Endicott, John Winthrop, or Cotton Mather as persecutors, Puritan authorities—even when acting *qua* authorities—typically described themselves as beleaguered victims of a persecuting majority. The people whom history has come to see as the dissenters (such as Anne Hutchinson, Mary Dyer, or the victims of the witchcraft persecution) are placed in the role of members of some grand conspiracy to martyr the Massachusetts Bay Colony.

This assigning of roles accounts for one of the more disturbing aspects of Puritan accounts of the persecutions. As the New England authorities banish someone, or order the execution of a Friend, or defend judicial anarchy, they feel sorry for *themselves* and describe themselves as martyred by a noble commitment to duty and persecuted by the Devil. They are persecuted by being forced to bore holes through tongues, cut off ears, and listen to the counter-arguments of the victims. It is this tendency that Delbanco has referred to as "the strategy of rendering New England as a colony of heroic sufferers" (97). It may seem hyperbolic (if not simply silly) when John Cotton compares Williams to the Egyptians for publishing pamphlets, but it makes sense in the context of the Puritan insistence on suffering.

This strategy was so common because Puritan doctrine dictated that members of the elect would suffer. Because one must undergo a scourging and chastening experience in order to reach God, chastening is a necessary step in the process of salvation. One must, as does Christian in *A Pilgrim's Progress,* walk past the lions, up the hills, and through the Valley of Death. Those who evade some of the difficulties (by trying to climb over walls, for example) are destined not to reach

heaven. Increase Mather, as did most ministers, uses typology in order to insist upon this point: "As the children of *Israel* went through
the Red Sea, and through the Wilderness, before they could enter into
Canaan, so must we wade through a Red Sea of Troubles, and pass
through a Wilderness of Miseries, e're we can arrive at the heavenly
Canaan" (emphasis in original, "Day of Trouble" 3). John Cotton says,
"It never fell out otherwise, but as sure as thou art sprinkled with
the water of Baptisme, so sure thou shalt be drenched in affliction"
(quoted in Miller, *Seventeenth Century* 36). Hooker says, "So it shall be
Spiritually, the Valley of Consternation, perplexity of Spirit, and bro-
kenness of heart, is the very gale and entrance of any sound hope, and
assured expectation of good" ("Heart Must Be Humble" 6). Shepard
describes the pain that people feel upon losing their houses and their
goods, saying, "But know it, thou must mourn here or in hell. If God
broke David's bones for his adultery, and the angels' backs for their
pride, the Lord, if ever he saves thee, will break thine heart too" (1: 93).
Bradstreet tells her children, "If at any time you are chastened of God,
take it as thankfully and Joyfully as in greatest mercyes, for if yee bee
his yee shall reap the greatest benefitt by it" (181). Because the elect had
first to be punished, God sends affliction to those whom he particularly loves; Rowlandson says, "For whom the Lord loveth he chasteneth
and scourgeth every son whom He receiveth" (75).

One of the most famous chastening and scourging narratives is
Mary Rowlandson's, originally published as *The Soveraignty and Goodness of God, Together, with the Faithfulness of His Promises Displayed; Being a Narrative of the Captivity and Restauration of Mrs. Mary Rowlandson*.
Rowlandson's narrative perfectly exemplifies the sin isolation-
humiliation-temptation-redemption-uncertain assurance pattern of
the conversion experience. She describes that her life was happy and
comfortable, such that she had become somewhat negligent in her ob-
servation of the Sabbath, when her home was attacked by Indians. Several members of her family are killed and wounded in front of her,
and she and her remaining children are taken captive. As they travel
deeper into the wilderness, one child dies in her arms, and the others
are separated from her. She describes her primary temptation as despair. When she turns to a Bible that she has miraculously been given,
she repents her former negligence and turns to God. Her travails do
not end immediately, but she is not as tortured by temptations to despair. When she is finally ransomed from the Indians, she returns
home permanently changed. Chastened, yet grateful for her affliction,

she has a greater awareness of the fragility of human-created happiness, thereby becoming more appreciative of God's bounty and more aware of his sovereignty and providence. As Calvin says, the effect of this experience is *"first,* to teach us reverence and fear; and, *secondly,* to induce us, under its guidance and teaching, to ask every good thing from [God], and, when it is received, ascribe it to him" (emphasis in original, *Institutes* 1: 41).[3] Therefore, although being chastened is painful, it is not bad, for it is a necessary preparation for redemption. Hooker says, "They that sow in teares, shall reape in joy" and recommends being grateful for such afflictions as illness: "Happely God layeth a man upon his sicke bed, and awakeneth his conscience" (*Implantation* 27, 10). He lists lack of trouble as one of the signs of damnation; speaking to the haughty sinners, he says, "You were never brokenhearted here for your abominations, know assuredly that you will burn for them one day; your proud hearts were never abased, and laid in the dust, the Lord will ruinate both you and them" ("Heart Must Be Humble" 11). Willingness to suffer is a sign that one is "on God's side," so one should be "glad that he may honour God, by being himself dishonoured, and exposed to the Contempt and Reproaches of the World" (I. Mather, "Greatest Honour" 17). John Cotton defines affliction as a sign of God's mercy and goodness because "the greater and deeper your troubles be, the deeper you drink of Christs cup, the more sweete it will bee in the bottome" ("Saints Deliverance" 38). Cotton Mather recommends that one not look on affliction as punishment for past behavior but as a cleansing that prepares one for salvation: "If any Afflictions come upon [the virtuous woman], they are not vindictive or destructive, but purely medicinal; she sees they are to do her good in the latter End; they are to make her Partaker of God's Holiness; they are to work for her a far more exceeding and eternal Weight of Glory" (emphasis removed, *Ornaments* 43). Increase Mather refers to afflictions as "Physick for the Soul" ("Day of Trouble" 8). In this regard, both Rowlandson and Increase Mather cite Scripture: "And I hope I can say in some measure, as David did, 'It is good for me that I have been afflicted' " (Rowlandson 75; I. Mather, "Day of Trouble" 14).

Puritans believed that if left alone in pleasant circumstances, human beings would deceive themselves about their own goodness and mistakenly think themselves the author of destiny. The chastening experience was necessary to break the subject out of complacency, the tendency that Puritans believed people have to imagine that they are not so very bad or that they are doing all that can be expected. For example, it was not until the Indians threatened to kill Rowlandson for wanting to keep the Sabbath holy that she realized how lax she had become before her captivity. The Puritan belief in dualities (which will be discussed below) ensured that human beings would be continually falling short of righteous behavior; they abhorred self-righteousness and required constant self-examination. The chastening was the impetus for that examination.

Increase Mather says that there are four benefits of affliction: probation, instruction, correction, and purgation. There is another one: that one has been tested may be a sign that one is among the chosen: "By this means the Lord Trieth the sincerity and fidelity of his Servants; yea, and what measure of grace they have too. If they faint in the day of adversity, their strength is small; but they that hold out faithfully and couragiously in times of great trouble, have received a good measure of grace" ("Day of Trouble" 17). Bradstreet explains that she has "more circumspection in my walking after I have been afflicted. I have been with God like an untoward child, that no longer than the rod has been on my back (or at least in sight) but I have been apt to forgett him and myself too. Before I was afflicted I went astray, but now I keep the statutes" (181). Rowlandson tells what she learned from her captivity: "The Lord hath showed me the vanity of these outward things. That they are the vanity of vanities and vexation of spirit, that they are but a shadow, a blast, a bubble, and things of no continuance. That we must rely on God himself and our whole dependence must be upon Him" (75). As Patricia Caldwell and Morgan have each argued, the Puritans had a morphology of conversion—one that prescribed instruction, correction, and purgation. These stages, which are brought on by travails and troubles, are necessary for causing an individual to recognize one's innate depravity and God's complete sovereignty.

Due to the place of chastening in the conversion process, it was sometimes interpreted as a sign of election. And because chastening was often interpreted as one of the signs of election, it was not uncommon for Puritans to desire affliction or worry if their lives were pleasant. Edwards says, "I have greatly longed of late for a broke heart and to lie low before God" (*Basic Writings* 87). Bunyan says that when Christian and Faithful are threatened with martyrdom, "each man secretly wished that he might have that preferment" (141). Rowlandson says that "before I knew what affliction meant, I was ready sometimes to wish for it. When I lived in prosperity . . . and yet seeing many whom I preferred before myself under many trials and afflictions . . . I should be sometimes jealous lest I should have" (75).

The public and private importance assigned to chastening shaped Puritan notions about what would happen if one participated in public discourse. This chastening was public, often verbal, and was at the hands of some dreadful and powerful tool of the forces of Satan. Like the pilgrim fighting Apollyon, they are instances of the individual fighting against a much larger entity. Rowlandson does not individuate the Indians who took her captive, just as the authorities did not individuate the Antinomians, and the Antinomians did not individuate the authorities. The righteous individual—like the American saints in Mather's *Magnalia Christi Americana*—will someday be forced to stand firm against a group of persecuting sinners who verbally abuse the saint.

Also like Christian's battling with Apollyon, Satanic attack is as much discursive as physical—Apollyon begins by posing various arguments intended to weaken Christian's faith. When Hooker describes the process of conversion, he emphasizes, as an instance of *affliction,* the verbal mocking that a person might receive from the reprobate: "thy drunken companions revile thee for the same, and say, art turned a Puritan now?" (*Soules Implantation* 104). Calvin's summary of the stoning of Stephen emphasizes that Stephen suffered from what people said to him and tells how they reacted to what he said: "He saw himself beset round with raging enemies; the goodness of his cause was oppressed, partly with false accusations and malice, partly with violence and outrageous outcries; he was environed with stern countenances on every side; he himself was haled unto a cruel and horrible kind of death; he could espy succour and ease no where" (Calvin, *Acts* 1: 313). Although taking the role of martyr is certainly nothing new in the history of Christianity, what distinguishes Puritan notions of the regenerate self from, for instance, Catholic tales of martyrdom is the extent to which Calvinist descriptions of struggle and persecution are discursive and the equation of physical and verbal "attack."

This literalizing of metaphors of verbal attack, coupled with the assumption that the elect individual will be persecuted, contributes to the ironic situation that the individuals who have come to typify Puritan orthodoxy and repression, such as John Winthrop and Cotton Mather, adopt the same ethos as those who are often taken to typify

America's history of individualism, such as Anne Hutchinson and Roger Williams. They all represent themselves as does Williams: "witnesses of the Lord presenting light unto them," who are persecuted by the fallen community to whom they present the light for fearlessly speaking the truth (Williams 1: 325). How Williams characterizes his situation is typical: he says that he is a humble man who merely desired "in meeknes and patience to testifie the truth of Jesus," but his opponent John Cotton is "swimming with the stream of outward credit and profit" (Williams 1: 339). Thrust into a "howling wilderness" for having spoken the plain truth, Williams does not mind: "fellowship with the Lord Jesus in his sufferings is sweeter than all the fellowship with sinners, all the profits, honours, and pleasures of this present evill world" ("Examined and Answered" in Williams 1: 315, 319; see also 1: 337, 338, 340, 342). Of course, "howling wilderness" is precisely the phrase used by Bradford, Hooker, Cotton and Increase Mather, Wigglesworth, and others to describe that to which the Puritans were driven by their enemies—people like Williams.[4]

Williams declares that although he has suffered greatly for his love of truth, he knows that he will triumph: "I hope the act of the Lord Jesus sounding forth in me (a poore despised Rams horn) the blast that shall in his owne holy season cast down the strength and confidence of those inventions of men in the worshipping of the true and living God. And lastly, his act in inabling me to be faithfull in any measure to suffer such great and mighty trials for his names sake" (Williams 1: 325). John Cotton responds to Williams by claiming for himself the position of the martyr for the sake of truth: "It will behoove Mr. *Williams* in Conscience to understand, that himselfe is the Persecutor, as of other servants of God, so of my selfe especially" (Cotton, in Williams 2: 26). He cites the above speech of Williams and says that "this speech of his is a blast of blasphemy against the Lord Jesus" (in Williams 2: 55) because Williams was never persecuted. "Persecution," he says, "is the affliction of another for Righteousnesse sake" and Williams's cause is not righteous (in Williams 2: 26). He refuses to grant Williams the role of martyr, instead claiming it for himself. What Williams has done to him (that is, publish pamphlets), Cotton claims, is a form of persecution worse than "*Aegyptian* bondage" and "more then Pharaonicall tyranny" (Cotton, in Williams 2: 42). Similarly, when Cotton Mather narrates his grandfather's life, he too makes Hutchinson a type of persecutor and describes John Cotton as martyred by her. Cotton Mather also takes the role of martyr for himself, saying that he knows that he will be persecuted for having written *Magnalia Christi,* but that his duty to truth required that he do so.

Other scholars have argued that the Antinomians represent a particular strain in American culture—the tendency to praise the individual who declares the individual as the basis of authority in the midst of a fight against society. And I agree that there is such a strain and that it is most often represented as the voice crying in the wilderness. Although this strain is Antinomian—in the sense that it is the way the Antinomians presented themselves—it is also Puritan. That is, the dissenters like Hutchinson were most Puritan in their moment of dissent.

The issue is one of identity, resulting from a way of imagining public relations that had very few roles available: if there are only two kinds of audiences (essentially those who are with one and those who are against one) then public disagreement means that there are two sides to every question. One side is the noble victim being persecuted for speaking the truth that everyone knows, and the other side is the persecutor operating from base and sinful motives. So, as with the Cotton/Williams exchange quoted above, the major controversies often turned on the question of who typifies what role, and it was argued about by disputing the personal and literal significance of the Scriptural type. By taking the role of martyr, Hutchinson not only cast the authorities in the role of Satanic persecutors but also threatened to prevent their being able to claim for themselves the place of being the righteous dissenter.

Arguing about identity took the form of arguing about the typology of experience, with the notable consequence being that the same signs were used for opposite interpretations. Whereas Cotton claimed that he was the anti-type of the persecuted Israelites because Williams had published pamphlets, Roger Williams interpreted his having been laid low with an illness and then banished from Massachusetts as Christ-like suffering, making himself the anti-type. John Cotton interpreted those same incidents as punishments from God (and therefore proof that Williams was a sinner). Hutchinson interpreted her trials and examinations as afflictions that confirmed her special status and the truth of her side; Winthrop interpreted the whole Antinomian controversy as a trial and affliction for the New England community, thereby proving its special status and the truth of the authorities' position (see, for example, "Examination" in Hall, *The Antinomian Contro-*

versy 339). Bradford interprets the illness and death aboard ship of a cursing sailor as punishment for wickedness, whereas he interprets the same illness and death aboard ship of Lady Arbella as proof of her election (*Plymouth Plantation*).

David Hall's *Worlds of Wonder* explores the Puritan fascination with providence tales, much of which concern interpretations of signs. And in fact, the diaries and journals of Puritans show a fascination with recording signifying events. They might be as minor as a chamberpot that breaks during the night, or as tragic as an attack by Indians. As Hall has noted, they were sometimes neighborhood incidents and sometimes republished stories from much older books, providing (in their republished form) among the most popular reading of early New England. The tales tend to be stories of instant punishment or miraculous rescues—drunkards and blasphemers who are struck dead, good church goers who are saved from a capsized boat. They are also tales about identity: the drunkard is proven to have a certain standing with God by being struck down, just as God proves who the church goers really are by saving them. And much of the sinning and saving is discursive: the drunkards and blasphemers insult the church goers, the church goers say something just before being saved.

My point is that Calvinist martyrdom is a process of verbal dissent, which teaches that a member of the elect should expect to be forced into a discursive battle at some point in the process of conversion. The "persecution" that Winthrop, Increase Mather, John Cotton, and Cotton Mather claim to have undergone is all discursive. They were argued with, criticized, and reproached. It is specifically this incident of dissent and verbal persecution that demonstrates the individual's commitment to Christ, that is, the person's integrity and authenticity.

This requirement of dissent reveals that the relation of Puritan ideology and independence is considerably more complicated than one might gather from interpretations of the political significance of Puritan theories of conversion. Schweitzer, for instance, concludes that: "Submission to a higher power allows people to accept without question or resistance a morphology of conversion that demands humiliation, abjection, and complete self abasement. . . . Patriarchal culture, with its roots in Puritan ideologies of redeemed subjectivity, and its gender and racial hierarchies, is committed to protecting and preserving the fathers' rule and the sons' obedience" (235). The problem with this interpretation is that it ignores the extent to which Puritanism insists upon the creation of a dissenting self that is humiliated, abject, and abased toward God but continually resistant against something else. Submission *and* resistance were signs of election.

Puritan thought did not permit ways to imagine communal conflict as beneficial. The irony is that Puritanism also imagined that each individual would come into conflict with a group. So, the apparently monologic system continually created a kind of dissent it could not manage with anything other than repression.

III

It is difficult for scholars to know how to talk about the relationship of Puritanism and dissent. Puritans were dissenters in search of religious freedom who treated their own dissenters with no mercy and forbad religious freedom to everyone else. It is hard to look at that situation and not characterize it as hypocrisy. The charge, an old one, is not just a result of their political institutions, but also due to their reliance on dualities in regard to the material world, wealth, the body, sex, and so on. The image of the hypocritical and repressive Puritans, as most famously depicted in Hawthorne's *Scarlet Letter,* continues to typify the Massachusetts Colony settlers, despite the efforts of scholars like Perry Miller and Edmund Morgan to present a more accurate picture of the complexity of Puritanism. Miller tried to refute the charge of hypocrisy by arguing that Puritans' simultaneous pursuit of spiritual piety and worldly wealth was not, in the New England mind, a contradiction. The Puritans, he argued, set for themselves the task of walking along a razor's edge: to pursue worldly success, but not for the sake of that success; to fulfill all one's duties, but never to rest in one's duties; to strive to make every enterprise financially profitable, but never so much that one is even momentarily distracted from God. Morgan referred to this same characteristic as the Puritan dilemma, "the paradox that required a man to live in the world without being of it" (*Puritan Dilemma* 31). One cannot reject the world and try to live as an ascetic; one cannot ignore the soul and live completely in the world. And one cannot try to mediate the demands of the flesh and the spirit by a compromise—the Puritans reserved their most powerful vitriol for those who suggested that piety could or should be diluted. One must live "soberly, righteously, and godly in this present world" (Perkins, "Vocations or Callings" 48). Morgan's argument in *The Puritan Dilemma* has been so pervasive that the title has become a catchphrase in discussing the American Puritans. Yet his (and Miller's) interpretation of the significance of conflict in the Puritan self does not prevent scholars from continuing to misinterpret the Puritan use of dualities as a sign of psychological or philosophical conflict with (or individual rebellion against) an oppressive and hegemonic creed.

The irony is that the first move in making this argument is to transform Puritan ideology into a hegemony and then interpret all the instances of multiple voices as non-Puritan deviations. On the contrary, as argued above, Puritanism was never actually hegemonic in the very simple sense that it *required* a degree of dissent it could not manage. There are two other areas in which Puritan ideology created places of indeterminacy that unravel the neat weaving of direct epistemology, hermeneutic certainty, and static ontology that together contributed to the early New England tendency to resort to coercive solutions to discursive controversies. One of these is the Puritan use of dualities—the insistence that true piety is a balancing of competing demands. These dualities are more often misunderstood as contradictions. The second area—Puritan use of typologies—will be discussed in the next section.

One can see this tendency to misunderstand Puritan dualities as instances of resistance against a simplistic ideology in writings on Anne Bradstreet, in which, at least since Josephine Piercy's 1965 monograph, she is generally interpreted as continually struggling to repress some kind of natural desire that is in conflict with Puritan dogma. This perception of a constant and sometimes unsuccessful attempt at repression is generally taken to demonstrate that Bradstreet is an atypical Puritan; she is thereby made into a typical (in the Puritan sense) dissident. This more or less vague notion of an individual struggling to stand against Puritan repression pervades scholarly discussions of poems like Bradstreet's "The Flesh and the Spirit." The narrator overhears two sisters, Flesh and Spirit, who have met "in secret place" to discuss things past and future (line 1). Their discussion, on a theme similar to Paul's discourse in Romans 8, begins with Flesh attempting to persuade Spirit that "worldly wealth and vanity" provide greater recompense in honor, fame, riches, and pleasure than does meditation (*Poems* 6). Spirit responds that she lives on things of which Flesh is unaware, that the riches and pleasures of heaven are far greater than anything Flesh could offer. This opposition of the pleasures of the flesh and the rewards of the spirit is a common topic in Christian doctrine, as is the juxtaposition of Flesh's temporal (and temporary) pleasure and Spirit's eternal reward. Even the conceit, having the poem a debate between the two, is a traditional medieval pattern. The argument that Spirit puts forward seems to confirm conventional stereotypes of the Puritans—as ascetic and dour people who have rejected the world, the body, and the natural environment.

But because several readers have found Spirit's apparent triumph in the argument less than conclusive, it has been suggested that the poem is evidence of Bradstreet's inability to reconcile herself with the asceticism and antienvironmentalism that Puritan dogma is assumed to have demanded. Richardson's reading is typical: "The poem raises more questions than it settles, and we may fairly wonder whether Spirit deserves to win the debate" (Richardson 105). Josephine Piercy sees the poem as a sign of "a troubled conscience" resulting from Bradstreet's passion for her husband; Elizabeth White reads it as an indication that Bradstreet had difficulty rejecting "love of living, among the good and pleasant aspects of her earthly lot, that the austerity of her creed condemned" (340). Others infer a conflict between Bradstreet's role as a poet and her beliefs as a Puritan, or "between her acceptance of Puritan dogma, and her own warm personality" (Stanford 80). It should be noted that it is those readers who assume that Spirit "has taken the proper Puritan attitude toward earthly things" who describe Bradstreet as being in conflict with Puritan theology (Stanford 82).

The fit reader does indeed have trouble granting Spirit's victory because the arguments that Flesh puts forward have considerable strength. After all, the earth does have "more silver, pearls, and gold, / Than eyes can see, or hands can hold" (lines 31–32). Bradstreet has Earth make the same point in her poem "The Four Elements." That "Industry hath its recompense" was a Puritan doctrine (line 22); the frequency and popularity of funeral elegies in Puritan communities demonstrated that honor and fame could indeed be acquired. Most striking, the rhetorical questions with which Flesh begins her argument echo Puritan criticisms of overly speculative theology: "What liv'st thou on / Nothing but Meditation? / Doth Contemplation feed thee so / Regardlessly to let earth goe? / Can Speculation satisfy / Notion without Reality?" (lines 9–14).

This is not to say that Flesh wins the debate but that her points are true in the context of this world. In this world, one cannot live on airy speculation, industry does provide recompense, one can achieve honor and rewards, and there are riches. In the context of eternal reward, however, most of Spirit's argument (but not all) display points of

Puritan theology: that the riches of the earth are nothing compared to those in heaven; that Spirit finds contemplation more rewarding than earthly pleasures; that Spirit shall be free from sickness and bodily infirmity; and that Spirit can live on the Word of God. Although Spirit says she will triumph over Flesh, the poem itself resists any simple triumph of either sister, leaving the reader in the same position as the narrator—one who has heard the arguments of both sides, but not chosen. That the poem frustrates readers' expectations that it endorse one side and condemn the other makes the inconclusiveness of the debate a "problem" that must be solved.

This problem is especially highlighted when considering Bradstreet's poems to and about her husband because they make no effort to hide the fleshly pleasure of their marriage. "Phoebus make haste" describes her envy of the sun because "once a day, thy Spouse thou mayst imbrace; / And when thou canst not treat by loving mouth, / Thy rayes afar, salute her from the south" (22–24). When her husband is gone, Bradstreet desires "the fervor of his ardent beams" (35). Her children she refers to as "those fruits which through thy heat I bore" ("A Letter to Her Husband" line 14) and to herself as "flesh of thy flesh, bone of thy bone" ("Letter" 25). Critics cannot help but remark on the passion and eroticism of these poems; this eroticism, is, however, a conundrum if one stereotypes the Puritans as opposed to the sensual world.

Although some scholars have pointed to the high birth rate, the number of pregnant brides, the recurrence in Jeremiads of the theme of sexual incontinence, and the frequency of prosecution for sexual crimes as indications that the Puritans were well aware of the pleasures of the flesh, at least in practice, others have argued that an examination of Puritan sermons and doctrine shows that they treated sex "with wariness, distaste, even horror, as a virtual invitation to damnation" (Verduin 223). Puritan theology is infamous for its condemnations of "this world" as when John Cotton stated that "there is another combination of vertues strangely mixed in every lively holy Christian, And that is, Diligence in worldly businesses, and yet deadness to the world" (Cotton, in Miller, *Seventeenth Century* 42). This apparent breach between practice and doctrine leads to the charge of hypocrisy or to the slightly more subtle accusation that the Puritans were self-deluding. The powerful eroticism is then taken as a moment when the Puritan "betrays his deepest self" (Verduin 235).

As with reading Bradstreet, this interpretive "problem" results from our assumption that the Puritans must categorically praise one thing and condemn the other or betray themselves as hypocrites. It is, in essence, our determination to see the Puritans as monologic that creates the expectation that describing the flesh as dangerous is necessarily the same perception as damning it as sinful.[5]

Although I agree that Bradstreet is, in fact, in deep conflict, I do not agree that it is between her sensuality (or her love for her husband, or her role as a poet) and Puritanism. Bradstreet is most Puritan when she expresses inner conflict, when she engages in an unresolved dialogue that ends praising a difficult balancing of dual positions. The oppositions that figure so significantly in Puritan writings (such as those in the above quote from Cotton) should not be read as antitheses (this world versus the next) that Puritans failed to resolve, but as dualities whose apparent conflict results from man's fallen nature. In a state of grace, the apparent paradoxes dissolve, but in this world we must hear the voices from both sides. Thus, rather than see Bradstreet as in a battle with the dominant theology, I suggest that the unresolved conflicts and doubts should be read as expressions of Puritan notions about the relation of the true self and the role of this world in spiritual development.

The centrality of conflict in Calvinist notions of piety is indicated in Calvin's definition of genuine religion: "confidence in God coupled with serious fear" (*Institutes* 1: 42). This definition is a perfect instance of Puritanism. A person is expected to believe simultaneously two concepts that the fallen understanding keeps trying to perceive as antithetical. This sense of dual concepts is indicated in the Puritan use of oxymoron to describe religious experiences. Jonathan Edwards, for instance, describes his feelings while walking in a field: "There came into my mind so sweet a sense of the glorious *majesty* and *grace* of God, as I know not how to express—I seemed to see them both in a sweet conjunction; majesty and meekness joined together: it was a sweet, and gentle, and holy majesty; and also a majestic meekness; an awful sweetness; a high, and great, and holy gentleness" (*Basic Writings* 84–85). It is important to understand that the terms in these oxymorons (fear and confidence; majesty and meekness; mercy and justice) are not, as they have been termed, "warring contraries." They are neither extremes that one should moderate, nor contraries between which one must choose. They should not be moderated, both because moderation is one of the easy roads to hell (Shepard 1: 68–69), and because it is impossible to have an immoderate amount of any of the virtues related to piety (e.g., fear of God). They are not contraries between which one must choose because they are always completely present: "God is not all mercy and no justice, nor all justice and no mercy" (Shepard 1: 17).

In a state of grace, one transcends the appearance of opposition by perceiving the two qualities as a union—the meekness is majestic, the sweetness awe-inspiring, the gentleness high and great. Similarly, genuine religion is feeling perfect confidence and complete fear toward God; the regenerate Christian would be completely and constantly looking toward the next world while fulfilling one's duties in this world; the spirit and the flesh will be as one when raised by Christ. One cannot continually maintain such a state of grace; being human, one is bound to slip. But while one is in this state, one feels reconciled, one feels "a calm, sweet abstraction of soul from all the concerns of this world; and sometimes a kind of vision, or fixed ideas and imaginations, of being alone in the mountains, or some solitary wilderness, far from all mankind, sweetly conversing with Christ, and wrapt and swallowed up in God" ("Personal Narrative" in *Basic Writings* 84). If one has the appropriate attitude, then the apparent contradictions dissolve. Edwards describes feeling so much at peace with God that he is not frightened, even by the typical sign of God's omnipotence:

> And scarce any thing, among all the works of nature, was so sweet to me as thunder and lightning; formerly nothing had been so terrible to me. Before, I used to be uncommonly terrified with thunder, and to be struck with terror when I saw a thunder storm rising; but now, on the contrary, it rejoiced me. I felt God, if I may so speak, at the first appearance of a thunder-storm; and used to take the opportunity, at such times, to fix myself in order to view the clouds, and see the lightnings play, and hear the majestic and awful voice of God's thunder, which oftentimes was exceedingly entertaining, leading me to sweet contemplations of my great and glorious God. While thus engaged, it always seemed natural for me to sing, or chant forth my meditations; or, to speak my thoughts in soliloquies with a singing voice. (*Basic Writings* 85)

Edwards's description of this experience emphasizes what came to be called the sublime—the feeling of awe at manifestations of God's sovereignty. One who is full of awe is also full of confidence. One sings or chants in the middle of something that would terrify the unregenerate.

This is also a perfect description of how Puritans theorized the moment of grace, that one could maintain apparently conflicting emotions or demands.

To abandon either of the seemingly conflicting demands is to sin. And one can see that sense of abandonment as sin in Bradstreet's "Flesh and the Spirit," which critics typically read as an argument for abandoning the flesh in favor of the spirit. This reading, however, ignores that Spirit makes two doctrinal errors. She announces that Flesh has too often made her a slave, and that in the Celestial City (where Flesh is forbidden as an unclean thing) she will triumph. Spirit thereby attempts to blame her falls from grace on Flesh, and she suggests that Flesh is banned from the eternal life.

It is important to understand that the Puritans did not identify bodily desire as the source of sin. They described engaging in adultery, sodomy, or excessive lust as the sign that one was sinful, and the result of a degenerate will or understanding. Attempting to blame one's body for one's inability to resist sin was itself one of the seven "distempers" of the mind, which the Puritan theologian Shepard defined as, "judging the striving of conscience against sin to be the striving of the flesh against the spirit; and hence come these speeches from carnal black mouths; the spirit is willing, but the flesh is weak" (Shepard 1: 79). That is, if the poem's stance and Spirit's stance were the same, if Bradstreet were suggesting that Spirit did have the appropriate attitude toward worldly things, then Bradstreet would have been in conflict with Puritan dogma.

She was not. Critics assume that their discomfort with Spirit's argument is a sign of flaws in the poem, but I would suggest that such is exactly the reaction that Bradstreet intended. We are supposed to be troubled by Spirit's argument, to see her explanation as inadequate and deceptive. We are supposed to see that Spirit falls because she is weak, not because of Flesh, and that her attempting to blame Flesh is one of the signs of her unregenerate nature. In this sense, the reader who desires to believe Spirit's argument—that flesh is the cause of falls from grace—falls for the same sin, and does so through attempting to deny responsibility for having chosen sin.

Recognizing that one has chosen sin is the first step in the conversion experience. A person in the sinful states is "so full of self-love that he is loth to pass a sentence against his own soul" (Hooker, "Heart Must Be Humble" 8). One must be humbled before God and forced to look clearly at the sins one has committed, taking "a full view of thy misery" (Shepard 1: 93). This recognition is almost always brought about by what John Cotton called a "tribulation," a deep and sore sickness in body, spirit, or estate ("Saints Deliverance" 45), such as illness (Bradstreet's "Upon a Fit of Sickness, Anno 1632" and "For Deliverance from a feaver"), captivity by Indians (Mary Rowlandson), or economic loss (this is Cotton Mather's interpretation of the benefit of Bradford having lost money in England). Spirit (like the reader who believes her) has not yet taken this step of critical self-examination.

Spirit's second error is describing heaven as a place forbidden to Flesh. The Puritans believed in the physical resurrection of the body on Judgment Day; in "Weary Pilgrim, Now At Rest" Bradstreet expresses that doctrine: "A Corrupt Carcasse down it lyes / a glorious body it shall rise" (lines 35–36). In this world, because of our flawed judgment and sinful natures, our bodies are corrupt and seem to be in conflict with our spiritual desires, but when they have been "rais'd by Christ," "Then soule and body shall unite" ("Weary Pilgrim" 38, 39). That is, the very conflict between soul and body is one of the signs of our distance from grace. It is not a conflict that will end with the triumph of the spirit, but with the union of spirit and flesh. Were our minds purer, we would be able to see the body for what it is: a "Temple of GOD" that "ought for ever to be beheld and employed, as designed for an *holy Temple*" (quoted in C. Mather, *Christian Philosopher* 222; Mather makes clear he agrees with the quote).

In this world, and with our fallen understandings, however, we are left with the conflict of trying to see the body as a temple when our minds want to make it the excuse for sin. And every individual must feel exactly this conflict; to claim not to do so would be a lie. Calvin says that because "thoughts and affections are so rebellious against the righteousness of God. . . . we must strive" (*Sermons on Ephesians* 652). The early American Puritans did not present themselves as continually maintaining the right attitude, being perfect Christians, or having been raised by Christ. They insisted that all human beings are bathed in sin: "The end of our creation and redemption was, that we might have communion with God; but all of us have played the adulteresses, wee have had our wicked lovers" (Hooker, *Implantation* 36). As Calvin said, "All are so degenerate, that in no part of the world can genuine godliness be found" (*Institutes* 1: 46), and "It is a hard thing to walk arights, for we shall have as many hindrances as can be" (*Sermons on Ephesians* 652). Because human beings are so utterly depraved, one should never fall for the temptation of thinking that one is free from sin. Being certain that one was saved is another of the easy roads to hell: "the way of presumption" (they presume too soon that they are saved) (Shepard 1: 65–68). It is one of the things that "harden the heart" against redemption: "False hope, whereby a man hopes he is not so bad as indeed he is" (Shepard 1: 93). Thinking that the regenerate would always feel assured was identified as among the errors of the Antinomians.

Since the various oppositions seem to be in conflict when one is not in a state of grace, and since it would be the sin of presumption or complacency to act as though one were always in a state of grace, the sincere Puritan would often describe feeling conflict. Because "The gate is strait, and therefore a man must sweat and strive to enter; both the entrance is difficult, and the progress of salvation too" (Shepard 1: 64), the good Christian might narrate moments when the apparent oppositions are transcended (Edwards in the field or Bradstreet in her poem "Contemplations") but would never claim to be able to maintain such a feeling. This is to say that the position of the narrator (not Spirit) in "The Flesh and the Spirit" is the one doctrinally recommended: she stands and listens to the arguments of each sister and is left contemplating the debate.

Similarly, the stance that the narrator takes in "Upon the burning of our house, July 10th 1666" does not demonstrate conflict with Puritan expectations, it fulfills them. The narrator relates her struggle with reconciling herself to having lost her home and everything in it. After two stanzas in which she describes all that is lost, she has three stanzas in which she chides herself for having fixed her "hope on mouldring dust" (line 39) and having made "the arm of flesh" "thy trust" (line 40). She reminds herself that she has another house, "Fram'd by that might Architect, / With glory richly furnished" (lines 44–45) and ends by praying "The world no longer let me Love, / My hope and Treasure lyes Above" (lines 53–54). Like "The Flesh and the Spirit," the poem is convincing in its portrayal of the draws of this world—the home, the things that were in it, the pleasures they brought—and the pull she feels from the permanent home. Although she hopes to reconcile herself to the loss, she does not deny that she feels it. Feeling the draw does not make her a sinner, nor does it prove she is not a saint because, as Calvin says, even the saints felt such conflict: "I say, that if we go back to the remotest period, we shall not find a single saint who, clothed with a mortal body, ever attained to such perfection as to love the Lord with all his heart, and soul, and mind, and strength; and, on the other hand, not one who has not felt the power of concupiscence" (*Institutes* 1: 303). Increase Mather insists that "spiritual troubles" may happen to anyone: "They may be molested with Satans temptations, the best Saint upon earth may [be] so, as Paul was" ("Day of Trouble" 5). Norton says that everyone must have spent at least some amount of time in sin's captivity: "It cannot be expected, according to the ordinary dispensation of God, that the Soul should be made partaker of the liberty of the Gospel by faith in Christ Jesus, without some foregoing sense of the bondage, servitude, sting and captivity of sin and the Curse" (135).

This is not to say that Puritans always behaved in the ways that Bradstreet described. The Puritans seem to have continually transformed the desire to be for God into assuming the position of being a representative of God. Rowlandson was so secure that she was being chastened for entry into the elect that the various moving ironies in her captivity never occurred to her—that she, who was mourning the death of her child, was callous at the death of her Naragansett mistress's child; that her captors treated her neither better nor worse than most Puritan servants were treated; that she was forced to eat disgusting food because her own people had destroyed her captors' food supply. When Cotton told Williams that the New England congregations were capable of seeing (and ejecting) all sinners, he ignored the doctrinal insistence on skepticism in such matters (in Williams 1: 300). Cotton Mather thanked God for having made him a "Partaker" of God's grace (thereby claiming to know that he was a member of the elect) and claimed to be grateful for having been made to abhor anything other than closeness with God—before promptly going on to thank God for making him such a good minister, so popular among the good people, and for having "a *Library*, exceeding any man's, in all this Land" (*Diary* 1: 77). In theory, Puritans were never supposed to make such claims for themselves, but in practice, the sense of ethical certainty (being certain that others are sinning) slips into spiritual pride (being certain that one is not sinning).

IV

Finally, the one-to-one explanation of linguistic reference is belied by the Puritans themselves in the theory of meaning put forward in typology. New England divines read the Old Testament as a layered prefiguration of Christ and his redemption of the chosen people; this prefiguration occurs through types, which Norton defines as: "a

person, action, or thing (whether having or not having any physical
aptness thereunto) by divine institution appointed and declared, to
signifie, testifie, and oft times to exemplifie some spiritual truth"
(*Orthodox Evangelist* 133).[6] Some types prefigure Christ himself—
"Divines generally make *Samson* a Type of Christ, there is such a fair
and full Analogy in sundry particulars of his Life and Death between
him and Christ" (emphasis in original, S. Mather 54–55). Some typify
an aspect of Christ's relationship to human beings—Adam's relation
to the rest of mankind (his "headship," as Edward Taylor says) prefigures Christ's being "the First the Spring, & Well Head of Christian
Kinde" (Taylor *Types*, 1: 36). Some types dictate Christian policy: issues
regarding who could and could not participate in communion were debated in terms of exactly what was typified by the ceremonial laws in
the Old Testament. Some Old Testament narratives prefigure periods
in the history of the true Christian Church: "As the Deliverance out of
Egypt and *Babylon*, if we read the History thereof in the Old Testament,
and compare it with the Prophesies in the New Testament, concerning the Churches Deliverance from Antichristian Bondage, we shall
clearly see, that it was a Type thereof" (emphasis in original, S. Mather
54). And some types prefigure the process of conversion of each member of the elect: Norton explains that Isaac's being born by virtue of
God's promise (long after Sarah could naturally conceive) is a "Type of
the Regeneration and Conversion of the Elect. . . . As therefore the
birth of *Isaac* was not by the strength of Nature, . . . but by virtue of the
Promise, after a supernatural manner, upon sensibleness of barrenness
and impotency to such a birth foregoing thereunto: So, seemeth it to be
according to ordinary dispensation proportionably, and in measure,
with every one that is born of the Spirit, in respect of their new birth"
(*Orthodox Evangelist* 133). Because the Puritans saw the world as the
other book written by God, they sometimes read it typologically: Anne
Bradstreet's "Contemplations" makes the oak and sun types of God,
the river a type of life narrative; Edward Taylor's poetry is largely
meditations on various types (a wasp is his soul, the polestar is God,
his head has the same relation to his body that God has to the true
church). What gives all things, events, and experiences (a wasp, a
house burning down, Indian captivity) importance is their ability
to signify one's relationship to Christ, and through that signification,
to bring about a closer relationship to him. By representing some re-
minder of Scriptural dicta, such types help to effect the conversion of
the fit reader.

One can see in these examples the two ways in which the theory of meaning suggested by Puritan typology violates the name-to-thing referentiality implicit in Puritan attitudes toward rhetoric: first, the meaning in the type is not in the name (Moses) but in the narrative (his leading the children of Israel out of captivity); second, these types are explicitly polysemous. In other words, what gives the type its ability to signify truly is not that it refers to another thing. It is not the word "Moses" that signifies Christ, but the narrative of Moses' actions. And it is not that "Moses" refers to a thing that gives the type meaning, but that it refers to another narrative—the narrative of Christ. The sign is not a word, and the signified is not a thing. The Puritan theory of typology suggests a conception of reference that violates the explanation of reference at the heart of the denigration of rhetoric—that meaning relies on a word to thing correspondence.

The theory of meaning suggested by Puritan typology is a much more dynamic one than that suggested by the one-to-one (word-to-thing) theory of reference. Typology makes metaphor, not simply an ornament hung like a Christmas ball onto a meaningful proposition, but the very nature of reference. Most important, the theory of linguistic reference implied by typology is explicitly polysemous: first, because most types refer to Christ *and* God *and* some narrative, every sign has (at least) three referents; second, because God is signified in nearly infinite ways, a referent may have a nearly infinite number of signs available.

This multiplicity of reference explains the Puritan tendency to treat the world as a text, and vice versa. Tony Tanner has referred to the "rampant hermeneutic activity" that gave "the conditions for an unchecked (even paranoid or megalomaniac) semiology. Crudely speaking, everything could be a type or an anti-type, could signify, something else. The Puritans lived in a hopelessly over-interpretable world. There was a continuous excess of significance and signification. Everything meant too much. Nothing was simply what it was" (19). In short, the American Puritans had two theories of reference. One of them—the one-to-one, word-to-thing reference behind the calls for plain language—contributes to the denigration of rhetoric, the restriction of the discipline to the ability to put the minimal appropriate clothing on the body of theology. That denigration and restriction of rhetoric may not have caused the violence of Puritan public discourse, but it certainly contributed to the habit of ambiguity and the inability to incorporate difference. The other theory of reference—the dynamic polysemous theory implied by typology—did lead to the rich poetry of Bradstreet and Edward Taylor, and could have led to a richer theory of rhetoric, truth, and discourse. It might have led to an embrace of the discipline of rhetoric, to an expansion of its domain, or a sense that it teaches the art of public discourse. Or, this other theory of reference might have led to the belief that different uses of language do not represent the presence of the Devil as much as they are the natural result of the variety of signs available in a community of discourse. It might have led to an ideal of public discourse grounded in the participation of different views. It did not. There are two consequences of this referential multiplicity. First, it represents yet another way that Puritanism failed to be monologic in practice because typology assumes that within each act of reference there is the possibility of a different one.

Second, it indicates another way that Puritanism is misrepresented. It has become commonplace to assert that the Puritans were hostile to the material world, and this hostility is part and parcel of the Puritan repression of dissent, indigenous peoples, and the natural environment. This latter view has been most famously argued by Roderick Nash, whose extremely influential book *Wilderness and the American Mind,* insists that the Puritans propagated "the belief that good Christians should maintain an aloofness from the pleasures of the world" (19). This antipathy toward the physical world is supposed to have led the Puritans to perceive the wilderness as a "dark model for all that was depraved," "as the symbol of anarchy and evil to which the Christian was unalterably opposed"—"to hate wilderness" thereby starting Americans on an errand of destroying the wilderness (Worster 177; Nash 34, 35).

Like the arguments which treat Puritans as hypocritical regarding sex, this interpretation of Puritanism necessitates imposing a simplistic antithesis on their ideology: either they praised everything about nature, or they must have hated it. One of the more obvious problems with this imposition of a binary opposition is the importance to Puritans of typological readings of the natural world. Edward Taylor's meditative poetry is full of metaphors drawn from nature: wasps; polestars; flowers; the sun. Edwards' narrative of spiritual conversion repeatedly describes walking through fields and woods in order to be closer to God, and when he imagines being as one with Christ, he imagines himself in the mountains or wilderness. Just as Edwards walks in his father's pasture and contemplates God's meekness and majesty, the speaker of Bradstreet's "Contemplations" walks in an un-named natural landscape and contemplates various oppositions that resolve themselves as she meditates upon them. The poem does not de-scribe the conflict between the things of the material world (an oak, the sun, a river, a nightingale) and spiritual topics (Cain and Abel, human mortality, spiritual immortality) but threads seamlessly among them. The narrator contemplates the majesty of an oak and is thereby led to contemplate the excellence of God; she admires the sun and is led to admire the glory of God; she desires to sing a song in praise of God but feels incapable of it until inspired by a grasshopper and cricket; medi-tating upon the unhappiness of human life relative to the earth and heavens causes her to remember the possibility of human immortality; watching a river leads her to think of her desire to be with her children in God's mansion; envying the merry nightingale reminds her that the fall was fortunate, that the cares and losses of life prepare one for heaven's bower.

The oak, fishes, nightingale, and so on function as emblems that en-able Bradstreet to read the landscape as she would the Bible. In doing so, she does what Calvin recommends: she aids her "inward knowl-edge" by reading "the creatures in which, as in a mirror, the perfec-tions of God may be contemplated" (*Institutes* 1: 27). Cotton Mather's long description of the various sorts of animals in *Christian Philosopher* is interspersed with the message that one is supposed to draw from a study of animals; he includes such exclamations as, *"Great GOD, Thou art the Father of all things; even the Father of Insects, as well as the Father of Spirits: And Thy Greatness appears with a singular Brightness in the least of Thy Creatures!"* (emphasis in original, 146). It is not simply the crea-tures that mirror God: "The elegant structure of the world [serves] us as a kind of mirror, in which we may behold God, though otherwise invisible" (Calvin *Institutes* 51). It is because God's message is in-scribed throughout the universe that contemplating any part of it leads to contemplating God: One can read God's will in the world because God himself is everywhere: "True it is that the Lord fills Heaven and Earth with his presence, yea, the Heaven of Heavens is not able to con-tain him . . . His infinite Being is every where, and one and the same every where in regard of himself; because his being is most simple, and not subject to any shadow of change, being all one with himself" (Hooker, "Heart Must Be Humble" 3–4). Edwards considers the stars; Edward Taylor meditates on a warming wasp; Mather suggests that even contemplating the wonder of one's own eye might lead one to

God: "None less than GOD could contrive, order, and provide an Organ as magnificent and curious as the Sense is useful. And Sturmius had reason enough to say, he was fully persuaded, that no Man who sur-vey'd the Eye could abandon himself to any Speculative Atheism" (em-phasis removed, C. Mather, *Christian Philosopher* 244). God's will is also manifest in worldly events. Incidents as grand as wars and epidemics or as particular as a broken chamber pot should lead a pious individ-ual to contemplation.

This is not to say that the Puritans "enjoyed" the wilderness or con-sidered it unequivocally pleasant; rather, they saw it (quite literally) as significant. What is signified in the natural environment is God's will: his power, wisdom, and goodness (C. Mather, *Christian Philosopher* 296).[7] As Calvin writes, if one observes the world, one sees God: "at one time making heaven reverberate with thunder, sending forth the scorching lightning, and setting the whole atmosphere in a blaze; at another, causing the raging tempests to blow, and forthwith, in one mo-ment, when it so pleases him, making a perfect calm; keeping the sea, which seems constantly threatening the earth with devastation, suspended as it were in air; at one time, lashing it into fury by the im-petuosity of the winds; at another, appeasing its rage, and stilling all its waves" (*Institutes* 1: 55). If we experience terror of God's justice (as made manifest in the sublime), it is because we are guilty and afraid of being punished. But a true Christian would never try to evade God's punishment: "Nevertheless, he is not so terrified by an apprehension of judgment as to wish he could withdraw himself, even if the means of escape lay before him" (*Institutes* 1: 42).

This sense that one should not fear God so much as to run from him indicates that the Puritans did not believe wilderness (or nature) was necessarily an Edenic garden in which one should wander. The Puritan wilderness is not a garden of peace and love; Cotton Mather's analysis of it, for example, describes insects, reptiles, death, and destruction. Even these aspects, however, prove God's wisdom: "That the Numbers of Insects and Vermin may not be too offensive to us, Providence has ordained many Creatures, especially such as are in superior Orders to make it their business to destroy them, especially when their Increase grows too numerous and enormous . . . The Destruction and Death of Animals does proclaim the Fame of the Divine Wisdom in adjusting of it!" (emphasis removed, *Christian Philosopher* 161).

The Puritans described the natural environment as sometimes threatening, often harsh, usually awe inspiring (or awful). Precisely for these characteristics the natural environment was significant in the Puritans' sense of individual and communal development. Like God, it threatened to punish those who were weak; like God, it could be very harsh; through it, one was continually reminded of the awe that one should feel toward God. The wilderness thereby signified God, as well as serving as the place for the rite of passage for an individual through which one was (somewhat) assured of one's membership in the community of the elect.

Because the true Christian is not terrified, such a person will welcome the chastening and scourging experience, an experience in which wilderness (physical or spiritual) must be the scene: "When the Lord will come to the soul, and draw it into communion with himself; he will have his way hereto prepared in the Desert; not in the throng of a City, but in a solitary Desert place, he will allure us, and draw us into the wilderness, from the company of men, when he will speak to our heart, and when he prepares our heart to speak unto him" (Bulkeley 34–35). In one sense, therefore, Puritanism makes the wilderness richly significant: it was absolutely necessary that the Puritan community and the individuals within it experience the same kind of isolation, hostility from heathens, and redemption in the same kind of wilderness as had the Israelites: "This was typified in the passage of the Children of Israel towards the promised Land; they must come into, and go through a vast and roaring Wilderness, where they must be bruised with many pressures, humbled under many overbearing difficulties, they were to meet withal before they could possess that good Land which abounded with all prosperity, flowed with Milk and Honey" (Hooker, "Heart Must Be Humble" 5; see also *Implantation*, 4; S. Mather, *The Figures or Types*). This notion of religious and political destiny made the wilderness tremendously significant. On the other hand, it made the actual characteristics of this wilderness, this experience, and these native inhabitants irrelevant. They were (because they must be) exactly like their types in the Old Testament. And like Scripture, the flesh, or anything else, the wilderness *qua* wilderness had no inherent value; it was valuable only insofar as one's use of it led to the greater glory of God.[8]

The wilderness that Wigglesworth describes in "Gods Controversy with New England" is a tool that God uses to instruct His Chosen People. Because it signifies God, it is by definition good, although due to nothing inherent in its nature. That is, nothing has any value separate from its signification of God's glory or his use of it in instructing the Chosen People. This is true of nature as well as of the people within it; the people of the New World, for example, do not will evil against the Puritans—Indians and devils have no spiritual desire for good or evil—but are used by God to punish the "stiff-neckt" and backsliding Christians or to demonstrate the Puritans' status as the Chosen People.

This notion of God using enemies to prove his love for his people is a complicated one, but it is essentially the same as the perception that God demonstrates his love for an individual by chastening and scourging. Calvin argued that God hardened the heart of Pharoah so that it would clearly take a miracle for the Israelites to leave Egypt, "because the tyrant must be gloriously conquered, and overwhlemed in so many hard-fought engagements, that the victory might be more splendid" (*Four Last Books of Moses* 1: 101). If the Pharoah had set the people free the first time that Moses asked, there would have been no need for the miracles of prophecy and salvation that Pharoah's hard heart required (the locusts, diseases, and pass over of the Hebrew children). If the Pharoah had not pursued the Israelites, there would have been no need for the parting and closing of the Red Sea. If the Israelites had not nearly starved or died of thirst, there would have been no need for the miracles of water and manna that God sent. So, God sends the nearly disastrous situation in order to free his people from it by a miracle that can be seen by all people. This miracle awes everyone; as Wigglesworth says: "The fame of thy great acts, o Lord, / Did all the nations quell. / Some hid themselves for fear of thee / In forrests wide and great: / Some to thy people croutching came, / For favour to entreat" ("Gods Controversy" lines 55–60). In this sense, the hardship is as much a part of the miracle as is the rescue: When Rowlandson lists the miracles made manifest in her experience, she discusses those events that prolonged her captivity, such as the Indians being able to cross a river that the English pursuers could not, being able to eat despite their food being destroyed, and the dogs being silent when the Indians attacked (see, for example, pages 68, 70).

This is the sense in which Puritans (ranging from Milton to Bradstreet) have been categorized as pantheists: God is everywhere, and everything says the same thing over and over if one is pure enough to read it correctly. This belief in the universality of the text of the Book of Nature could equally lead to opposing attitudes toward observing the natural world; it could foster the scientific pantheism of Jonathan Edwards (and his insistence on accuracy) or the highly inaccurate nature writings of Anne Bradstreet (whose panegyrics to nature sound more like the European countryside of her readings than the New England flora and fauna through which she was walking).[9] If the people inhabiting the wilderness of the New Israelites are essentially the same as those who fought (and were conquered by) the other Israelites, then one can learn about them either through studying the customs of the people who presently exist or by reading the Bible: one can try to convert them (as did John Eliot), or one can refer to all of them by the names of the hostile tribes in the Old Testament (as did Michael Wigglesworth).

Again, one sees the Puritan evasion of difference of opinion: the Puritans maintained this faith in the universality of the book of nature's message in the face of tremendous disagreement about just what it is that the book says. It was clear, for example, that one could contemplate the history of the colonies in order to see God's message, but the various authors who did so had quite different narratives of that history. Bradford's history *Of Plymouth Plantation* describes the early years of the colony as struggles against starvation and illness and the middle years as filled with conflicts with hostile inhabitants, legal problems, and moral degradation. Wigglesworth describes that first period as vanishing quickly and the second as a time of peace and piety: "So that through places wilde and waste / A single man, disarm'd, / Might journey many hundred miles, / And not at all be harm'd. / Amidst the solitary woods / Poor travellers might sleep / As free from danger as at home, / Though no man watch did keep" ("Gods Controversy" lines 97–104). My point is not simply that the Puritans had different narrations of the history of their plantation, but that they maintained these different histories in the face of theories that their history was teleological, emblematic, and that it unarguably communicated one clear message. And willed ignoring of an obvious contradiction is one of the most important characteristics of the early American Puritans in regard to their attitudes toward public discourse. The presence of dispute and controversy regarding the meaning of Scripture did not prevent individuals from describing their own interpretations as undeniable and indisputable.

It is extremely easy to misstate this point. I am not making the rather obvious argument that Puritanism, like any other set of beliefs, is imperfectly systematic. Puritan theology is, explicitly and avowedly, elitist. Very few people can be Jonathan Edwards or Anne Bradstreet, can feel perfect confidence and serious fear at one and the same moment, can see God's justice and mercy as noncontradictory, and can sincerely and convincingly admit their slips and confusions. It is easier to see the dualities as antitheses—to talk about God's justice and forget his mercy, to hate this world in order to love the next, to congratulate oneself about one's righteousness and forget one's sins.

The Puritans believed that we are particularly given to such antitheses because we are generally in a fallen state. So it should be no surprise that many members of the Puritan communities failed to live up to the extremely high standards that Puritan theology set. From the beginning, they were aware that their errand might fail, that they might turn into a laughingstock and a byword rather than an inspirational example of the perfect Christian community. One of the more intriguing paradoxes about the Puritans is that they tried to establish communities on the basis of rules that they themselves said very few people could follow. To put it bluntly, ideas have consequences, but the same set of ideas does not always have the same set of consequences. That was not something that the Puritans acknowledged: in the middle of disputes about the meaning of history, the natural world, a Scriptural passage, both parties would insist on the indisputability of their readings.[10] Nevertheless, disagreements and inconsistencies did exist. For example, the Puritans said that man is the highest being in creation (so that the world was created for him) *and* that man is the lowest being in creation (and the world was created for God's greater glory).

The notion that man is the highest creation was often associated with the Great Chain of Being. Cotton Mather, for example, says: "There is a Scale of Nature, wherein we pass regularly and proportionably from a *Stone* to a *Man,* the Faculties of the Creatures in their *various Classes* growing still brighter and brighter, and more capacious, till we arrive to those noble ones which are found in the *Soul* of MAN; and yet MAN is, as one well expresses it, *but the Equator of the Universe"* (emphasis in original, *Christian Philosopher* 292–93). Man is halfway between a stone and God (or, sometimes, between Satan and God)—he has the physicality of the material world "below" him, but the mind and understanding of the spiritual "above" him.[11] He is God's highest creation. Since man is the highest, and since "as we know that it was chiefly for the sake of mankind that the world was made, we must look to this as the end which God has in view in the government of it" (Calvin, *Institutes* 1: 177; see also 1: 157). We are therefore justified in considering all nature in terms of how useful it is for human beings, in measuring its value by how it pleases or helps humanity.

But human beings are the lowest in all creation. When man fell, he brought sin upon himself. Although he brought misfortune and death upon the "innocent creatures," they neither participated in nor received any part of human sin (Calvin, *Institutes* 1: 292). The Puritans insisted that sin is not external to human beings—it does not reside in the flesh, the world, or Satan—but it is in the human mind. In regard to what we call the works of Satan, Calvin says, "the cause of which is not to be sought in anything external to the will of man, in which the root of the evil lies, and in which the foundation of Satan's kingdom, in other words, sin, is fixed" (*Institutes* 1: 266). Whatever faculties we may have that the creatures lack, we also have sin, which the creatures also lack. In many ways, then, human beings are the lowest; we are, as Calvin says (over and over), worms.

Determining the appropriate relation of human beings to nature is further complicated by the Puritans' indecision as to whether the world did participate in man's fall; the variation in the Hebrew Scripture (some texts say that the ground was cursed for man's sake and some say that it was cursed in man's toil) led to variation in Christian commentary.[12] It was quite common to argue that the world remained in a prelapsarian state and that we became alienated from it in our fall. Therefore, the Biblical injunctions to have dominion over nature may not apply quite as clearly when humanity is fallen but nature is not: "It is very certain our Dominion over the Creatures is very much impair'd by our Fall from God" (emphasis removed, Mather, *Christian Philosopher* 220). Calvin, saying that a human being may desire to be thought of as a rational creature and master of nature, "but if he were to be worthy of such honor, he would have to be sent to school to the beasts, he has so perverted everything" (quoted in Bouwsma 140).

Finally, Puritan ideology was profoundly inconsistent in regard to the self in several important ways. In addition to the conflicting model of dissent and conflict (that each member of the elect will have conflict with his or her community and that the perfect community will have no conflict), Puritanism describes the self as both very strong and very weak. As Christopher Felker has said, "The Puritan self, at once assertive and submissive, was an unstable construct" (645). In some contexts, such as discussions of predestination, Puritanism describes a self that is static, that has a single identity (elect or reprobate), and that cannot be changed by anything human. In other contexts, however, such as discussions of religious toleration or heresy, Puritanism presumes a very fragile self, which can be easily led astray. That is, in Puritanism, the self can and cannot be changed by what other people say.

The Puritan model of the self both condemns and causes the sin of spiritual pride. Ever since Augustine, Christians had talked in terms of two churches: the visible one, made up of sinners and saints; the invisible church, made up of saints alone. The American Puritans set out to make those churches as one, to form a visible church that had nothing but saints. If the church is made up of visible saints, then it would be extremely difficult for an individual not to consider oneself saved.

Immediately prior to Miller's work on the Puritans, Progressive historians had been very interested in condemning the Massachusetts Bay Puritans for the various contradictions in that ideology: their having been victims of and then engaging in religious persecution; their working so hard at prosperity while valorizing constant piety; the ambiguities and inconsistencies in American Calvinist articulations of the doctrine of predestination; and so on. Miller, in his attempt to respond to such condemnations (and condescensions) by emphasizing the piety, learning, and sincerity of the Puritans, may well have made their efforts seem too consistent and their system too unified. Nevertheless, it is difficult to be entirely fair to the people who settled the Massachusetts Bay Colony, to give a good sense of the considerable differences and disagreements and yet the remarkable consistency in doctrine. This is not to say that the Puritans always agreed upon doctrine, but that they were surprisingly consistent in their repeated reliance on certain assumptions within specific contexts. When discussing predestination, Puritan theologians and ministers were very consistent about the self being static; when discussing conversion experiences, they were consistent in the belief that the self changes.

Between contexts, in other words, Puritans appealed to contradictory assumptions. When discussing public argumentation, the discipline of rhetoric, the role of the minister in conversion, and the correct relationship of the government and the public, Puritan ideology describes a still and certain world in which one can know with great certainty everything one needs to know. In those contexts, there is perfect submission to a static authority, an authority that demonstrates propositions that everyone immediately recognizes to be true. When discussing the conversion experience, chastening and scourging, natural or Scriptural typology, however, Puritans assume contingent balances, a dynamic process of imperfect reference, and continual resistance.

6

Arguments with Voices
in the Wilderness

I was having problems with a student in one of my classes, who continually insulted his opposition when writing what was supposed to
be persuasive papers. When I tried to explain to him that this was not
rhetorically effective, he was outraged. "How can you say I'm not persuasive?" he demanded, "No one I know will argue with me because I
always win!"

Earlier, I said that this book attempted to answer an altered version
of the central question for Habermas's historical work: What are the
social and intellectual conditions that prevent a rational-critical debate
about public issues by private persons intending to let arguments and
not statuses determine decisions? At least one answer is presented
by the Puritan attempt to create a monologic public sphere. A hetero-
geneous public sphere cannot function discursively (it will continually
stagger into violence of one form or another) when it is premised on a
static notion of truth, an epistemology that assumes easy and direct
access to that static truth, a vision of language that dictates that words
can and should accurately represent what one gains from that easy and
direct access, and a uniform model of the self. These premises are especially problematic when they coexist with the concept that spiritual pride is a sin, that one sees through a glass darkly, that the self
changes, and that God's word is sometimes ineffable. There are, finally,
three consequences of these premises: the community will continually
have dissension; it will have no discursive method of resolving that
dissension; and the intellectual system itself will not provide a method
of critical self-reflection that might enable the community to see what
is going wrong.

Having begun like a good Puritan minister with my thesis, I should
end with an exhortation, and I will. But I want to vary from the form
somewhat, in that I want to exhort the readers as to the importance of

the question itself. My intention is not so much to persuade readers to accept dialogic rhetoric into their hearts, as much as it is to persuade proponents of dialogism to take instances of monologism seriously as systems of thought. Or, in simpler terms, dialogism needs to find a way to include monologism in its own dialogue about rhetoric.

I agree with the proponents of dialogic discourse that dialogic rhetoric is, as Walker says, "ethically and intellectually responsible" (62), and it is the form of discourse that I try to teach in my writing courses. But I have been continually haunted by two questions: What is the most useful and accurate description of dialogic discourse (or rhetoric, or consensual communication) for distinguishing it from monologic discourse (or demonstration, or strategic action)? And if it is so clear that dialogue is more ethically and intellectually responsible, why is it so hard to teach? That is, what is so attractive about monologic discourse? Answering these two questions helps to explain why it is worth worrying about a discourse community some three hundred years old.

A description of dialogic rhetoric must be both accurate and useful—accurate in effectively distinguishing monologic from dialogic and useful in enabling critical self-reflection. Therefore, a useful definition should enable people who are engaging in monologic discourse to see that they are doing so, and it should also help persuade them why they should change. It should be descriptive, normative, and persuasive. But being able to persuade people to change from one form of discursive practice to another requires that their reasons for preferring monologic discourse be understood and acknowledged.

I

I have argued that the Puritans are an ideal case to think carefully about what promotes or prevents an inclusive and discursive public sphere, for the Puritans constituted a highly educated and self-conscious community that repeatedly chose to promote monologic discourse as the ideal form of public discourse. Their sometimes spectacular failures—such as the Halfway Covenant, the Williams-Cotton debate, their difficulty with renewing their charter, the Salem witch-hunting debacle, and even the Great Awakening—indicate some of the ways in which their choice grieved them. The problem with investigating the public sphere through the Puritans, however, is that they can seem much more distant than they are. It is not simply the genuinely vexing problem that the Puritans are attributed all sorts of qualities they did not have—hatred of the body, sex, women, the material world, and the environment—but also the odd place that religion has come to have in American politics. When teaching about the Puritans, I have found that students (and colleagues) typically assume that a historical and rhetorical connection exists between the seventeenth-century Puritans and current religious fundamentalists; hence, many of the attributes that may be true of the contemporary blend of politics and religion are pushed backwards onto the Puritans. On the contrary, the Puritans would have banished and hung such enthusiasts at the first opportunity. What Puritan thinkers would find most offensive about current fundamentalists is the rejection of rationality, the assumption that religion and informed logical thought are necessarily opposed. Yet, because people know that fundamentalists are zealous about religion, and they know that the Puritans were zealous about religion, they assume that the two groups must be similar. They are not. When I listen to televangelists or read pamphlets or tracts that are published by the current religious right, I am rarely reminded of the American Puritans; current religious debates seem to me far more influenced by American Romanticism and sentimentalism than by Calvinism.

This is not to say that the Puritan influence on any form of current thought is negligible; the efforts by various scholars to see Puritanism in American literature, politics, foreign policy, and identity are quite persuasive. It is to say that American Puritanism was secularized, so that one should look for current instances of it outside of religion. To put it somewhat cryptically, religious fundamentalists are not the heirs of Puritanism but the Enlightenment is. One can see similar endeavors to Puritanism in various forms of what is sometimes called the Enlightenment Project—the attempt to make Reason paramount in public life. Despite the poststructuralist attack on that project, one can see it in several forms, ranging from Habermas's "communicative action" to the place that "facts" have in popular culture. For both cases, the failure of the Puritan public sphere remains an important critique.

It may seem actively impish to compare someone like Jürgen Habermas to the American Puritans, but the results are instructive. Habermas's work, in general, has two aspects. First, in much of his work, he describes and argues for a rational-critical public sphere, a discursive realm with three characteristics. It is a public sphere that at least in theory disregards status in favor of rationality; the discussion within this realm is the domain of "common concern," including criticism of the governmental authority; finally, the realm is perfectly inclusive (at least in principle) "for it always understood and found itself immersed within a more inclusive public of all private people, persons who—insofar as they were propertied and educated—as readers, listeners, and spectators could avail themselves via the market of the objects that were subject to discussion" (*Structural Transformation* 37). Christopher Norris has characterized this aspect of Habermas's project as "the 'unfinished project' of modernity, conceived as the potential for emancipating science (or practical-cognitive interests) from the dominance of a reified means-ends rationality imposed by narrowly positive conceptions of knowledge, method and truth" (101). Because it intends to be completely inclusive, and because it depends upon discourse (rather than coercion), categorizing Habermas's project as a kind of dialogic rhetoric seems fair.

The second general aspect of Habermas's work is to respond to the post-structuralist critique that discourse (let alone rationality) can never serve the liberatory function described above, for there is no possibility of freeing oneself from one's prejudices, narrow condition, and assertion of self interests. Stanley Fish, for example, has argued that the goal of self-reflective critical practice of any sort (including Habermas's communicative action) requires that one be able to "see through" historical and cultural forces: "But that is the one thing a historically conditioned consciousness cannot do—scrutinize its own beliefs, conduct a rational examination of its own convictions; for in order to begin such a scrutiny, it would first have to escape the grounds of its own possibility, and it could only do that if it were not historically conditioned and were instead an acontextual or unsituated entity of the kind that is rendered unavailable by the first principle of the interpretivist or conventionalist view" (245).

For critics like Fish, all discourse is strategic action, with the essentially coercive nature of interpretation often hidden due to the existence of discourse communities. Habermas has long been concerned with this notion—that rationality is itself a kind of language game, the rules of which are culturally constructed—and the second aspect of his project has been to find some ontological grounding for rationality. He has drawn on psychoanalysis, history (especially in *Structural Transformation*), and beginning with *Communication and the Evolution of Society,* speech act theory. This last area—specifically the work of Austin and Searle—has enabled Habermas to argue that the basic pieces of communicative action are a necessary part of the use of language. That is, people who speak together make and fulfill certain validity claims, or they no longer communicate: understandability (that what they are saying is meaningful); honesty (that what they are saying is an accurate representation); sincerity (that they believe what they are saying); finally, whatever obligations pertain to the particular speech act in which they are engaging (that they intend to fulfill their word if they are making promises, and so on). If a participant makes an assertion to which another participant will not assent, then communication ceases, or s/he needs to redeem it in some manner. In communicative action, it is redeemed through further assertion; in other kinds of action (such as strategic action) the speaker may gain assent through rhetoric (by which Habermas means something akin to propaganda) or some kind of coercion.

Habermas's project is distinguished from other dialogic rhetorics in several ways: most obviously, he is critical (if not dismissive) of the discipline of rhetoric (accepting the narrow definition of rhetoric as a kind of slick monologism); his arguments for communicative action are grounded in the Kantian tradition (rather than some version of the classical, as most defenses of rhetoric are); he wants to claim for rationality a status outside culture and history (whereas other notable defenses of dialogic rhetoric are typically made on pragmatic grounds, leaving aside the issue of ontology).

This last characteristic gives Habermas's work an attractive thoroughness, a kind of philosophical systematicity, which rhetoric often lacks. For good reason, it is a convention to set rhetoric in opposition to philosophy, and one of the more common grounds for that distinction is the difference in the ways the two disciplines treat categories. Whereas philosophy attempts to lay out taxonomies that accurately represent reality, for the rhetorician, categories are useful as heuristics or rhetorical structures. One of the lines of argument, categorizing is a figure of thought (divisio) that might serve as the basis for a method of proof (as with expeditio or antithesis) or as a means for distributing off those parts of the argument that are irrelevant, problematic, or misleading (distributio) or as a way of defining the subject at hand (especially with some form of a genus-species argument). The resulting taxonomy is contingent and particular: the same topic would be divided differently depending upon which of these functions the act of categorizing was intended to serve. And that is the main complaint that philosophy has long had about rhetoric: that when it comes to evaluating taxonomies, rhetoric is more concerned with what is useful than what

is true. For many philosophers (and some rhetoricians) this hierarchy of priorities seems to mean that rhetoric is not at all concerned
with what is true. Yet, although there are modern-day sophists like
Stanley Fish, who seem quite comfortable equating discourse and
coercion, there are also modern day rhetoricians like Wayne Booth or
Martha Nussbaum, whose skepticism about language contributes to
an inclusive discursive theory but who are not nihilistic about truth.

Habermas's project seems to me a recent version of what George
Kennedy has famously called philosophical rhetorics. It is a theory of
public argumentation with a philosophical basis. Numerous critics of
his project have focused on that basis, but the pragmatic aspect seems
more important to me, and more problematic. For an inclusive theory
of public discourse to lead to an inclusive practice, any attempt to articulate the characteristics of a liberatory and inclusive discourse
must itself fit two criteria: first, it must be inclusive in its definition of
rationality; second, it must contribute to self-reflection. On both
counts, Habermas's project has the same problems as does American
Puritanism.

For both Habermas and Puritanism, the definition of rationality is
both circular and elusive, and, thereby, it functions to exclude genuinely different points of view. One can see the problems by compar-
ing Habermas's discussion of the eighteenth-century *philosophes* with
the American Puritans. As I argued in an earlier chapter, Habermas's
description of what made the eighteenth-century public sphere a
rational-critical public sphere fails to distinguish it from the American
Puritan public sphere. The American Puritans intended to establish a
realm of discourse that would disregard the status of the person speaking in favor of the force of the argument, one in which all topics would
be open for discussion and one that would be open to anyone who met
what appeared to be minimal standards of rational behavior. It is, of
course, that last criterion that is so subject to misuse. It *seemed*, to both
the *philosophes* and the Puritans, that all of their respective exclusions
were on the basis of rationality. That is, the gender and ethnocentrism
of the *philosophes* seemed not to be an exclusion on the basis of status
but on what appeared to be the inherent irrationality of women and
nonwhites; similarly, the Puritans' exclusion of anyone who disagreed
with their supposedly self-evident propositions was not on the basis of
the person's status but on what seemed to authorities to be the clear
irrationality of such disagreement.

The *philosophes*, as Habermas grants, practiced exclusion in fact, but he wants to subsume that fact to the equally important fact of their intentions. The Puritans practiced exclusion in fact, yet it is logical to grant them the same exception given to the *philosophes*. If one does so, and there is no good reason not to, one seems forced to conclude that the Puritans had a rational-critical public sphere. And that conclusion is absurd: the Puritans tortured religious and political dissenters, and they only altered the practice when they had religious toleration forced on them. Whatever the flaws of the *philosophes*, they never engaged in that degree of repression. In short, granting exceptions on the basis of intention does not help to distinguish an inclusive from an exclusive sphere. Good intentions are not good enough.

In fact, as James Kastely has argued, well-intentioned exclusion is *the* problem for theorists of the public sphere: "However upsetting is the conscious use of race, gender, class, or creed to deny a person a voice, the more disturbing insight is that we undoubtedly exclude others from the community not because we wish to do them injury or because we possess despicable motives but because we are trapped in our own languages" (44). The problem, for both the *philosophes* and the Puritans, is that Habermas's theories do not provide a way for a well-intentioned but self-deceived person to recognize that s/he has made the same error that both groups made. The important moment in an argument is when what seems to one person to be an obvious premise is rejected by the other person. Habermas says that one should redeem this premise through rational argumentation, and if this is impossible, one resorts to strategic action. As I argued earlier, this was exactly the procedure followed by the Puritans. People like John Cotton went to great trouble to demonstrate the rationality of their premises. Only when (and even sometimes after) the interlocutor demonstrated his/ her willful irrationality did the authorities resort to torture or banishment.

Therein lay the problem. Instead of trying to demonstrate the rightness (and righteousness) of their premises, the failure to reach agreement should have been a moment when the authorities questioned those premises; that is, questioned their own rationality. And this is the sense in which Habermas's theories fail to create a self-reflective praxis. Because the definition of rationality is so easily self-serving, Habermas's theories of communicative action fail to help an individual distinguish between moments when discourse is failing because his/her interlocutor is being irrational and those moments when discourse is failing because the individual is the one being irrational. This, then, is one pragmatic problem with Habermas's project; in his terms, any project must "provide a critical standard, against which actual practices—the opaque and perplexing reality of the constitutional state—could be evaluated" (*Between Facts and Norms* 5). People must be able to engage in critical self-evaluation, and it is precisely that which Habermas's project fails to provide.

Perhaps because I have continually been teaching writing (and teaching the teaching of writing), I have increasingly come to value the rhetorical consequences of visions of the dialogic public sphere. That is, the issue to which I keep returning is which visions *persuade* people to abandon seeing discourse as a form of force. Or, to put it another way, Kenneth Burke has remarked that any governmental system will work if one begins with the premise that people will be good to each other. Similarly, if as Habermas assumes, participants in discourse engage with complete goodwill such that they will cheerfully and carefully redeem all questioned claims and pursue no goals but intersubjective agreement, then any discourse system will work. Habermas asserts that "Communicative freedom exists only between actors who, adopting a performative attitude, want to reach an understanding with one another and expect one another to take positions on reciprocally raised validity claims" (*Between Facts and Norms* 119). There are, I have been arguing, two problems: first, as a critique, Habermas's model does not provide a way for someone who was unintentionally engaging in strategic action to reflect critically on his/her own practice (that is, it provides no grounds by which individuals can evaluate their practices; they are likely instead to conclude that the other person is being irrational); second, as a practice, it is restricted to an extremely small arena. Communicative freedom, as Habermas defines it, is rare.

These problems are not limited to Habermas but may be most obvious in his work because he has tried to establish an ontological rather than simply pragmatic basis for his project. I first ran across both of these problems as an undergraduate tutoring persuasive writing. I was in a program that emphasized dialogic discourse (mostly based in neo-Aristotelians like Kenneth Burke and Wayne Booth) and was deeply moved by the effectiveness of this form of discourse in my own life. But as I said, I often found myself working with students who refused to adopt the worldview (skepticism about one's own rightness, a sense of the contingency of any particular resolution, respect for the opposition, a desire for discursive reciprocity) necessary for even wanting to learn what dialogism might be. Ironically enough, even using dialogic rhetoric with these recalcitrant students often failed to persuade them of its merits; that is, I had found the limits of dialogism. Often it was institutional coercion that changed their practices, for they had to begin treating the opposition with respect in order to get the grades they wanted. Sometimes that experience caused a kind of conversion in them, so that they went on to become interested in dialogism; sometimes, of course, it did not.

Dialogism seemed especially limited in regard to environmental issues, for this was an area in which opponents disagreed about practical issues because they had fundamentally incompatible but deeply held views. In a notable failure of my own, I discovered that such a specific issue as whether an urban park should be designed more for human use or wildlife habitat quickly moved to questions about the right relationship among God's will, the purpose of Nature, and human re-creation. The task appeared to be to find a method of dialogism that would work under those conditions, and it initially seemed to me that Habermas's communicative action provided just such a method. I became interested in exploring the problem of persuasion in the face of recalcitrance by looking at an especially striking case: John Muir's attempt to prevent the damming and flooding of the Hetch Hetchy Valley in Yosemite National Park. Muir, although a well-known public figure, lecturer, and popular naturalist, was more or less ridiculed during the 1914 Congressional debate, and his arguments against the dam were disregarded as ill-informed and irrelevant because he was a man without a college degree who was disagreeing with engineers. Yet on the contrary, the promises made by the dam proponents—that camping would never be restricted, that recreation on the lake would be encouraged, that the hydroelectric power would never be sold to a private company, that they would build a hotel and a road around the lake— were utterly impractical and could not be fulfilled. In fact, there is no hotel or road, camping and recreation are restricted or forbidden, and the power is sold to a private company. In addition, the dam cost about three times as much as was estimated, and that cost difference was not entirely due to unforeseen problems; the costs of materials in the official report were inconsistently compared so that the Hetch Hetchy *seemed* the least expensive option when it was not. As such, the controversy perfectly exemplified the practical consequences of public discourse grounded in the strategy of exclusion. The dam was built because the reservoir opponents' arguments were excluded from the discourse due to narrow conceptions of rationality and excessive (and inappropriate) attention to speaker status.[1]

It had seemed that such an example would function as a case study that might be used to evaluate various models of inclusive public discourse, but it did not. As I said, at the time that I was working with the Hetch Hetchy material, I was most attracted to Habermas's theory of consensual communication, and I had hoped that the controversy would serve as an argument to support Habermas's theories. Although it perfectly exemplified his critiques of positivism and strategic action, however, it seemed almost irrelevant to his positive program of communicative action.

Given that dam proponents used misleading numbers, one could hardly argue that they were fulfilling their obligations to sincerity and honesty; given that Muir compared them to Satan, one would probably not want to argue that he was fulfilling his obligations to provide rational support for his questioned assertions. In short, the Hetch Hetchy debate typified the failure of consensual communication—a circumstance under which Habermas recommends that participants resort to rhetoric (meaning propaganda) to restore premises. Muir and the other preservationists put out pamphlets, engaged in letter-writing campaigns, and generally did everything possible to propagandize the sense of nature that would convince people to prevent the damming of the valley, but they were unsuccessful. Thus, resorting to "rhetoric" (in Habermas's sense) under such circumstances also does not improve the quality of debate in the public sphere—nor does it ensure good policy decisions. One can infer two points regarding a Habermasian analysis of a controversy like the debate over the Hetch Hetchy: first, a study of such a controversy does not succeed in providing a useful evaluation of consensual communication, as no one involved can be argued to have attempted such a form of discourse; second, Habermas's positive project does not imply a useful set of recommendations for participants in political controversy in which major assumptions are at issue. This latter point now seems to me to be a significant critique of Habermas's project, in that the Hetch Hetchy debate exemplifies most political debates: there are multiple sides, with conflicting conceptions of rational argumentation, whose arguments are grounded in incompatible premises. If Habermas's project has little relevance for such situations, then it has little relevance for the bulk of political discourse.

II

As Charles Taylor has argued when looking at a set of ideas that constitute a sense of self for an era or culture, one can pose either of two questions. One might ask a question of historical genesis and tradition: *Why* did this particular identity arise; that is, what specific historical forces caused it to become part of a tradition? Such a question would necessitate demonstrating the historical, material, and cultural forces that caused both its formation in one era and its transformation(s) in others. If, for instance, one were to demonstrate that the Jeremiad began with the American Puritans of the seventeenth century, one would also need to show how it was transmitted from one generation to another such that students in a course in persuasive writing would still find it meaningful. This is not the errand of this book. The second question is not to ask what caused the identity to arise, but, instead, what seemed to make it attractive. My study should be understood as pursuing that second kind of question. A close examination of Puritanism helps to define what seems so attractive about monologic discourse: Why would intelligent (and even well-intentioned) people promote a system of public argumentation that cannot discursively resolve difference?

The cultural phenomenon with which I am interested is the notion that one participates in public discourse by announcing one's stance, listing one's arguments, and condemning one's opposition. This notion about what argument is results in the paradox of the American public sphere: in a democracy, which puts tremendous importance on public discourse, it is considered extremely bad taste to disagree about politics or religion face to face.

Americans have long been noted for our inability to keep political differences from getting personal if not physical. In Anthony Trollope's *The American Senator,* the senator is ridiculed for his continually offending people through his unnecessarily confrontational method of argument. H. L. Mencken noted this tendency in American politicians toward demonizing the opposition: "Every great campaign in American history, however decorously it started with a statement of principles, has always ended with a violent pursuit of hobgoblins"

(353). Charles Dickens was (ironically enough) burned in effigy for having remarked on the hypocrisy of Americans' bragging about free speech when silencing dissent through tarring and feathering, stoning, or even lynching vocal dissenters.

This tendency to react with violent repression to speech was particularly true of the seventeenth-century Americans. Anne Hutchinson, Roger Williams, and Friends (Quakers) were banished from the colony for espousing their beliefs; Friends who returned might be additionally fined, maimed, whipped, or have their children sold into servitude. It was not infrequent for authorities to slit the noses of other kinds of dissenters, bore holes in their tongues, have them whipped through several towns, banish them in the middle of winter, confiscate their property, or take their children away to be raised by someone considered more appropriate. Robert St. George has counted 856 cases of prosecution for "heated speech" between 1640 and 1680 in Essex County alone. "Heated speech" includes blasphemy, sedition, and "creating social damage," and punishment for such speech included public confession, wearing a paper that described the offense, spending one half to one hour in the stocks, being whipped, or going to jail.

Why does this happen? Why do Americans have so much trouble disagreeing productively?

There is no shortage of models of productive methods of argumentation. As has often been remarked, the history of rhetoric is largely the history of various models by which people who disagree about fundamental things can argue without engaging in verbal or physical violence. In the popular sphere, too, there are notions like "empathic listening," "Getting to Yes," or "Win/Win" models of interaction, all of which describe how people can resolve conflict. Why do so many people remain hostile to such models?

One way that Americans disagree unproductively is to assume that Isaiah is the ideal public speaker. The phrase "voice crying in the wilderness" remains a term of praise, used approvingly as the title for the autobiographies, biographies, or essay collections for such incongruous figures as a nuclear physicist involved in arms control, a Soviet dissident, the president of a black college, nineteenth-century nature writers, Edward Abbey, and Albert Schweitzer.[2] It has also been used by or on behalf of James Baldwin, William Jennings Bryan, George Bush, Martin Luther King, Jr., Huey Long, and John Muir.

The ubiquitousness of this phrase is in the Puritan sense significant, typifying a vision of the role that an individual should have in the community and the impossibility of the public sphere serving as a locus of inquiry and intellectual change. To invoke the "voice crying in the wilderness" ethos is to summon up an entire relationship of public argumentation as a battleground of good and evil. For instance, a socialist pacifist William Robinson used the term as the title of his journal begun to protest American entry into World War I. In the first article, Robinson explains his mission:

> Yes, we, the few who remain true to the ideals of liberty, truth and humanity, cannot help a feeling of despair. But while despairing we must not fold our arms and do nothing. We must not sulk and grieve in our tents. We must not let the forces of darkness and cruelty run over the world unopposed; we must not be silent, even tho our voice be a voice in the wilderness; if we are to be destroyed, let us be destroyed fighting, with our boots on.
>
> . . . So the only thing left for me to do is to found another organ in which I can express my opinions without any apologies to anybody, and to make my appeal to people who are willing and anxious to listen to all sides of a question.
>
> If I were to consult my personal comfort, my finances, my time, I would not do it. But Duty tells me to go ahead.
>
> . . . I know what it means to make yourself a *persona non grata* to the powers that be. . . . Their power to injure the individual is unlimited. But with all the disagreeable possibilities in sight, I must go ahead. I can do no other. (Robinson 2)

This ethos is the same adopted by Hutchinson, Winthrop, Cotton, Hooker, and the Puritans involved in the major controversies: wronged and persecuted, self-sacrificing and heroic, so dedicated to the hard truth that they refuse to compromise, no matter how great the threat.

This is not simply a definition of the speaker's role, however. Prophetic rhetoric has a limited number of roles for anyone who participates in public discourse: the good, the bad, and the neutral. The argument itself has two sides, which are engaged in a life or death battle. Although on the side of the good and battling against the evil, Robinson is not actually speaking to those people whom he is fighting; his intended audience is, as he says, made up of the neutral people who are willing to listen to all sides of a question.

What is less remarked is that prophetic rhetoric leaves one with no way of imagining public discourse as a form of *inquiry*. Fundamental to prophetic rhetoric is the limitation of all questions to two sides, either of which is formed outside of the public sphere (through a conversion experience, if it is the right side, and through a submission to Vanity Fair, if it is the wrong side). The public sphere is simply the place where the two sides fight, with any change of position seen as an admission of defeat or a move in realpolitik. A politician who changes positions may be portrayed as a waffler (as was Carter) or as a realist (as was Nixon), but never as someone whose stance was appropriately changed because of having heard convincing reasons.

Perhaps what is most inhibiting about prophetic rhetoric is that it amounts to a very short list of qualities required for a good person. Foremost on that list is a determined intransigence, such that it seems to be a point of honor to be unable or unwilling to include an intelligent and informed opposition in one's deliberation process. The practical consequence is that we have a public sphere made up of Isaiahs, that we cannot imagine public argument as anything other than taking stances and listing reasons for the benefit of some fictional "neutral" audience and the confirming of others on our side.

It seems quite reasonable to suggest that the problems in our practice of public argument might be connected to our methods of training, that is, in how we teach students to engage in argument. Such an origin is especially likely considering that for some time argumentation has had a problematic status in contemporary composition courses. As Janice Lauer has said, "Writing persuasively about issues in the public world has marginal status in many composition classes both in high school and college today" (63). Halloran has bemoaned the replacement of "the rhetoric of citizenship" with writing pedagogies that focus exclusively on the personal and professional. Kate Ronald has pointed to the division of argumentation in many curricula (as a separate and often more advanced course) as indicating the false assumption that public writing is somehow opposed to personal writing. Not everyone is made unhappy by the restriction of argumentation into a special course. Some feminists have justly criticized the tendency for the teaching of persuasive writing to inculcate an aggressive attitude toward discourse, for teaching communication as another form of force. Miriam Brody refers to "The Ciceronian notion of persuasion as muscular and male" (192), a notion that she argues results in "a repression of the feminine" whether the feminine is "imagined as weakness or as the open, generous-hearted flexibility that Peter Elbow advised preceded well-honed argument" (192). Elisabeth Daümer and

Sandra Runzo have said that "even when we diligently and conscientiously urge our students to write about issues of significance, we still primarily teach a style, whose distinctive features are detachment from others, suppression of emotion, a 'logical'—i.e., hierarchical—organization, 'appropriate' topic and word choice, persuasive strategies, and reliance on rules" (52). The argument is that this male, agonistic, and confrontational approach to discourse excludes many students, whereas it reinforces and legitimates fundamentally coercive societal and institutional structures.

Argumentation has been portrayed as an assertion of self, a display of knowledge, and therefore in contrast to exploratory writing, it is characterized as a static form that does not enable students to learn through the process of writing. Paul Connolly has said:

> In argument, I marshall my ideas and regiment them into a case; I plot strategy; it is like drilling an army on a parade ground. But always, or almost always, in arguing I am working with knowns, givens, with counters: rooks and pawns. All the cards are in my hand, all the players are on the board—or, again, almost all. The point is, argument is something you do after you've called up your forces. . . . But when I am not arguing—as I am not here—writing is actually exploring, examining, thinking alive. It is a dynamic, not a static, activity. I am, literally, making ideas, concepts—which is quite a different matter from ordering ideas into arguments. (78–79)

There is something confusing here about the implicit definition of argumentation. In what sense is Connolly *not* arguing? He is asserting propositions, making claims about the nature of reality, using figures of argument such as antithesis, correctio, apostrophe, and division.

One might even suggest that Connolly is using the argumentative fallacy of the straw man—setting up a version of argumentation that is easy to knock down, that is not a real opponent—were it not that many proponents of argumentation do characterize the activity in militaristic, male, and competitive metaphors. Walter Ong has claimed it necessarily has an essentially combative nature, arguing that public argumentation is a form of male symbolic display, much like sports (*Fighting for Life*). The insistence upon some sort of equivalence among these realms—male aggression, sports, and public argumentation—has a long history. Aristotle compares rhetorical skill to boxing, Gorgias compares it to rape, Puritan ministers equate giving a sermon with attacking listeners, and as George Lakoff and Mark Johnson have pointed out, most metaphors for public discourse are militaristic (one undermines, attacks, or shoots down an argument). The assumption is that the speaker (who is, for most of western European history, male) enters the field of combat with one argument (which might have three supporting reasons), and that this person will leave the field victorious or defeated. To leave with a different relationship toward that initial argument—to reconsider it, for instance—is to be defeated.

This is a model for participating in public discourse that is essentially static: one displays one's knowledge, presents one's evidence, possibly with the hope that others might be persuaded, but with no intention of changing one's own position. If not militaristic, the metaphors are often ones of display (showing what one means, presenting evidence) rather than ones that might indicate a more dynamic view of discourse (such as metaphors of exploration, exchange, or dialogue). The composing process in such a discourse is assumed to be neatly linear: one determines one's own position; *then* one considers the potential audience; *then* one decides which concessions to make to that audience; *then* one arranges one's argument; *then* one uses style to ornament one's points most effectively. One's thesis, stated clearly at the beginning of the argument and restated at the end, is more or less the position with which one began the process of composing. Ideas are given objects that can be moved around, enlarged, reduced, ornamented, and then displayed for the audience.

In its uglier forms, such discourse can feel like a kind of dishonesty (or coercion) because winning an argument is the goal of the discourse, and this goal determines the means. One's purpose in expanding a particular section of an argument, for example, is not that such an expansion would be most accurate, but most effective. As the Puritan logician Alexander Richardson complained, orators "referre all to victory; they are like Lawyers, and therefore think they may lye at pleasure: therefore they will place their strongest arguments first, that their auditors may chew the cud upon them: and then they put out their meane arguments in the middle, whilst their auditors are meditating on the first; and then at last by that time the auditors have well thought of the first, they bring out one or two strong ones more, to make their auditors beleeve that they in the middle were like to the first, and last" (340). Such changes in arrangement are not made with an eye to incorporating one's audience's potential objections or points of view, but in order to mislead or distract them away from weaknesses in one's argument. In other words, triumphing over the opponent, rather than being accurate or fair, is both the goal of the interaction with others and the only criterion for success.

But what does it mean to "win" an argument by misleading, coercing, intimidating, or distracting one's audience? No one pretends that such strategies move intelligent readers whose disagreement is grounded in an informed but different understanding of the situation. They would know the issue so well that they would not be deceived by the positioning of weaker arguments. Such an approach to discourse might confirm the opinions of those who already agree and, temporarily at least, gain the assent of the uninformed. But in general, monologic discourse simply alienates or enrages the intelligent and informed opposition. In this sense it is not persuasive discourse. I want to insist on this very narrow definition of persuasive discourse—a use of language that causes informed listeners or readers to *change* their understanding of a situation. In such discourse, it is not simply that the rhetor hopes that listeners might be changed during the discourse, but that the discourse is shaped in ways that incorporate the listener's ideas such that genuine persuasion of informed and intelligent people is likely. But this sense of argument as simple assertion in which the relationship of speaker and argument remain static is only one form, and it is the form that is most often criticized by proponents of the teaching of persuasion. Variously called monologic discourse, strategic action, eristic rhetoric, this approach to discourse makes objects of audience and knowledge: the purpose of engaging in communication is to transmit the speaker's knowledge into the mind of the audience.

One of the paradoxes that quickly struck me when I began teaching writing was that although some students (and teachers) were insistent upon using and praising monologic discourse, they did not claim ever to have been persuaded by instances of such writing. They may have admired it when the writing promoted a stance that they already shared, but they were rarely moved to a new understanding of an important issue through such discourse. Instead, when they described the forms of discourse that actually caused them to change their minds (assuming that they could think of such a piece of writing), they cited examples of fiction, exploratory writing, personal narrative, or dialogic discourse.

Dialogic discourse (variously called consensual communication or controversial thinking) is a dynamic form that incorporates various points of view into a multiply voiced dialogue oriented toward a better understanding. Chaim Perelman's distinction is typical: "Dialogue, as we consider it, is not supposed to be a *debate*, in which the partisans of opposed settled convictions defend their respective views, but rather a *discussion*, in which the interlocutors search honestly and without bias for the best solution to a controversial problem" (emphasis in original, 37).

Philosophical foundations for such discourse have been placed in Mikhail Bakhtin (Clark), Aristotle (Gage, Walker), Cicero (Sloane), Carl Rogers (Hairston, Young), and Immanuel Kant (Habermas). Although significant differences exist between and among these figures, the concepts shared among these theorists of argument are several. First, they agree that public discourse should include dissent—not simply in the sense that the public sphere as a whole should permit dissenters to speak, but that each speaker should consciously strive to consider, understand, and include dissenting opinions in his/her discourse. Second, this inclusion should not be merely at one (fairly late) stage in the linear process of composing, such that one might list an objection in order to contradict it, but in a dynamic and recursive process of coming to an understanding. Third, one considers several positions while one comes to one's own, and one's own position is held somewhat contingently: given what the speaker understands about the situation at that moment, this is the best position, but that position may change if the speaker's understanding of the situation changes.

These distinctions are specific descriptions of the most important difference between monologue and dialogue, which is the difference in intention: one enters what one perceives as an open-ended conversation with an open mind. Perelman insists that argumentation requires a particular attitude toward one's interlocutor: "One is not regarding him as an object, but appealing to his free judgment. Recourse to argumentation assumes the establishment of a community of minds, which, while it lasts, excludes the use of violence. To agree to discussion means readiness to see things from the viewpoint of the interlocutor" (55).

Clark says that the assumptions behind dialogic rhetoric "demand that any rhetor function as but one voice in a pluralistic process of collaborative exchange through which a community of equals discover and validate what they can collectively consider true" (21). Walker has argued for pedagogies that possess a "tendency to emphasize the dialogic relation between writer and audience by requiring the writer to include the audience's thinking in the invention process, rather than merely 'adapting' the discourse to an audience considered after the fact or considered only as an external 'other' to be manipulated, or accommodated by the writer's unilateral, monologic action" (47). As Clark has noted, this approach to the teaching of writing is unusual: "This dialogical stance is very different from the stance that most of us are taught to take when we write, one that allows us to objectify the people we address as uninformed beings we must attempt to inform with the truth" (3).

In a sense, the problem at the heart of my research into the Puritans is implied in Clark's comment. The dialogic approach to discourse *is* different from what we are normally taught; it is the exception to common practice. Yet, if dialogic discourse is, as so many theorists argue, obviously better than monologic discourse—if it promotes learning through writing, a sense of community, and a noncoercive way to resolve disagreement—why are so many students and teachers hostile to it?

I have argued that the American Puritans found monologic discourse convincing because it flowed from and reinforced various central assumptions that they made about knowledge, power, language, and interpretation. That is, they responded to dissent with repression and force because they could imagine no other response. And what one sees in Puritanism, especially in contrast to almost any form of dialogic rhetoric, is that it is a system, whereas rhetoric tends to be a quilt. Monologism promises intellectual certainty and security, whereas rhetoric is a useful patchwork. It seems to me that it is unwise for proponents of dialogism to ignore how attractive that certainty and security are. The attraction that monologism held for Puritans (and for many people today) is at least partially indicated in the above. Unlike rhetoric, monologism promises a way to present what is True such that any moderately intelligent person must assent, whereas rhetoric seems unconcerned with truth. That is a very attractive promise.

The oddest quality about monologic discourse is that as in the Puritan public sphere it continually fails to fulfill that promise. Quite simply, monologism does not work. Proponents of monologism are often open about that failure; they admit that it does not work with people who are committed to opposing the policy or proposition under consideration. In fact, proponents of monologic discourse, like the Puritans, begin by excluding such members of the audience. Whereas the Puritans divided the audience into two parts so that the exclusion left a rhetor only with members of the elect, modern monologism adds a third kind of audience and describes them as the intended object of persuasion—some more or less hypothetical neutral or uncommitted audience. It is common, for instance, for instructors and textbooks to recommend that students not try to reach the people who are genuinely opposed to one's position because, as one textbook says, "dyed-in-the-wool opponents of your view . . . are not likely to be won over, no matter what you say" (Cooley 297). Instead, an author should merely attempt to persuade those who do not disagree, yet do not agree—the "uncommitted reader" (Cooley 297; see also, Hirschberg 85).

What gets distributed out of the argument about argument with this move of excluding the committed opposition is that any resulting community of discourse is one grounded in exclusion. That is an obvious point but one worth insisting upon over and over. Monologic discourse is effective only insofar as the community of discourse is constituted by excluding points of view that are substantially different. It cannot therefore serve as the model for a public sphere that might be genuinely inclusive.

As in the Cooley quote, it also leads to a circular argument: because monologism is ineffective with committed and intelligent oppositions, it announces that there is no way of reaching such audiences. Again, as with Puritanism, rather than see such a failure as a reason to doubt the efficacy of the method, the continual persuasive failure of monologism is used as a basis for a kind of rhetorical determinism. The Puritan authorities did not doubt their own methods of discourse when (even though) they continually failed to find discursive methods of conflict resolution, but instead blamed the hard-heartedness of those who would not be persuaded.[3]

On a simpler level, monologism cannot even serve as an effective pedagogical practice for enabling students to manage the kinds of arguments that they are likely to face in their lives. The advice that they ignore the committed opposition, although common, is extremely impractical because it is based on a false model of audiences: there are very few topics of public debate on which people are uncommitted. Members of the public may be committed to conflicting propositions— freedom of the press *and* suppression of child pornography; low federal budget *and* expansion of expensive federal programs; no affirmative action *and* lower college entrance standards for athletes—but they are committed. They have not been trained as debate judges who will try to evaluate the conflicting arguments purely on the merit of the arguments presented; the general public does not see its role in public discourse as the same as a judge in a trial. Teaching students to participate in public discourse by using methods that will only work with an uncommitted audience is teaching them to speak to people who do not exist.

On the contrary, most of the instances of argumentation in which students are likely to participate involve being literally or figuratively face-to-face with their opposition. They might, for example, need to persuade their parents to permit a fifth year of college, or a change of major, or time off from school. They might need to persuade a roommate to change behavior, a teacher to alter some policy, or a friend to reconsider a decision. In these situations, a form of argumentation based in excluding the opposition is ineffectual at best and disastrous at worst. The parent, roommate, teacher, or friend *is* committed to some course of action; the person whom the student needs to persuade *is* the opposition. If students are not taught how to persuade a person committed to an opposing position, then like the Puritans, they are left without options for discursively resolving such situations. This form of discourse teaches students to take a stand and list their reasons; it teaches them to behave like Old Testament prophets crying in the wilderness.

That limitation of method leaves communities with two ways to deal with genuine difference of opinion: they can resolve the conflict through some form of coercion; they can avoid the conflict. If one raises the level of abstraction, one sees a depressing view of culture: we have a public sphere in which people must deny difference or resolve it through force. We have a culture that cannot imagine discursive methods of conflict resolution when the differences are substantial. So we must keep breaking the larger sphere into smaller ones made up of people who have only minor disagreements, or we continually evade public argument on topics on which people disagree, or we keep resorting to forms of coercion. As Farrell has said, "a critically reflective rhetoric is necessary in order to mediate among the normative contents of any community" (153–54). Voices in the wilderness are not critically reflective, and they never mediate.

I said earlier that the American Puritans of the seventeenth century function as a case study of the sort of public sphere that relies on monologic discourse. Intelligent and well-educated people, they were continually confronted by the limitations of their form of discourse, yet they refused to acknowledge these confrontations or consider alternate models. If the question is, "What made monologic discourse so attractive?" the answer is that it promised and premised stability and certainty. The ontology promises a stable world that can be known; the epistemology describes a method of knowing that world with certainty; the theory of language says that what one knows can be easily stated and accurately represented in language; the hermeneutics premises a method of knowing with certainty exactly what someone else has meant; the theory of identity presumes a stable self that is revealed through how one reacts to statements of the truth.

If one slightly rephrases the initial question, and asks, "What makes dialogic discourse so unattractive to some people?" one gets a similar answer. It is often that they are wedded to some part of the above system and therefore reject any part of dialogism that would confront those parts. For instance, in the 1970s and 1980s, one form of dialogic discourse that was promoted in some textbooks used what was called Rogerian argument. Loosely based in the kind of therapy described and promulgated by Carl Rogers, it was supposed to encourage "empathy instead of opposition, dialogue instead of argument" (Lassner 220). Phyllis Lassner's critique of that form of argument, based in her examination of its use by a group of women students, argues that marginalized groups are further hindered by Rogerian argument's prescription to use neutral language: "In the experience of many no language is neutral, nondirective, or nonjudgmental" (223).

The most difficult hindrance, according to Lassner, is the recommendation that dialogic discourse involves recognizing the feelings of others and potentially changing one's own. For several of Lassner's students, this turned into the fairly threatening prescription that "they must change their way of thinking in order to be part of the majority culture," and such a method "would simply mean that women will repress their authentic feeling and comply with values and expectations of what others wish them to be, not with what they feel themselves to be" (227). Lassner and other critics of similar forms of argumentation say that such an approach feels doubly false: it apparently turns the real self into a false one; it apparently makes the rhetor say things that s/he does not believe.

This is, obviously, the Puritan objection as well, and it appeals to the same oddly contradictory view of the solidity of the self—expressivist and social constructivist at the same time. The self, which has a true form, is corrupted by contact with the other. Thus, it both is and is not constituted by discourse. Or perhaps more accurately, it is constituted by experience and then corrupted by discourse. The assumption is that contact with the argument of the other—such as listening to it carefully enough that one might be able to paraphrase it accurately—threatens the integrity of the very self. Like Calvin's objection to the Corinthians, this fear is that the true identity will be covered over by the wrong language. Like Ward's objection to discourse with sinners, this fear is *also* that such contact will change the very identity of the body, that bad ideas are diseases we catch through listening. Or to use another metaphor common in the history of rhetoric, if we get too close to those bad ideas, they will seduce us.

In addition, as argued in the first and second chapters, any set of criteria dependent upon the speaker's intention is deeply problematic. It is not simply that any piece of discourse is threaded with multiple (even conflicting) intentions, nor that mind reading is notoriously difficult. The problem is that categorizing discourse dependent upon speaker's intention becomes virtually meaningless when working with speakers who do not recognize the possibility of public discourse as inquiry. Historical or theoretical work with such an approach has the same problem as that mentioned in regard to Habermas: it neither promotes nor permits critical self-reflection because it describes as a flaw something that the opposition sees as a virtue, and it describes as a goal something that they see as either nonexistent or undesirable. Thus, like Puritanism, it works only insofar as one is not trying to reach the opposition.

Pedagogically, any taxonomy of discourse based in intentions has the same problems as the above. It also raises the ethical dilemma of seeming to require that we muck around in the hearts and souls of our students. We are not simply requiring that they behave in a certain way, but appear to be saying (if we are going to be consistent) that students will be graded on what intentions they have. It is no wonder that critics of argumentation have failed to see dialogism as anything other than another form of coercion. If we define the project of engaging in argument as having a particular set of motives, then we must put students in a discursive Panopticon.

There is a slightly different problem with dialogism grounded in Bakhtin's theory, a problem suggested in hearing multiple voices and a dialogic quality to Hooker's sermon. Certainly such a sermon is amenable to a Bakhtinian reading and thus to the characterization of being dialogic. But if Hooker is dialogic, then dialogic discourse is not necessarily liberatory. One can make this same argument at an even more general level. If all discourse is in fact dialogic, then either all discourse is liberatory, or dialogism and liberation are not causally connected. A study of Puritanism is a strong case for the second.

Yet Bakhtinian dialogism may indicate one way out of monologism. It may be that as others have argued, pointing out that language is inherently dialogic is one way to persuade monologists that their premises are wrong. That is, the monologism of, for instance, the Puritans appears to be a hegemonic system of interlocking ontology, epistemology, soteriology, and linguistic theory. Demonstrating that it is not actually hegemonic *might* be the first step in demonstrating that monologism is not simply undesirable but actually inaccurate; it is certainly not an inherently liberatory theory, however.

It would be self-contradictory were a form of dialogic discourse, or a way of teaching it, to preclude the theoretical or pedagogical adoption of another. So a Bakhtinian critique of discourse is not necessarily the only step. In addition, the notion of controversia seems a rich way to categorize discourse. Some pieces of discourse begin and end at the same place and mention oppositions only as parts of antitheses; other pieces of discourse incorporate alternate points of view into the process of coming to an argument. Inferring the process by looking at the product (and paying attention to the process of reading) seems to me an appropriate way to pay attention to discourse. Although it does not involve either mind reading or mucking in students' hearts and souls, it does accurately point to an experiential distinction.

There are several other models as well: Arendt's concept of the work of a public sphere, Brian Vicker's defence of rhetoric, the Rogerian rhetoric of Young and Hairston, the work of legal rhetoricians like Perelman, and Kastely's notion of a "rhetoric of class." This is not to say that all the models are equal or that no difference among dialogisms exists, as much as that any form of dialogism must itself be capable of understanding just how seductive the certainty and stasis of monologism can be. That is, dialogism must itself be able to include monologism in a dialogue about discourse.

Notes

1. Ghost in the Sphere

1. The story is about a man Thomas Morton calls Innocent Faircloath, who had complained that a church member would not pay a debt (Morton, bk. 3, chaps. 25, 170). Faircloath, whose real name was Philip Ratcliffe, had lost his temper with the debtor and insulted him and the church that would have him as a member. He was punished in the manner Morton describes.

2. Ramus's complete exclusion from general histories of rhetoric makes more sense than his inclusion in the Renaissance era. Although Ramus was influential among American Puritans, with his theories of rhetoric and logic dominating the American curriculum until the eighteenth century, his influence was minor (if not negligible) in English and Continental rhetoric.

3. The notable exception to this generalization is Warren Guthrie's series of articles in *Speech Monographs* in the late 1940s. Although he did trace the use of textbooks in rhetoric courses from 1635 to 1850, he did not connect that practice either to later composition pedagogy or to Puritan discursive practice. Other historians of rhetorical practice have not been concerned with the academic discipline, as much as with the history of a public sphere of argumentation. Like the historians of the discipline, however, such scholars generally ignore the Puritan era, either moving from the Roman Republic to the eighteenth century (Arendt) or beginning their narrative in the eighteenth century (Sennett, Habermas).

4. For the argument about Puritanism in *Uncle Tom's Cabin*, see Lang, "Feel Right and Pray" in *Prophetic Woman*, and Tompkins, "Sentimental Power: *Uncle Tom's Cabin* and the Politics of Literary History" in *Sensational Designs*.

2. The Ontic Logos, Predestination, and Aims of Probability

1. Like many other writers on early American Puritans, I should explain my intentionally vague use of categories. As will be discussed in the fourth

chapter, there were considerable differences of doctrine and theology among the early ministers and public officials in seventeenth-century New England; it was not, in fact, an instance of hegemonic discourse (for more on this see Hall's *Worlds of Wonder,* especially "The Mental World of Samuel Sewall" 213–38). One of many interesting qualities of those American writers who are loosely called Puritans is that they *wanted* hegemonic discourse, which perhaps contributes to one's sense that there were also considerable points of agreement among them. For most of this book, I am interested in those points of agreement, so I quote from several generations of American Puritans. I do recognize that the varied historical and natural experiences of the settlers resulted in doctrine that sometimes shifted, but as I said, my interests for the most part are with those points of doctrine that remained. Similarly, I also draw upon writers who were not American but whose writings directly or indirectly influenced the American writers—including John Calvin, Peter Ramus, William Perkins, and William Ames. For all of these sorts of people, I tend to use the terms *Calvinist* and *Puritan* interchangeably. This is not to suggest that there is no difference between the two terms, but that the differences are not important for this argument.

2. To some extent, the argument concerning heterodoxy and conformity in early New England is definitional, with different scholars having narrower or broader bands of inclusion. Shipton, for instance, in arguing for diversity, points to the existence of "Quakers, Baptists, and Presbyterians" at town meetings (138). To me this seems an extremely narrow range of practices, for the groups he lists are closely related forms of English Reformation Puritanism. It seems especially odd considering that neither the Quakers nor Baptists could practice their forms in public without risking banishment or torture.

3. Recantation did not necessarily mean that the authorities neglected punishment, but it does seem to have made banishment less likely. In a situation in which it was not strictly heresy (as when Ratcliffe insulted a church member), it does not appear that the process was very different from the more famous cases. What does distinguish the Antinomian controversy is that the dissenters were the authorities for a brief moment in time and that they had themselves followed legal procedures. There has been an impressive amount of scholarship on the Antinomian controversy, with the most fair and thorough account being David D. Hall's prefatory material in *The Antinomian Controversy.*

4. For all these texts, including John Cotton's, I am using the editions collected in *The Complete Writings of Roger Williams.*

5. See, for example, Coddington's speech during her examination in "The Examination of Mrs. Anne Hutchinson at the Court at Newtown" in

Hall, *The Antinomian Controversy* 344–45. The New England authorities were repeatedly rebuked for their high-handedness in these matters, and *Winthrop's Journals* notes several instances when friends at court had to intervene. There is some indication that there were threats to the charter due to how dissent was handled, and religious toleration was forced on the colony when the charter was revoked and reinstated. Bradford's *Plymouth Plantation* and *Winthrop's Journals* are both mostly concerned with various legal problems, many of which were caused by extra-legal procedures for dissenters like Williams, Ratcliffe, Hutchinson, and others.

6. And I cannot help but point out that it is highly reminiscent of the Puritans. They too believed that one could not have an effective public sphere if the people participating were simply trying to use that arena to further their own narrow ends. People who participate should be, they insisted, sincere, disinterested, and willing to accede to the better argument.

7. See especially *Institutes,* bk. 1, chap. 15; bk. 2, chap. 5; bk. 3, chaps. 15, 16, and 23. For more on Calvin's theory of predestination, see Bouwsma 172–73, 180–84.

8. Calvin's commentaries on the Bible will be listed by the name of the Biblical book in italics. Quotes from the Bible will be listed without italics. So, for example, *Hebrews* is from Calvin's *Commentaries on the Epistle of Paul the Apostle to the Hebrews,* and Hebrews is from Scripture.

9. It is also important as a kind of warning to modern readers. It seems to me that one of the reasons modern readers often misunderstand the Puritans is that we impose back on them some of our own dichotomies—such as rationality versus religiosity. The Puritans were fanatically religious *and* better trained in logic than most modern scholars.

10. The external moving cause of an oak tree would be the rain and sunlight that enabled the acorn to sprout; the material cause would be the wood, chlorophyll, and so on; the formal cause would be the branch, roots, and leaves (the shape the tree takes).

11. The final cause is not the most important for Aristotle, but for the Aristotelian tradition within Christianity. For a clear explanation as to exactly how the final cause functioned in Aristotle's thought, see Randall 225–29.

12. And it is interesting to note that Norton assumes that his audience (probably other ministers) will follow his argument. He neither explains his terms nor cites any information on causality.

13. In addition, seeing it as a theory of causality (and therefore one kind of determinism) raises the question of the general relationship between determinism and prophetic rhetoric. It is all very fine for moderns to snicker at predestination, but as Wayne Booth long ago argued, this is the century of deter-

minism. It is simply that our determinisms may look like biochemical, cognitive, or psychological theories.

14. This is an example of what I mean by saying that the repression of the Puritan public sphere comes from a failure of imagination. The model of power that one continually sees in Puritan discussion of topics as apparently disparate as predestination and discourse suggest that they had no image available for thinking of dissent as anything other than an attempt to resist God's will. They could not imagine that God's will might come from multiple sites.

15. Perkins's "Arte of Prophecying" is available in an easy-to-read but abridged form in *Work* and in a complete but difficult-to-read original publication. Whenever possible, I have cited from the edited version, and so indicated by referring to it as *Work*. When citing from the complete version, I refer to it as "Arte."

16. Perkins says that "The elect, having the Spirit of God, do first discern the voice of Christ speaking in the scriptures" (*Work* 335). They are moved through reading Scripture, and their sanctity is confirmed through listening to sermons.

17. Arnauld was neither American nor Puritan, but a French Jansenist. I refer to him, however, throughout the book when discussing Puritan theories of logic because his *Port-Royal Logic* directly and indirectly influenced American Puritanism. Not only were English translations of Arnauld's texts used in the English Dissenting Academies that trained so many American divines but also they formed the basis for such American logic texts as Brattle's *A Compendium of Logick* and Morton's *System of Logick*. For more on the relationship between Arnauld and American Puritan logic texts, see Rick Kennedy, "The Alliance Between Puritanism and Cartesian Logic."

18. This is a rejection of the argument put forward in Cicero's *De Oratore* that it is precisely through consideration of conflicting proposals that one might come to discover the best.

19. For more on the decline and fall of the ontic logos, see Charles Taylor 146–58.

20. As I have indicated, dialogic discourse (what I have slipped into calling rhetoric) is generally defined by speaker motive, something that is virtually impossible to identify very clearly. The elusiveness of speaker motive would seem to suggest that we cannot actually distinguish dialogic from monologic discourse, but obviously there is something experientially different about monologic and dialogic discourse. It may be that speaker motive is not the best criterion but that the issue of ontology indicates a more productive means of making the distinction between the two: Although monologic dis-

course posits one (and only one) ontology, rhetoric permits people with different theories of reality to engage in noncoercive discourse.

21. It is interesting to point out that Hooker does not mention effectiveness as a virtue.

3. The Place of the Opposition

1. Nor is the controversy between an orderly and disorderly process new to the Renaissance humanists and Puritans. Cicero outlines a process in *De Inventione* that is so systematic that he more or less recants it in *De Oratore*. One of the controversies in classical rhetoric was that some sophists taught simple formula for inventing speeches, whereas others claimed that the art of creating a speech was a complicated process.

2. This ghost of Ramus remains in the advice we give students regarding outlines and arrangements. The traditional outline is essentially Ramistic, and our insistence on a subpoint having at least two points comes from Ramus. This outline form is very amenable to a list structure but quite difficult to use for arguments that are not simply accretions of reasons.

3. In addition, this presumes the possibility of getting a single answer that will suffice for all people and all times, and such an answer is the goal of logical analysis and genesis. Logic loses its role as a heuristic or as the skill that enables one to understand the route by which different people come to the same conclusion.

4. Leon Howard's essay on Ramistic arrangement in English Puritanism indicates that the British Puritans may have been more flexible on this point, or that practice deviated more than it did in the American colonies.

5. For more on the history of the concept of synderesis, see Robert Greene. Greene's history of the term traces its use in British intellectual history, so he ignores Ames—who was very important to American Puritans, but of little interest to European scholars.

6. As will be discussed in a later chapter, this point has interesting implications for thinking about language, especially about ornamentation in style. For the Puritans, what made rhetoric so dangerous is that it continually presented this problem: it might serve as a vessel for carrying God's Word, or it might serve as a container which actually enclosed and hid God's Word.

7. There is a slight problem with the Puritan insistence that one cannot blame sin on ignorance, since they also insisted that one cannot understand spiritual truths unless one has received the spirit of God (see, for example, Hooker, "No Man" 6). The ignorant sinners' argument (to which

Wigglesworth's Jesus does not really reply) is that they are being punished for certain actions which they could not have prevented: they are going to hell because Jesus chose not to save them. The American Puritans tried to answer yes and no to this objection—saying that humans can and cannot understand spiritual truths.

8. Engaging in moral actions includes educating himself as much as possible about religion.

9. In a later sermon, *The Soules Ingraffing Into Christ*, Hooker seems to contradict this argument, by seeming to suggest that one is guaranteed grace by appropriate preparation. In other words, like Morgan, I would argue that Hutchinson was right, and that Puritan doctrine changed on this point, so that the doctrine of signs did move awfully close to a doctrine of works (*Visible Saints*).

10. Later, he says, "Our mind [should] be content with this, namely, that it hath so pleased God to illuminate some unto salvation, and blind some other unto death; and not seek for any cause above his will" (Calvin, *Romans* 265).

4. Sugaring of Rhetoric

1. "What purpose, then, is served by exhortations? It is this: As the wicked, with obstinate heart, despise them, they will be a testimony against them when they stand at the judgment-seat of God; nay, they even now strike and lash their consciences. For, however they may petulantly deride, they cannot disapprove them. . . . Had exhortations and reprimands no other profit with the godly than to convince them of sin, they could not be deemed altogether useless. Now, when, by the Spirit of God acting within, they have the effect of inflaming their desire of good, of arousing them from lethargy, of destroying the pleasure and honeyed sweetness of sin, making it hateful and loathsome, who will presume to cavil at them as superfluous?" (Calvin, *Institutes* I:276, 277).

2. It has become a convention to divide the teaching of writing on the basis of whether pedagogies teach writing as a process or product. This distinction usually means one determines whether writing instruction spends most of the time presenting and admiring models of the final product or actually teaches students various strategies for inventing, arranging, and revising a piece of writing. Here, I am suggesting that there is a similar distinction which should be made regarding theories of audience—a distinction which is not sufficiently explicit in modern composition theory.

3. It is also a somewhat unfortunate convention to refer to this tradition

as humanist, unfortunate because it implies some distinction between this tradition and more recent developments in feminist rhetorics, when the two are
actually quite compatible.

4. For this interpretation see, for example, Wilson, *The Pulpit in Parliament*, especially chapter 5.

5. And as Ann Kibbey has shown in *The Interpretation of Material Shapes
in Puritanism*, the Puritans did use figures of speech. Sargent Bush's *The Writings of Thomas Hooker* also spends considerable time showing Hooker's reliance
on various kinds of metaphor.

6. Kenneth Cmiel has discussed this confusion in regard to nineteenth-
century rhetoric, arguing persuasively for a distinction between the plain and
colloquial style; see especially 239–57.

7. It is also interesting to point out that the vagueness of the rules tends
to make clearer what one should not do (have sermons like John Donne's)
rather than what one should do. This may well be the genesis of the modern
tradition of teaching style by teaching editing—giving students a series of sentences that are wrong in some way and requiring that the students correct
them. The approaches to teaching style that do not rely on teaching avoidance
(e.g., sentence embedding, imitation) seem to have come and gone.

8. There is a paradox here that I will mention briefly: it is conventional
to define metaphor as marked language use; therefore heavily metaphorical
language is the most marked. Yet, Puritan language use was marked in
Elizabethan England by its *lack* of metaphor. To preach a certain way was to
identify oneself as having a particular theological and political stance.

9. There is something commonsensical about associating vividness and
specificity of reference. For instance, that assumption is made throughout
George Orwell's essay "Politics and the English Language," an essay that is
probably one of two or three included in virtually every anthology intended
for freshman writing. Orwell bemoans the use of such phrases as "ring the
changes on" and "ride roughshod over" on the grounds that the people who
use them generally have no idea what the phrases actually mean, so "it can be
taken as certain that the writer is not seeing a mental image of the objects he is
naming; in other words he is not really thinking" (361). Significantly, he says
that the result is that one ends up "almost unconscious of what he is saying, as
one is when one utters the responses in church" and that such vagueness is
both the sign and cause of insincerity (362). The four things that Orwell connects are: mental images; language as naming things; conscious thinking as
seeing those mental images that one names through correct use of words; and
sincerity. Those are precisely the same things the Puritans connected.

10. Before pursuing exactly what is misleading about seeing metaphor as pure ornamentation, I want to mention that it is still common. It is behind the calls for plain speech and plain speaking, the equation of simple language with accuracy, and the faith that it is harder to lie in plain language. Behind our cultural sense that the high style is always an attempt to be evasive is a simple faith that language is something that gets between the listener and the truth; the more language, the more covered the truth.

11. This is the problem with the fantasy—the mind's capacity to create ideas that have no referents (e.g., a centaur): some people might use that capacity to contemplate things that have no true existence in God's world. They might theoretically be thinking of non-things. This is what I mean when I say that the goal of Puritan communal discourse—univocality—is simultaneously a theory of linguistic reference: every thing should have one referent; and every referent should have one name; every speaker should use that one name. As will be discussed in the next chapter, although Puritans made this assertion in the context of discussions of Scriptural interpretation, of Christian doctrine, of public discourse, and of rhetoric, they made virtually the opposite assertion regarding linguistic reference in their own methods of interpreting the Bible and in much of their poetry.

12. It should be mentioned that New England courts did not go quite this far, saying that servants could sue at court for unjust punishments, but then too, obedience was continually recommended.

13. Paul's skill with rhetoric is so marked that several scholars have inferred that he must have attended one of the many schools of rhetoric then flourishing. See, for example, George A. Kennedy's, *Classical Rhetoric and Its Christian and Secular Tradition from Ancient to Modern Times* (Chapel Hill: U of North Carolina P, 1980) 130–32; F. Forrester Church, "Rhetorical Structure and Design in Paul's Letter to Philemon," *Harvard Theological Review* 61 (1978): 17–33; Raymond Humphries, "Paul's Rhetoric of Argumentation in I Corinthians 1–4," Ph.D. diss. Berkeley, 1979.

14. Such a point obviously contradicts the very notion of metaphor being discussed. The Corinthian display was not, in fact, purely display but was deeply meaningful.

15. Sennett, of course, is discussing Western Europe of one century later, but the economic conditions that cause precisely the changes he describes occurred in New England in the seventeenth century, as did the issues of false signification raised by social mobility.

16. One can get a clear sense of just how limited those choices were by looking at texts like Ward's *Simple Cobler*—a document that, significantly

enough, condemns excessive ornamentation in clothing *and* religious tolerance.

17. It is interesting to note that this very argument (that style can be feminine) has a long tradition within rhetoric. As early as Cicero, there is the argument between Attic and Asiatic forms of style, with the Asiatic considered the effeminate (and foreign and excessive) whereas the Attic is spare, hard, and masculine.

18. This issue of the femininity of rhetoric is paradoxically related to the modern issue of feminist responses to argument in composition. For the Puritans, rhetoric is the ornamentation of an argument (and therefore associated with feminine qualities of vanity and excess), but in modern conventional usage, rhetoric is argumentation, and argumentation is presumed to be void of ornamentation. Ornamentation is, on the contrary, assumed to be a quality of literature or literary writing—thus indicating the extent to which the Puritan equation of style and fiction has triumphed.

19. It is this anxiety that Lassner points to in attempting to use Rogerian methods of discourse as a feminist.

20. The process of invention being taken over by theology has been narrated by many scholars—Richard McKeon's landmark article "Rhetoric in the Middle Ages" *Speculum* 17.1 (January 1942): 1–32 is still probably one of the best introductions to the topic.

21. And here is the dichotomy that continues in modern theories of rhetoric—a rather simplistic assumption that argument is opposed to the work of the imagination and affections. This dichotomy means that people assume that processes of the imagination are irrelevant to inventing or understanding an argument, that literature and literary devices are not arguments, and that emotions are somehow destructive to the preparation and presentation of an argument.

22. See "The Referential Imperative" in Kibbey's *The Interpretation of Material Shapes in Puritanism*. First, it inadvertently favors the ranters, due to the argument that an effective minister must be divinely inspired and the equation of rhetorical effectiveness with inspiration. Since such self-consciousness is inferior to divine inspiration, formal artistry (or reliance on the human art of rhetoric to help one prepare) seems to be something one only uses when inspiration is absent. It is tempting to infer that any sign of preparation is therefore a sign of the speaker's lack of inspiration. According to the Puritan argument, if he is not inspired, he should not be preaching. The irony is that preparation is not forbidden, but that any sign of it is. As mentioned earlier, Puritanism often presumed a dichotomy, with some things assumed to be deep (theology)

and others to be shallow (rhetoric). Preparation, then, is deep, and signs of preparation are shallow.

In practice, Puritan ministers relied on conscious art *and* divine inspiration, but their defenses of rhetoric provided no strong reasons for seeing the relation of rhetoric and spirit as a duality or mutually supportive means to grace. Even Puritan defenses of rhetoric make the disipline a crutch to be concealed as much as possible. What begins with the Puritans as a sense that rhetoric (i.e., self-conscious consideration of the available means of persuasion) may be an aid to inspiration quickly becomes an antithesis—rhetoric versus inspiration. In other words, Puritanism sowed the seeds of antirhetoricalism, albeit unintentionally.

23. Hooker says that affliction enables one to contemplate what a minister has said. Sermons on conversion tend to follow Hooker's argument. Conversion narratives, however, often neglect to mention the role of preaching. The affliction causes one to think about God, but the authors do not usually mention a particular sermon that comes to mind. For more on the role of the heart in preparation in Hooker's theology, see Pettit 96–101.

5. Prophets in a Howling Wilderness

1. Despite postmodernist claims that we are in a logocentric era, rationality is not much valued in current discourse. The appearance of rationality in the form of the use of numbers is promoted, but not rational critique. The public sphere largely consists of people taking stands that claim to be, more or less, in isolation of anyone else's; hence, careful and self-reflective critique has no place.

2. For more on the role of typology in early American thought and literature, see especially Brumm's *American Thought and Religious Typology*, Bercovitch's *American Jeremiad*, and Miller's "Errand into the Wilderness" and "The End of the World" in *Errand into the Wilderness* 1–15, 217–39. Delbanco has criticized Bercovitch's and Miller's reading of New England's political use of typology, but not in ways that affect my argument (see especially Delbanco's "Errand Out of the Wilderness" in *Puritan Ordeal*).

3. Note that my argument is in contrast to Slotkin's interpretation of Mary Rowlandson's experience as an incomplete reintegration into her white community because she has been partially captivated by the natural world (Slotkin, *Regeneration Through Violence*). Although I agree that her reintegration into the human community is incomplete, I do not agree that she is partially Indianized. The experience has, as all good chastening experiences

should, weakened her ties to the civil life and strengthened those to the invisible community of the spiritually elect. It has made her more capable of the Puritan balance.

4. The reference is to Deuteronomy 32.10 ("He found him in a desert land, and in the waste and howling wilderness; he led him about, he instructed him, he kept him as the apple of his eye"). To have been chased into a howling wilderness is to be a child of the true house of Israel, one who has been chastened but will be redeemed as one of God's Chosen People.

5. This supposition is multiply ironic. By making this assumption about what the Puritans should believe, we can (at one and the same time) condemn them as ascetics immune to the beauty of this world and as hypocrites who failed to practice what we think they should have preached. We can thereby lay at their door responsibility for environmental destruction and sexual repression at the same time that we make them seem very different from (and very inferior to) us. It is, of course, precisely the move for which many people hostile to the Puritans condemn them—the tendency to demonize the Other by blaming them for all of our faults.

6. Samuel Mather defines it as follows: "A Type is some outward or sensible thing ordained of God under the Old Testament, to represent and hold forth something of Christ in the New" (emphasis removed, *The Figures or Types* 52). Edward Taylor's definition is: "A Type is a Certain thing Standing with a Sacred impression set upon it by God to Signify Some good to come as Christ, or the Gospell Concerns in this Life" (*Types* 1: 3).

7. Calvin lists "compassion, goodness, mercy, justice, judgment, and truth" (*Institutes* 1: 88).

8. Hooker compares the world to land that a prince leases out. He might even lease portions of it "to the Devil and his Angels, and instruments, reserving a Royalty and Prerogative to himself" ("Heart Must Be Humble" 3).

9. One can also see how this insistence that the Book of Nature and the Book of Scripture say the same thing, could be taken so far as to ignore the second book. Although the Book of Nature may well prove the existence of God, as Bradstreet points out, it does not prove that "he is such a God as I worship in Trinity" (182). In short, as Miller says, it is not really so far from Edwards to Emerson.

10. It is also important to correct the misunderstanding that the Puritans hated nature or the material world; they did not. Some were not very interested in it (Bradford's history of the Plymouth Plantation only has one passage describing the natural environment); some praised it tremendously (an early letter from Higginson makes it sound like an Eden); some paid careful attention

to it (such as Edwards, Cotton Mather, or Edward Taylor). Thus, it simply does not make sense to attribute the Puritan tendency to repression and violence to hatred of the natural or material world.

11. Calvin also refers to the Scale of Nature; see especially *Institutes* 1: 179. See also Samuel Mather, *The Figures or Types* 46–47.

12. My argument on this issue is strongly influenced by Marjorie Nicolson's *Mountain Gloom and Mountain Glory*.

6. Arguments with Voices in the Wilderness

1. For more on this subject, see Holway Jones and Ben Martin.

2. Bernard Feld, *A Voice Crying in the Wilderness: Essays on the Problems of Science and World Affairs* (New York: Pergamon Press, 1978); Jacob L. Reddix, *Voice Crying in the Wilderness: The Memoirs of Jacob L. Reddix* (Jackson: UP of Mississippi, 1974); Charles F. Parham, *Voice Crying in the Wilderness* (1902); Edward Abbey, *Voice Crying in the Wilderness* (New York: St. Martin's Press, 1989); Hermann Hagedorn, *Prophet in the Wilderness: The Story of Albert Schweitzer* (New York: Macmillan, 1947).

3. It may be tempting to blame this move on the zealotry of the Puritans, but one sees the same move in defenders of Habermas's communicative ethics. Böhler, for instance, when faced with disagreement regarding what constitutes the heart of the argument, attributes this disagreement to ignorance on the part of his opposition: "What could be more characteristic of the oblivion of reflection in parts of contemporary philosophy . . . than that one must first show and explain to philosophical opponents the genuine philosophical battleground, the problem of reflection?" (123)

Works Cited

Puritan Primary Material

Ames, William. *Of Conscience and the Cases Thereof.* London, 1639.

———. "Marrow of Theology." *The Workes.* London, 1629. Rpt. in *The Marrow of Theology.* Trans. and ed. John Eusden. Boston: Pilgrim Press, 1968.

———. *Technometry.* 1633. Trans. Lee W. Gibbs. Philadelphia: U of Pennsylvania P, 1979.

Arnauld, Antoine. *The Port-Royal Logic.* Trans. Thomas Spencer Baynes. 7th ed. Bks. 1 and 3. Edinburgh: W. Blackwood, 1874.

"Body of Liberties, 1641." *A Bibliographical Sketch of the Laws and the Massachusetts Colony from 1630 to 1686.* Ed. William H. Whitmore. Boston: Rockwell and Churchill, 1890.

Bradford, William. *Of Plymouth Plantation, 1620–1647.* New York: Random House, 1981.

Bradstreet, Anne. *Poems of Anne Bradstreet.* Ed. Robert Hutchinson. New York: Dover Publications, 1969.

Bulkeley, Peter. "Gospel-Covenant; or, the Covenant of Grace Opened." 1651. *Salvation in New England: Selections from the Sermons of the First Preachers.* Ed. Phyllis M. Jones and Nicholas R. Jones. Austin: U of Texas P, 1977.

Bunyan, John. *The Pilgrim's Progress.* London: Penguin Books, 1965.

Calvin, John. *Commentaries upon the Acts of the Apostles.* Trans. Henry Beveridge. 2 vols. Edinburgh, 1844.

———. *Commentaries on the Epistles of Paul the Apostle to the Corinthians.* Trans. John Pringle. 2 vols. Edinburgh, 1848.

———. *Commentaries on the Epistle of Paul the Apostle to the Hebrews.* Trans. Rev. John Owen. Edinburgh, 1853.

———. *Commentaries upon the Epistle of Saint Paul to the Romans.* Trans. Christopher Rosdell. Edinburgh, 1844.

———. *Commentaries on the First Book of Moses Called Genesis.* Trans. Rev. John King. 2 vols. Edinburgh, 1847.

―――. *Commentaries on the Four Last Books of Moses, Arranged in the Form of a Harmony.* Edinburgh, 1852.

―――. *Commentaries on a Harmony of the Evangelists, Matthew, Mark, and Luke.* Trans. Rev. William Pringle. 3 vols. Edinburgh, 1845.

―――. *Institutes of Christian Religion.* Trans. Henry Beveridge. 2 vols. Grand Rapids: Wm B. Eerdmans, 1975.

―――. *Sermons on the Epistle to the Ephesians.* Edinburgh: Banner of Truth Trust, 1973.

Cotton, John. "The Bloody Tenent, Washed and Made White in the Blood of the Lamb." 1646. *The Puritans in America: A Narrative Anthology.* Ed. Alan Heimert and Andrew Delbanco. Cambridge: Harvard UP, 1985. 201–6.

―――. *A Brief Exposition With Practical Observations, Upon the Whole Book of Canticles.* London, 1655. Research Library of Colonial Americana. New York: Arno Press, 1972.

―――. "Gods Mercie Manifest in His Justice." *Gods Mercie Mixed With His Justice; Or, His Peoples Deliverance in Times of Danger.* Ed. Everett H. Emerson. Gainesville, Fla.: Scholars' Facsimiles & Reprints, 1958. 51–72.

―――. "The Saints Deliverance Out of Tribulations." *Gods Mercie Mixed with His Justice; Or, His Peoples Deliverance in Times of Danger.* Ed. Everett H. Emerson. Gainesville, Fla.: Scholars' Facsimiles & Reprints, 1958. 27–50.

Edwards, Jonathan. *Jonathan Edwards: Basic Writings.* Ed. Ola Elizabeth Winslow. New York: New American Library, 1966.

―――. "Preaching the Terrors." *Theories of Preaching: Selected Readings in the Homiletical Tradition.* Ed. Richard Lischer. Durham, N.C.: Labyrinth Press, 1987. 100–105.

Higginson, John. "The Cause of God and His People in New-England, as it was Stated and Discussed in a Sermon Preached before the Honourable General Court of the Massachusetts Colony, on the 27 Day of May 1663." 1663. *Election Day Sermons, Massachusetts.* Ed. Sacvan Bercovitch. Vol. 1. A Library of American Puritan Writings. New York: AMS Press, 1984.

Hooker, Thomas. "The Heart Must Be Humble and Contrite." *Redemption: Three Sermons.* Ed. Everett H. Emerson. Gainesville, Fla.: Scholars' Facsimiles & Reprints, 1956. 49–64.

―――. "No Man By Nature Can Will Christ and Grace." *Redemption: Three Sermons.* Ed. Everett H. Emerson. Gainesville, Fla.: Scholars' Facscimiles & Reprints, 1956. 1–47.

―――. *The Soules Humiliation.* 1640. Ed. Sacvan Bercovitch. Vol. 16. A Library of American Puritan Writings. New York: AMS Press, 1981.

———. *The Soules Implantation into the Naturall Olive.* 1640. Vol. 17. A Library of American Puritan Writings. New York: AMS Press, 1981.

———. *Soules Preparation for Christ: Being a Treatise of Contrition.* London, 1638. Vol. 15. A Library of American Puritan Writings. New York: AMS Press, 1981.

Hubbard, William. *The Happiness of a People in the Wisdom of Their Rulers.* Boston, 1676.

Mather, Cotton. *The Christian Philosopher: A Collection of the Best Discoveries in Nature, with Religious Improvements (1721).* Ed. Josephine K. Piercy. Gainesville, Fla.: Scholars' Facsimiles & Reprints, 1968.

———. *Diary of Cotton Mather.* Ed. Worthington Chauncey Ford. New York: Frederick Ungar, 1957.

———. *Magnalia Christi Americana; or, The Ecclesiastical History of New England; From Its First Planting in the Year 1620 unto the Year of Our Lord 1698.* 2 vols. Hartford, 1820.

———. *Manuductio ad Ministerium: Directions for a Candidate of the Ministry.* 1726. New York: The Facsimile Text Society, 1938.

———. *Ornaments for the Daughters of Zion, or the Character and Happiness of a Virtuous Woman.* Boston, 1741.

Mather, Increase. "The Day of Trouble is Near." *Jeremiads.* Ed. Sacvan Bercovitch. Vol. 20. Library of American Puritan Writings. New York: AMS Press, 1985.

———. "The Great Blessing of Primitive Counselors." Boston, 1693. *Jeremiads.* Ed. Sacvan Bercovitch. Vol. 20. Library of American Puritan Writings. New York: AMS Press, 1985.

———. "The Surest Way to the Greatest Honour." 1699. *Jeremiads.* Ed. Sacvan Bercovitch. Vol. 20. Library of American Puritan Writings. New York: AMS Press, 1985.

Mather, Richard. "Church Government and Church Covenant Discussed, In an Answer to the Elders of Severall Churches in New England." 1643. Microform.

Mather, Samuel. *The Figures or Types of the Old Testament.* 1705. New York: Johnson Reprint Corporation, 1969.

Miller, Perry, and Thomas H. Johnson, eds. *The Puritans: A Sourcebook of Their Writings.* 2 vols. New York: Harper & Row, 1938.

Milton, John. *Paradise Lost.* Ed. Scott Elledge. A Norton Critical Edition. Bk. 4. New York: W. W. Norton, 1975.

Morton, Thomas. *New English Canaan.* Bk. 3. London, 1637.

Norton, John. *The Orthodox Evangelist.* London, 1654. Ed. Sacvan Bercovitch.

Vol. 11. A Library of American Puritan Writings. New York: AMS Press, 1981.

Perkins, William. "The Arte of Prophecying." *The Workes of William Perkins.* Cambridge, 1631.

———. "A Discourse of Conscience." *William Perkins, 1558–1602, English Puritanist.* Ed. Thomas F. Merrill. The Hague: N.V. Drukkerij, 1966. 1-78.

———. "A Treatise of the Vocations or Callings of Men, With Sorts and Kinds of Them, and The Right Use Thereof." *Puritan Political Ideas.* Ed. Edmund S. Morgan. Indianapolis: The Bobbs-Merrill. 35–73.

———. *The Work of William Perkins.* Ed. Ian Breward. The Courtenay Library of Reformation Classics. Appleford, England: The Sutton Courtenay Press, 1970.

Rainolds, John. *John Rainold's Oxford Lectures on Aristotle's Rhetoric.* Trans. Lawrence D. Green. Cranbury, N.J.: Associated University Presses, 1986.

Ramus, Peter. *Arguments in Rhetoric Against Quintilian: Translation and Text of Peter Ramus's* Rhetoricae Distinctiones in Quintilianum. Trans. Carole Newlands. DeKalb, Ill.: Northern Illinois UP, 1986.

Richardson, Alexander. *The Logicians SchoolMaster.* London, 1657.

Rowlandson, Mary. "The Sovereignty and Goodness of God." *Puritans Among the Indians: Accounts of Captivity and Redemption, 1676–1724.* Ed. Alden T. Vaughan and Edward W. Clark. Cambridge: Harvard UP, 1981. 33–75.

Sewall, Samuel. *The Diary of Samuel Sewall.* Ed. Harvey Wish. New York: Putnam, 1967.

Shepard, Thomas. *The Works of Thomas Shepard: First Pastor of the First Church, Cambridge, Mass., with a Memoir of His Life and Character.* 1853 ed. Vol 1. New York: AMS Press, 1967.

Smith, John, Gent. *Mysterie of Rhetoric Unvail'd.* 1657.

Synod at Cambridge. "A Platform of Church Discipline: Granted Out of the Word of God, and Agreed upon the Elders and Messengers of the Churches Assembled in the Synod at Cambridge, in New England." *Aspects of Puritan Religious Thought.* Ed. Sacvan Bercovitch. Vol. 6. A Library of American Puritan Writings. New York: AMS Press.

Taylor, Edward. *The Poems of Edward Taylor.* Ed. Donald E. Stanford. Chapel Hill: U of North Carolina P, 1989.

———. *Upon the Types of the Old Testament.* Ed. Charles Mignon. Vol 1. Lincoln: U of Nebraska P, 1989.

Ward, Nathaniel. *The Simple Cobler of Aggawam in America.* Ed. P. M. Zall. Lincoln: U of Nebraska P, 1969.

Wigglesworth, Michael. "The Day of Doom." *American Poetry of the Seventeenth*

Century. Ed. Harrison T. Meserole. University Park: Pennsylvania State UP, 1985.

———. "Gods Controversy with New England." *American Poetry of the Seventeenth Century.* Ed. Harrison T. Meserole. University Park: Pennsylvania State UP, 1985.

———. "The Praise of Eloquence." *The Puritans: A Sourcebook of Their Writings.* Ed. Perry Miller and Thomas H. Johnson. 2 vols. New York: Harper & Row, 1963.

Williams, Roger. *The Complete Writings of Roger Williams.* Vols. 1 and 2. New York: Russell & Russell, 1963.

Winthrop, John. "A Model of Christian Charity." *The Norton Anthology of American Literature.* 3rd ed. Vol. 1. New York: W. W. Norton, 1989. 31–42.

———. "A Short Story of the Rise, reign, and ruine of the Antinomians, Familists & Libertines, that infected the Churches of New England." 1644. *The Antinomian Controversy, 1636–1638.* Ed. David D. Hall. Durham: Duke UP, 1990. 199–310.

———. *Winthrop's Journals,* "History of New England." 1630–1649. Ed. James Kendall Hosmer. 2 vols. Original Narratives of Early American History. New York: Charles Scribner's Sons, 1908.

Other

Adams, John C. "Alexander Richardson's Puritan Theory of Discourse." *Rhetorica* 4 (summer 1986): 255–74.

———. "Linguistic Values and Religious Experience: An Analysis of the Clothing Metaphors in Alexander Richardson's Ramist-Puritan Lectures on Speech." *Quarterly Journal of Speech* 76 (February 1990): 58–68.

Alkana, Joseph. "Introduction: Cohesion, Dissent, and the Aims of Criticism." *Cohesion and Dissent in America.* Ed. Carol Colatrella and Joseph Alkana. Albany, N.Y.: State U of New York P, 1994. ix–xxi.

Arendt, Hannah. *The Human Condition.* Chicago: U of Chicago P, 1958.

Aristotle. *Nicomachean Ethics.* Trans. David Ross. Oxford: Oxford UP, 1990.

———. *The Rhetoric.* Trans. W. Rhys Roberts. New York: The Modern Library, 1984.

Augustine. *On Christian Doctrine.* Indianapolis: Bobbs-Merrill Educational Publishing, 1958.

Battis, Emery. *Saints and Sectaries: Anne Hutchinson and the Antinomian Controversy in the Massachusetts Bay Colony.* Chapel Hill: U of North Carolina P, 1962.

Bellah, Robert N., et al. *Habits of the Heart: Individualism and Commitment in American Life.* New York: Harper & Row, 1985.

Bercovitch, Sacvan. *The American Jeremiad.* Madison: U of Wisconsin P, 1978.

——. *The Puritan Origins of the American Self.* New Haven: Yale UP, 1975.

Berlin, James A. "Contemporary Composition: The Major Pedagogical Theories." *The Writing Teacher's Sourcebook.* Ed. Gary Tate and Edward P. J. Corbett. 2nd ed. New York: Oxford UP, 1988. 47–59.

——. *Writing Instruction in Nineteenth-Century American Colleges.* Carbondale: Southern Illinois UP, 1984.

Berry, Boyd M. *Process of Speech: Puritan Religious Writing & Paradise Lost.* Baltimore: Johns Hopkins UP, 1976.

Bizzell, Patricia, and Bruce Herzberg, eds. *The Rhetorical Tradition: Readings from Classical Times to the Present.* Boston: Bedford Books of St. Martin's Press, 1990.

Böhler, Dietrich. "Transcendental Pragmatics and Critical Morality: On the Possibility and Moral Significance of a Self-Enlightenment of Reason." *The Communicative Ethics Controversy.* Ed. Seyla Benhabib and Fred Dallmayr. Cambridge: MIT Press, 1990. 111–50.

Booth, Wayne C. *Modern Dogma and the Rhetoric of Assent.* Chicago: U of Chicago P, 1974.

Bouwsma, William. *John Calvin: A Sixteenth Century Portrait.* Oxford: Oxford UP, 1988.

Brody, Miriam. *Manly Writing: Gender, Rhetoric, and the Rise of Composition.* Carbondale: Southern Illinois UP, 1993.

Brumm, Ursula. *American Thought and Religious Typology.* New Brunswick, N.J.: Rutgers UP, 1970.

Burke, Kenneth. *The Rhetoric of Religion: Studies in Logology.* Berkeley: U of California P, 1961.

Bush, Sargent, Jr. *The Writings of Thomas Hooker: Spiritual Adventure in Two Worlds.* Madison: U of Wisconsin P, 1980.

Caldwell, Patricia. *The Puritan Conversion Narrative.* Cambridge: Cambridge UP, 1983.

Calhoun, Craig. Introduction. *Habermas and the Public Sphere.* Ed. Craig Calhoun. Cambridge: MIT Press, 1992. 1–48.

Cicero. *De Inventione* in *De Inventione, De Optimo Genere Oratorum, Topica.* Trans. H. M. Hubbell. Vol. 2. Loeb Classical Library. Cambridge: Harvard UP, 1949.

——. *De Oratore.* Vols. 3 and 4. Loeb Classical Library. Cambridge: Harvard UP, 1942.

Clark, Gregory. *Dialogue, Dialectic, and Conversation: A Social Perspective on the Function of Writing.* Carbondale: Southern Illinois UP, 1990.

———, and S. Michael Halloran, eds. *Oratorical Culture in Nineteenth-Century America: Transformations in Theory and Practice of Rhetoric.* Carbondale: Southern Illinois UP, 1993.

Cmiel, Kenneth. *Democratic Eloquence: The Fight over Popular Speech in Nineteenth-Century America.* Berkeley: U of California P, 1990.

Conley, Thomas M. *Rhetoric in the European Tradition.* New York: Longman, 1990.

Connolly, Paul. "Exploratory Writing to My Colleagues." *Pre/Text: A Journal of Rhetorical Theory* 11 (spring–summer 1990): 77–82.

Cooley, Thomas. *The Norton Guide to Writing.* New York: W. W. Norton, 1992.

Cowell, Pattie, and Ann Stanford, eds. *Critical Essays on Anne Bradstreet.* Boston: G. K. Hall, 1983.

Däumer, Elisabeth, and Sandra Runzo. "Transforming the Composition Classroom." *Teaching Writing: Pedagogy, Gender, and Equity.* Ed. Cynthia L. Caywood and Gillian R. Overing. Albany, N.Y.: State U of New York P, 1987. 45–62.

Davidson, Donald. *Inquiries into Truth and Interpretation.* Oxford, England: Clarendon Press, 1984.

Delbanco, Andrew. *The Puritan Ordeal.* Cambridge: Harvard UP, 1989.

Erikson, Kai T. *Wayward Puritans: A Study in the Sociology of Deviance.* New York: John Wiley & Sons, 1966.

Farrell, Thomas B. *Norms of Rhetorical Culture.* New Haven: Yale UP, 1993.

Feidelson, Charles. *Symbolism and American Literature.* Chicago: U of Chicago P, 1953.

Felker, Christopher D. "Roger Williams's Uses of Legal Discourse: Testing Authority in Early New England." *New England Quarterly* 63, no. 4 (December 1990): 624–48.

Fiering, Norman. *Moral Philosophy at Seventeenth-Century Harvard: A Discipline in Transition.* Chapel Hill: U of North Carolina P, 1981.

Fish, Stanley. *Doing What Comes Naturally: Change, Rhetoric and the Practice of Theory in Literary and Legal Studies.* Oxford, England: Clarendon Press, 1989.

Fitzgerald, Frances. *Cities on a Hill.* New York: Simon & Schuster, 1987.

Foster, Stephen. *Their Solitary Way: The Puritan Social Ethic in the First Century of Settlement in New England.* New Haven: Yale UP, 1971.

Gage, John. "An Adequate Epistemology for Composition: Classical and Modern Perspectives." *Classical Rhetoric and Modern Discourse.* Ed. Robert J. Connors, Lisa S. Ede, and Andrea A. Lunsford. Carbondale: Southern Illinois UP, 1984. 152–69.

Greene, Robert A. "Synderesis, the Spark of Conscience, in the English Renaissance." *Journal of the History of Ideas* 52, no. 2 (1991): 195–219.

Gura, Philip F. *A Glimpse of Sion's Glory: Puritan Radicalism in New England, 1620–1660.* Middletown, Conn.: Wesleyan UP, 1984.

Guthrie, Warren. "The Development of Rhetorical Theory in America, 1635–1850." *Speech Monographs* 13.1 (1946): 14–22.

Habermas, Jürgen. *Between Facts and Norms: Contributions to a Discourse Theory of Law and Democracy.* Trans. William Rehg. Cambridge: MIT Press, 1996.

———. *Communication and the Evolution of Society.* Trans. Thomas McCarthy. Boston: Beacon Press, 1979.

———. "Remarks on Discourse Ethics." *Justification and Application: Remarks on Discourse Ethics.* Ed. Ciaran P. Cronin. Cambridge: MIT Press, 1993.

———. *The Structural Transformation of the Public Sphere: An Inquiry into a Category of Bourgeois Society.* Trans. Thomas Burger. Cambridge: MIT Press, 1991.

———. *The Theory of Communicative Action: Reason and the Rationalization of Society.* Trans. Thomas McCarthy. Vol. 1. Boston: Beacon Press, 1984.

Hairston, Maxine. *A Contemporary Rhetoric.* Boston: Houghton Mifflin, 1974.

Hall, David D. *Worlds of Wonder, Days of Judgment: Popular Religious Belief in Early New England.* New York: Knopf, 1989.

———, ed. *The Antinomian Controversy, 1636–1638: A Documentary History.* 2nd ed. Durham, N.C.: Duke UP, 1990.

Halloran, S. Michael. "Rhetoric in the American College Curriculum: The Decline of Public Discourse." *Pre/Text: A Journal of Rhetorical Theory* 3 (fall 1982): 245–64.

Harrington, Mona. *The Dream of Deliverance in American Politics.* New York: Knopf, 1986.

Hirschberg, Stuart. *Strategies of Argument.* New York: Macmillan, 1990.

Hofstadter, Richard. *Anti-Intellectualism in American Life.* New York: Random House, 1962.

Holifield, E. Brooks. *Era of Persuasion: American Thought and Culture, 1521–1680.* Boston: Twayne Publishers, 1989.

Horner, Winifred, ed. *Historical Rhetoric: An Annotated Bibliography of Selected Sources in English.* Boston: G. K. Hall, 1980.

———. *The Present State of Scholarship in Historical and Contemporary Rhetoric.* Columbia: U of Missouri P, 1990.

Howard, Leon. "In Rightly Dividing the Word of Truth: Ramean Hermeneutics and the Commandment Against Adultery." *Essays On Puritans and Puritanism.* Ed. James Barbour and Thomas Quirk. Albuquerque: U of New Mexico P, 1986. 135–56.

Johnson, Nan. *Nineteenth-Century Rhetoric in North America.* Carbondale: Southern Illinois UP, 1991.

Jones, Holway. *John Muir and the Sierra Club.* San Francisco: Sierra Club, 1965.

Kastely, James L. *Rethinking the Rhetorical Tradition from Plato to Postmodernism.* New Haven: Yale UP, 1997.

Kennedy, Rick. "The Alliance Between Puritanism and Cartesian Logic at Harvard, 1687–1735." *Journal of the History of Ideas* 51 (October–December 1990): 549–72.

Kibbey, Ann. *The Interpretation of Material Shapes in Puritanism: A Study of Rhetoric, Prejudice, and Violence.* Cambridge: Cambridge UP, 1986.

Kinneavy, James. *A Theory of Discourse; The Aims of Discourse.* Englewood Cliffs, N.J.: Prentice-Hall, 1971.

Kneupper, Charles W. "The Tyranny of Logic and the Freedom of Argumentation." *Pre/Text* 5, no. 2 (summer 1984): 113–21.

Konig, David Thomas. *Law and Society in Puritan Massachusetts. Essex County, 1629–1692.* Chapel Hill: U of North Carolina P, 1979.

Lakoff, George, and Mark Johnson. *Metaphors We Live By.* Chicago: U of Chicago P, 1980.

Lang, Amy Schrager. *Prophetic Woman: Anne Hutchinson and the Problem of Dissent in the Literature of New England.* Berkeley: U of California P, 1987.

Lassner, Phyllis. "Feminist Responses to Rogerian Argument." *Rhetoric Review* 8.2 (spring 1990): 220–32.

Lauer, Janice. "Issues in Rhetorical Invention." *Classical Rhetoric and Modern Discourse.* Ed. Robert J. Connors, Lisa S. Ede, and Andrea A. Lunsford. Carbondale: Southern Illinois UP, 1984. 129–51.

Leverenz, David. *The Language of Puritan Feeling: An Exploration in Literature, Psychology, and Social History.* New Brunswick, N.J.: Rutgers UP, 1980.

Lowance, Mason I., Jr. *The Language of Canaan: Metaphor and Symbol in New England from the Puritans to the Transcendentalists.* Cambridge: Harvard UP, 1980.

Martin, Ben. "The Hetch Hetchy Controversy: The Value of Nature in a Technological Society." Ph.D. diss., Brandeis University, 1981.

McFague, Sallie. *Metaphorical Theology: Models of God in Religious Language.* Philadelphia: Fortress Press, 1982.

Mencken, H. L. *A Mencken Chrestomathy.* New York: Random House, 1949.

Miller, Joshua. *The Rise and Fall of Democracy in Early America, 1630–1789: The Legacy for Contemporary Politics.* University Park: Pennsylvania State UP, 1991.

Miller, Perry. *Errand into the Wilderness.* Cambridge: The Belknap Press of the Harvard UP, 1956. 244.

———. *The New England Mind: From Colony to Province.* Boston: Beacon Press, 1961.

——. *The New England Mind: The Seventeenth Century.* Cambridge: Harvard UP, 1939.

——, ed. *The American Puritans: Their Prose and Poetry.* New York: Doubleday, 1956.

Milton, John. *Paradise Lost.* Ed. Scott Elledge. A Norton Critical Edition. New York: W. W. Norton, 1975.

Morgan, Edmund S. *The Puritan Dilemma: The Story of John Winthrop.* Boston: Little, Brown, 1958.

——. *The Puritan Family: Religion and Domestic Relations in Seventeenth-Century New England.* New York: Harper & Row: 1966.

——. *Visible Saints: The History of a Puritan Idea.* New York: New York UP, 1963.

——, ed. *Puritan Political Ideas, 1558–1794.* Indianapolis: Bobbs-Merrill, 1965.

Nash, Roderick. *Wilderness and the American Mind.* 3rd ed. New Haven, Conn.: Yale UP, 1982.

Nelson, William E. *Dispute and Conflict Resolution in Plymouth County, Massachusetts, 1725–1825.* Chapel Hill: U of North Carolina P, 1981.

Nicolson, Marjorie Hope. *Mountain Gloom and Mountain Glory: The Development of the Aesthetics of the Infinite.* Ithaca, N.Y.: Cornell UP, 1959.

Norris, Christopher. *What's Wrong with Postmodernism: Critical Theory and the Ends of Philosophy.* Baltimore: Johns Hopkins UP, 1990.

Ong, Walter J. *Fighting for Life: Contest, Sexuality, and Consciousness.* Amherst: U of Massachusetts P, 1989.

——. *Ramus: Method, and the Decay of Dialogue.* Cambridge: Harvard UP, 1983.

Orwell, George. *Collected Essays.* 2nd ed. London: Secker & Warburg, 1961.

Perelman, Chaim, and L. Olbrecths-Tyteca. *The New Rhetoric: A Treatise on Argumentation.* Trans. John Wilkinson and Purcell Weaver. Notre Dame: U of Notre Dame P, 1969.

Pestana, Carla Gardina. "The City Upon a Hill Under Siege: The Puritan Perception of the Quaker Threat to Massachusetts Bay, 1656–1661." *New England Quarterly* 56 (September 1983): 323–53.

Pettit, Norman. *The Heart Prepared: Grace and Conversion in Puritan Spiritual Life.* Middletown, Conn.: Wesleyan UP, 1989.

Piercy, Josephine K. *Anne Bradstreet.* New York: Twayne Publishers, 1965.

Randall, John Herman, Jr. *Aristotle.* New York: Columbia UP, 1963.

Richardson, Robert D., Jr. "The Puritan Poetry of Anne Bradstreet." *Critical Essays on Anne Bradstreet.* Ed. Pattie Cowell and Ann Stanford. Boston: G. K. Hall, 1983. 101–15.

Ricoeur, Paul. *The Rule of Metaphor: Multidisciplinary Studies of the Creation of Meaning in Language.* Trans. Robert Czerny. Toronto: U of Toronto P, 1977.

———. "Word, Polysemy, Metaphor: Creativity in Language." *A Ricoeur Reader: Reflection and Imagination.* Ed. Mario J. Valdés. Toronto: U of Toronto P, 1991. 65–85.

Roberts, Patricia. "Habermas and the Puritans: Rationality and Exclusion in the Dialectical Public Sphere." *Rhetoric Society Quarterly* 26, no. 1 (winter 1996): 47–68.

———. "Habermas' Rational-Critical Sphere and the Problem of Criteria." *The Role of Rhetoric in an Anti-Foundational World.* Ed. Michael Bernard-Donals and Richard Glejzer. New Haven: Yale UP, 1998. 170–94.

Robinson, William J. *Voice Crying in the Wilderness.* 1917.

Ronald, Kate. "A Reexamination of Personal and Public Discourse in Classical Rhetoric." *Rhetoric Review* 9 (fall 1990): 36–48.

Rosenmeier, Rosamond. *Anne Bradstreet Revisited.* Twayne's United States Author Series. Boston: Twayne Publishers, 1991.

St. George, Robert. " 'Heated' Speech and Literacy in Seventeenth-Century New England." *Seventeenth Century New England.* Ed. David D. Hall and David Grayson Allen Hall. Boston: Colonial Society of Massachusetts, 1984. 275–322.

Schweitzer, Ivy. *The Work of Self-Representation: Lyric Poetry in Colonial New England.* Chapel Hill: U of North Carolina P, 1991.

Sennett, Richard. *The Fall of Public Man.* New York: Vintage Books, 1978.

Shea, Daniel B., Jr. *Spiritual Autobiography in Early America.* Princeton: Princeton UP, 1968.

Shipton, Clifford K. "The Locus of Authority in Colonial Massachusetts." *Law and Authority in Colonial America.* Ed. George Athan Billias. New York: Dover Publications, 1965. 136–48.

Sloane, Thomas O. *Donne, Milton, and the End of Humanist Rhetoric.* Berkeley: U of California P, 1985.

Slotkin, Richard. *Regeneration Through Violence: The Mythology of the American Frontier, 1600–1860.* Middletown, Conn.: Wesleyan UP, 1973.

Stanford, Ann. "Anne Bradstreet: Dogmatist and Rebel." *Critical Essays on Anne Bradstreet.* Ed. Pattie Cowell and Ann Stanford. Boston: G. K. Hall, 1983. 76–88.

Stout, Harry S. *The New England Soul: Preaching and Religious Culture in Colonial New England.* New York: Oxford UP, 1986.

Tanner, Tony. *Scenes of Nature: Signs of Men.* New York: Cambridge UP, 1987.

Taylor, Charles. *Sources of the Self: The Making of the Modern Identity.* Cambridge: Harvard UP, 1989.

Tobin, Lad. "A Radically Different Voice: Gender and Language in the Trials of Anne Hutchinson." *Early American Literature* 25 (1990): 253–70.

Tompkins, Jane P. *Sensational Designs: The Cultural Work of American Fiction, 1790–1860.* New York: Oxford UP, 1985.

Ulrich, Laurel Thatcher. *Good Wives: Image and Reality in the Lives of Women in New England, 1650–1750.* New York: Vintage Books, 1980.

Verduin, Kathleen. " 'Our Cursed Natures': Sexuality and the Puritan Conscience." *The New England Quarterly* 2 (June 1983): 220–37.

Vickers, Brian. *In Defence of Rhetoric.* Oxford, England: Clarendon Press, 1988.

Walker, Jeffrey. "The Body of Persuasion: A Theory of the Enthymeme." *College English* 56 (January 1994): 46–65.

Watkins, Owen C. *The Puritan Spiritual Experience.* New York: Schocken Books, 1972.

Weber, Max. *The Protestant Ethic and the Spirit of Capitalism.* Trans. Talcott Parsons. New York: Charles Scribner's Sons, 1958.

White, Eugene E. *Puritan Rhetoric: The Issue of Emotion in Religion.* Landmarks in Rhetoric and Public Address. Carbondale: Southern Illinois UP, 1972. 215.

White, Elizabeth Wade. *Anne Bradstreet: The Tenth Muse.* New York: Oxford UP, 1971.

Wills, Garry. *Inventing America.* Garden City, N.Y.: Doubleday, 1978.

Wilson, *Pulpit in Parliament: Puritanism During the English Civil Wars, 1640–1648.* Princeton: Princeton UP, 1969.

Worster, Donald. *Nature's Economy: A History of Ecological Ideas.* Cambridge: Cambridge UP, 1985.

Index

American Jeremiad, xi, 6, 167; and
community, 127; and complaints
against servants, 99; and conflict, 12–13; paradoxical nature
of, 12–13; sexual themes in, 139
Ames, William: on conscience, 53–
54, 76; on controversia, 82; on
epistemology, 54; on syllogism,
53–54, 61–62. *See also* Puritan
rhetoric
Antinomian controversy, 79, 134–35,
182 (n. 3); rhetorical patterns of,
19–20; similarities to Williams-
Cotton debate, 12, 16–21; summary of, 13–15. *See also* Conflict;
Winthrop, John
Antinomians, 55, 57, 109, 132, 134;
and typology, 120
Argument. *See* Conflict
Aristotle, 51, 92, 171; and emotion,
111; on invention, 48; and metaphor, 93, 95; on oppositional
thinking, 47–48. *See also* Rhetoric
Arminianism, 20; Covenant of
works, 14, 20. *See also* Predestination
Arnauld, Antoine: on epistemology,
55; relation to Puritans, 184
(n. 17); on rhetoric, 115; on style,
85, 92, 96–97; on syllogism, 53
Audience, 17, 19, 21, 23, 24, 31, 34,
38, 40, 47, 51, 57–59, 64, 66, 68,
71, 84–85, 106, 111, 113–14, 116–
17, 125–26, 134, 169–76, 186 (n. 2).
See also individual authors

Augustine, 156; on audience, 58; and
truth, 109. *See also* Rhetoric

Bakhtin, Mikhail, 126, 174, 179, 180
Bercovitch, Sacvan, xi, 3, 6, 12, 20,
120, 127. *See also* American
Jeremiad
Body of Liberties (1641), 10
Bradford, William: and history of
the colonies, 153; nature versus
spirituality, 153; and style, 74;
and typology, 135
Bradstreet, Anne, 145, 148, 152–54;
"Contemplation," 149; "The
Flesh and The Spirit," 137–39,
142, 143, 144; and natural desires, 137–40, 149; as Puritan dissident, 137; on suffering, 131;
and typology, 146
Bulkeley, Peter: on nature versus
spirituality, 151

Calvin, John, 74, 84, 100, 152; on conversion, 132; on epistemology,
56–57; linguistic reference, 116,
179; on logic, 59, 62, 69–70; nature versus spirituality, 149, 150,
154, 155; on sin, 143–45, 155; on
sinners, 64–65, 71, 106; on style,
87–89, 93, 97–98, 100–102. *See also*
Rhetoric
Calvinists, 57, 59, 64, 67, 72, 74, 84,
97. *See also* Predestination;
Rhetoric
Catholicism: compared to Puritanism, 110, 132; compared to Puri-

About the Author

Patricia Roberts-Miller is Assistant Professor of Rhetoric and Composition at the University of Missouri-Columbia. She earned her master's and doctorate degrees from the University of California, Berkeley. Under the name Patricia Roberts, she has published several articles as well as a chapter in *The Role of Rhetoric in an Anti-Foundational World*, edited by Michael Bernard-Donals and Richard Glejzer (1998).